Listed Volatility and Variance Derivatives

Listed Volatility and Variance Derivatives

A Python-based Guide

DR. YVES J. HILPISCH

WILEY

Registered office
John Wiley & Sons Ltd, The Atrium, Southern Gate, Chichester, West Sussex, PO19 8SQ, United
Kingdom

For details of our global editorial offices, for customer services and for information about how to apply
for permission to reuse the copyright material in this book please visit our website at www.wiley.com.

Library of Congress Cataloging-in-Publication Data is available

A catalogue record for this book is available from the British Library.

ISBN 978-1-119-16791-4 (hbk) ISBN 978-1-119-16792-1 (ebk)
ISBN 978-1-119-16793-8 (ebk) ISBN 978-1-119-16794-5 (ebk)

Cover Design: Wiley
Top Image: © grapestock/Shutterstock
Bottom Image: © stocksnapper/iStock

Set in 10/12pt Times by Aptara Inc., New Delhi, India
Printed in Great Britain by TJ International Ltd, Padstow, Cornwall, UK

Contents

PART THREE

Listed Variance Derivatives

Preface

Volatility and variance trading has evolved from something opaque to a standard tool in today's financial markets. The motives for trading volatility and variance as an asset class of its own are numerous. Among others, it allows for effective option and equity portfolio hedging and risk management as well as straight out speculation on future volatility (index) movements. The potential benefits of volatility- and variance-based strategies are widely accepted by researchers and practitioners alike.

With regard to products it mainly started out around 1993 with over-the-counter (OTC) variance swaps. At about the same time, the Chicago Board Options Exchange introduced the VIX volatility index. This index still serves today – after a significant change in its methodology – as the underlying risk factor for some of the most liquidly traded listed derivatives in this area. The listing of such derivatives allows for a more standardized, cost efficient and transparent approach to volatility and variance trading.

This book covers some of the most important listed volatility and variance derivatives with a focus on products provided by Eurex. Larger parts of the content are based on the Eurex Advanced Services tutorial series which use Python to illustrate the main concepts of volatility and variance products. I am grateful that Eurex allowed me to use the contents of the tutorial series freely for this book.

Python has become not only one of the most widely used programming languages but also one of the major technology platforms in the financial industry. It is more like a platform since the Python ecosystem provides a wealth of powerful libraries and packages useful for financial analytics and application building. It also integrates well with many other technologies, like the statistical programming language R, used in the financial industry. You can find links to all Python resources under http://lvvd.tpq.io.

I thank Michael Schwed for providing parts of the Python code. I also thank my family for all their love and support over the years, especially my wife Sandra and our children Lilli and Henry. I dedicate this book to my beloved dog Jil. I miss you.

YVES
Voelklingen, Saarland, April 2016

# One

Introduction to Volatility and Variance

Derivatives, Volatility and Variance

T he first chapter provides some background information for the rest of the book. It mainly covers concepts and notions of importance for later chapters. In particular, it shows how the delta hedging of options is connected with variance swaps and futures. It also discusses different notions of volatility and variance, the history of traded volatility and variance derivatives as well as why Python is a good choice for the analysis of such instruments.

1.1 OPTION PRICING AND HEDGING

In the Black-Scholes-Merton (1973) benchmark model for option pricing, uncertainty with regard to the single underlying risk factor S (stock price, index level, etc.) is driven by a *geometric Brownian motion* with stochastic differential equation (SDE)

$$dS_t = \mu S_t dt + \sigma S_t dZ_t$$

Throughout we may think of the risk factor as being a stock index paying no dividends. S_t is then the level of the index at time t, μ the constant drift, σ the instantaneous volatility and Z_t is a standard Brownian motion. In a risk-neutral setting, the drift μ is replaced by the (constant) risk-less short rate r

$$dS_t = r S_t dt + \sigma S_t dZ_t$$

In addition to the index which is assumed to be directly tradable, there is also a risk-less bond B available for trading. It satisfies the differential equation

$$dB_t = r B_t dt$$

In this model, it is possible to derive a closed pricing formula for a vanilla European call option C maturing at some future date T with payoff $\max[S_T - K, 0]$, K being the fixed strike price. It is

$$C(S, K, t, T, r, \sigma) = S_t \cdot \mathbf{N}(d_1) - e^{-r(T-t)} \cdot K \cdot \mathbf{N}(d_2)$$

where

$$N(d) = \frac{1}{\sqrt{2\pi}} \int_{-\infty}^{d} e^{-\frac{1}{2}x^2} dx$$

$$d_1 = \frac{\log \frac{S_t}{K} + \left(r + \frac{\sigma^2}{2}\right)(T-t)}{\sigma\sqrt{T-t}}$$

$$d_2 = \frac{\log \frac{S_t}{K} + \left(r - \frac{\sigma^2}{2}\right)(T-t)}{\sigma\sqrt{T-t}}$$

The price of a vanilla European put option P with payoff $\max[K - S_T, 0]$ is determined by put-call parity as

$$P_t = C_t - S_t + e^{-r(T-t)}K$$

There are multiple ways to derive this famous Black-Scholes-Merton formula. One way relies on the construction of a portfolio comprised of the index and the risk-less bond that perfectly *replicates the option payoff* at maturity. To avoid risk-less arbitrage, the value of the option must equal the payoff of the replicating portfolio. Another method relies on calculating the *risk-neutral expectation* of the option payoff at maturity and discounting it back to the present by the risk-neutral short rate. For detailed explanations of these approaches refer, for example, to Björk (2009).

Yet another way, which we want to look at in a bit more detail, is to perfectly hedge the risk resulting from an option (e.g. from the point of view of a seller of the option) by dynamically trading the index and the risk-less bond. This approach is usually called *delta hedging* (see Sinclair (2008), ch. 1). The delta of a European call option is given by the first partial derivative of the pricing formula with respect to the value of the risk factor, i.e. $\delta_t = \frac{\delta C_t}{\delta S_t}$. More specifically, we get

$$\delta_t = \frac{\delta C_t}{\delta S_t} = N(d_1)$$

When trading takes place continuously, the European call option position hedged by δ_t index units short is risk-less:

$$d\Pi_t \equiv dC_t - \delta_t S_t = 0$$

This is due to the fact that the only (instantaneous) risk results from changes in the index level and all such (marginal) changes are compensated for by the delta short index position.

Continuous models and trading are a mathematically convenient description of the real world. However, in practice trading and therefore hedging can only take place at discrete points in time. This does not lead to a complete breakdown of the delta hedging approach, but it introduces hedge errors. If hedging takes place at every discrete time interval of length Δt, the Profit-Loss (PL) for such a time interval is roughly (see Bossu (2014), p. 59)

$$PL_{\Delta t} \approx \frac{1}{2}\Gamma \cdot \Delta S^2 + \Theta \cdot \Delta t$$

Γ is the *gamma* of the option and measures how the delta (marginally) changes with the changing index level. ΔS is the change in the index level over the time interval Δt. It is given by

$$\Gamma = \frac{\partial^2 C}{\partial S^2} = \frac{N'(d_1)}{S\sigma\sqrt{T-t}}$$

Θ is the *theta* of the option and measures how the option value changes with the passage of time. It is given approximately by (see Bossu (2014), p. 60)

$$\Theta \approx -\frac{1}{2}\Gamma S^2 \sigma^2$$

With this we get

$$PL_{\Delta t} \approx \frac{1}{2}\Gamma \cdot \Delta S^2 - \frac{1}{2}\Gamma S^2 \sigma^2 \cdot \Delta t$$
$$= \frac{1}{2}\Gamma \cdot S^2 \left[\left(\frac{\Delta S}{S}\right)^2 - \left(\sigma \cdot \sqrt{\Delta t}\right)^2 \right]$$

The quantity $\frac{1}{2}\Gamma \cdot S^2$ is called the *dollar gamma* of the option and gives the second order change in the option price induced by a (marginal) change in the index level. $(\frac{\Delta S}{S})^2$ is the squared realized return over the time interval Δt – it might be interpreted as the (instantaneously) realized variance if the time interval is short enough and the drift is close to zero. Finally, $(\sigma \cdot \sqrt{\Delta t})^2$ is the fixed, "theoretical" variance in the model for the time interval.

The above reasoning illustrates that the PL of a discretely delta hedged option position is determined by the difference between the realized variance during the discrete hedge interval and the theoretically expected variance given the model parameter for the volatility. The total hedge error over $N = \frac{T}{\Delta t}$ intervals is given by

$$\text{Cumulative } PL_{\Delta t} \approx \frac{1}{2}\sum_{t=1}^{N} \Gamma_{t-1} \cdot S_{t-1}^2 \left[\left(\frac{\Delta S_t}{S_{t-1}}\right)^2 - \left(\sigma \cdot \sqrt{\Delta t}\right)^2 \right] \qquad (1.1)$$

This little exercise in option hedging leads us to a result which is already quite close to a product intensively discussed in this book: listed variance futures. *Variance futures*, and their Over-the-Counter (OTC) relatives *variance swaps*, pay to the holder the difference between realized variance over a certain period of time and a fixed variance strike.

1.2 NOTIONS OF VOLATILITY AND VARIANCE

The previous section already touches on different notions of volatility and variance. This section provides formal definitions for these and other quantities of importance. For a more detailed exposition refer to Sinclair (2008). In what follows we assume that a time series is given with quotes $S_n, n \in \{0, \ldots, N\}$ (see Hilpisch (2015, ch. 3)). We do not assume any specific model that might generate the time series data. The log return for $n > 0$ is defined by

$$R_n \equiv \log S_n - \log S_{n-1} = \log \frac{S_n}{S_{n-1}}$$

- **realized or historical volatility**: this refers to the standard deviation of the log returns of a financial time series; suppose we observe N (past) log returns $R_n, n \in \{1, \ldots, N\}$, with mean return $\hat{\mu} = \frac{1}{N} \sum_{n=1}^{N} R_n$; the realized or historical volatility $\hat{\sigma}$ is then given by

$$\hat{\sigma} = \sqrt{\frac{1}{N-1} \sum_{n=1}^{N} (R_n - \hat{\mu})^2}$$

- **instantaneous volatility**: this refers to the volatility factor of a diffusion process; for example, in the Black-Scholes-Merton model the instantaneous volatility σ is found in the respective (risk-neutral) stochastic differential equation (SDE)

$$dS_t = rS_t dt + \sigma S_t dZ_t$$

- **implied volatility**: this is the volatility that, if put into the Black-Scholes-Merton option pricing formula, gives the market-observed price of an option; suppose we observe today a price of C_0^* for a European call option; the implied volatility σ^{imp} is the quantity that solves *ceteris paribus* the implicit equation

$$C_0^* = C^{BSM}(S_0, K, t = 0, T, r, \sigma^{imp})$$

These volatilities all have squared counterparts which are then named *variance*, such as realized variance, instantenous variance or implied variance. We have already encountered realized variance in the previous section. Let us revisit this quantity for a moment. Simply applying the above definition of realized volatility and squaring it we get

$$\hat{\sigma}^2 = \frac{1}{N-1} \sum_{n=1}^{N} (R_n - \hat{\mu})^2$$

In practice, however, this definition usually gets adjusted to

$$\hat{\sigma}^2 = \frac{1}{N} \sum_{n=1}^{N} R_n^2$$

The drift of the process is assumed to be zero and only the log return terms get squared. It is also common practice to use the definition for the uncorrected (biased) standard deviation with factor $\frac{1}{N}$ instead of the definition for the corrected (unbiased) standard deviation with factor $\frac{1}{N-1}$. This explains why we call the term $(\frac{\Delta S_t}{S_{t-1}})^2$ from the delta hedge PL in the previous section *realized variance over the time interval* Δt. In that case, however, the return is the simple return instead of the log return.

Other adjustments in practice are to scale the value to an annual quantity by multiplying it by 252 (trading days) and to introduce an additional scaling term (to get percent values instead of decimal ones). One then usually ends up with (see chapter 9, *Realized Variance and Variance Swaps*)

$$\hat{\sigma}^2 \equiv 10000 \cdot \frac{252}{N} \cdot \sum_{n=1}^{N} R_n^2$$

Later on we will also drop the hat notation when there is no ambiguity.

1.3 LISTED VOLATILITY AND VARIANCE DERIVATIVES

Volatility is one of the most important notions and concepts in derivatives pricing and analytics. Early research and financial practice considered volatility as a major input for pricing and hedging. It is not that long ago that the market started thinking of volatility as an *asset class* of its own and designed products to make it directly tradable.

The idea for a volatility index was conceived by Brenner and Galai in 1987 and published in the note Brenner and Galai (1989) in the Financial Analysts Journal. They write in their note:

> *"While there are efficient tools for hedging against general changes in overall market directions, so far there are no effective tools available for hedging against changes in volatility. ... We therefore propose the construction of three volatility indexes on which cash-settled options and futures can be traded."*

In what follows, we focus on the US and European markets.

1.3.1 The US History

The Chicago Board Options Exchange (CBOE) introduced an equity volatility index, called VIX, in 1993. It was based on a methodology developed by Fleming, Ostdiek and Whaley (1995) – a working paper version of which was circulated in 1993 – and data from S&P 100 index options. The methodology was changed in 2003 to the now standard practice which uses the robust, model free replication results for variance (see chapter 3 *Model-Free Replication of Variance*) and data from S&P 500 index options (see CBOE (2003)). While the first version represented a proxy for the 30 day at-the-money implied volatility, the current version is a proxy for the 30 day variance swap rate, i.e. the fixed variance strike which gives a zero value for a respective swap at inception.

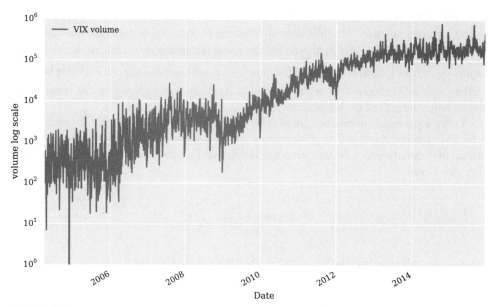

FIGURE 1.1 Historical volume of traded VIX derivatives on a log scale. Data source:
http://cfe.cboe.com/data/historicaldata.aspx

   Carr and Lee (2009) provide a brief history of both OTC and listed volatility and variance
products. They claim that the first OTC variance swap has been engineered and offered by
Union Bank of Switzerland (UBS) in 1993, at about the same time the CBOE announced the
VIX. These were also the first traded contracts to attract some liquidity in contrast to volatility
swaps which were also introduced shortly afterwards. One reason for this is that variance swaps
can be robustly hedged – as we will see in later chapters – while volatility swaps, in general,
cannot. It is more or less the same reasoning behind the change of methodology for the VIX
in 2003.

   Trading in *futures on the VIX* started in 2004 while the first *options* on the index were
introduced in 2006. These instruments are already described in Whaley (1993), although their
market launch took more than 10 years after the introduction of the VIX. These were not the
first listed volatility derivatives but the first to attract significant liquidity and they are more
actively traded at the time of writing than ever. Those listed instruments introduced earlier,
such as volatility futures launched in 1998 by Deutsche Terminbörse (now Eurex), could not
attract enough liquidity and are now only a footnote in the financial history books.

   The volume of traded contracts on the VIX has risen sharply on average over recent years
as Figure 1.1 illustrates. The volume varies rather erratically and is influenced inter alia by
seasonal effects and the general market environment (bullish or bearish sentiment).

   In December 2012, the CBOE launched the *S&P 500 variance futures contract* – almost
20 years after their OTC counterparts started trading. After some early successes in building
liquidity in 2013, liquidity has dried up almost completely in 2014 and 2015.

1.3.2 The European History

Eurex – back then Deutsche Terminbörse – introduced in 1994 the *VDAX volatility index*, an
index representing the 45 day implied volatility of DAX index options. As mentioned before,

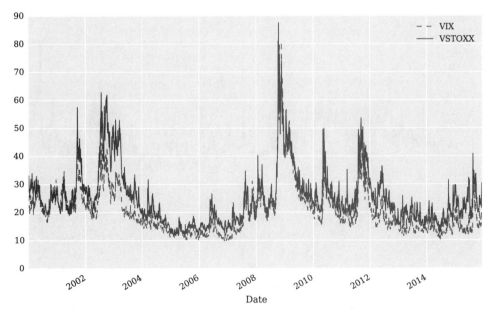

FIGURE 1.2 Historical daily closing levels for the VIX and the VSTOXX volatility indexes. Data source: Yahoo! Finance and http://stoxx.com

in 1998 Eurex introduced futures on the VDAX which could, however, not attract enough liquidity and were later delisted. In 2005, the methodolgy for calculating the index was also changed to the more robust, model-free replication approach for variance swaps. The index was renamed VDAX-NEW and a new futures contract on this index was introduced.

In 2005, Eurex also launched *futures on the VSTOXX volatility index* which is based on options on the EURO STOXX 50 index and uses the by now standard methodology for volatility index calculation as laid out in CBOE (2003). In 2009 they were re-launched as "Mini VSTOXX Futures" with the symbol FVS. At the same time, Eurex stopped the trading of other volatility futures, such as those on the VDAX-NEW and the VSMI.

Since the launch of the new VSTOXX futures, they have attracted significant liquidity and are now actively traded. A major reason for this can be seen in the financial crisis of 2007–2009 when volatility indexes saw their highest levels ever. This is illustrated in Figure 1.2 where the maximum values for the VIX and VSTOXX are observed towards the end of 2008. This led to a higher sensitivity of market participants to the risks that spikes in volatility can bring and thus increased the demand for products to hedge against such adverse market environments. Observe also in Figure 1.2 that the two indexes are positively correlated in general, over the period shown with about +0.55.

In March 2010, Eurex introduced *options on the VSTOXX index*. These instruments also attracted some liquidity and are at the time of writing actively traded. In September 2014, Eurex then launched a *variance futures contract* on the EURO STOXX 50 index.

1.3.3 Volatility of Volatility Indexes

Nowadays, we are already one step further on. There are now indexes available that measure the *volatility of volatility (vol-vol)*. The so-called VVIX of the CBOE was introduced in March

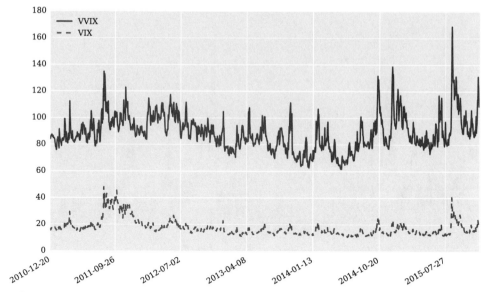

FIGURE 1.3   Historical daily closing levels for the VIX and the VVIX volatility (of volatility) indexes. Data source: Thomson Reuters Eikon

2012. In October 2015 the index provider STOXX Limited introduced the V-VSTOXX indexes which are described on www.stoxx.com as follows:

> *"The V-VSTOXX Indices are based on VSTOXX realtime options prices and are designed to reflect the market expectations of near-term up to long-term volatility-of-volatility by measuring the square root of the implied variance across all options of a given time to expiration."*

These new indexes and potential products written on them seem to be a beneficial addition to the volatility asset class. Such products might be used, for example, to hedge options written on the volatility index itself since the vol-vol is stochastic in nature rather than constant or deterministic.

The VVIX index is generally on a much higher level than the VIX index as Figure 1.3 illustrates. This indicates a much higher volatility for the VIX index itself compared to the S&P 500 volatility.

Over the period shown, the VVIX is highly positively correlated with the VIX at a level of about +0.66. Figure 1.4 plots the time series data for the two indexes on two different scales to show this stylized fact graphically.

1.3.4 Products Covered in this Book

There is quite a diverse spectrum of volatility and variance futures available. Out of all possible products, the focus of this book is on the European market and these instruments:

- VSTOXX as a volatility index
- VSTOXX futures
- VSTOXX options
- Eurex Variance Futures.

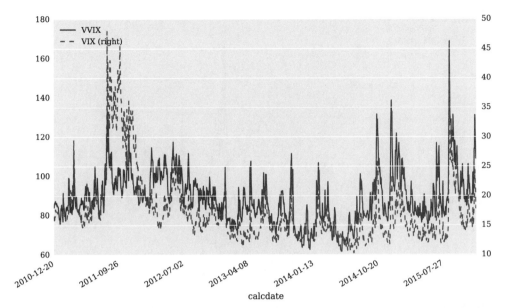

FIGURE 1.4   Different scalings for the VVIX and VIX indexes to illustrate the positive correlation. Data Source: Thomson Reuters Eikon

The majority of the material has originally been developed as part of the Eurex Advanced Services. Although the focus is on Europe, the methods and approaches presented can usually be tranferred easily to the American landscape, for instance. This results from the fact that some methodological unification has taken place over the past few years with regard to volatility and variance related indexes and products.

1.4   VOLATILITY AND VARIANCE TRADING

This section discusses motives and rationales for trading listed volatility and variance derivatives. It does not cover volatility (variance) trading strategies that can be implemented with, for example, regular equity options (see Cohen (2005), ch. 4).

1.4.1   Volatility Trading

It is instructive to first list characteristics of volatility indexes. We focus on the VSTOXX and distinguish between *facts* (which follow from construction) and *stylized facts* (which are supported by empirical evidence):

- **market expection** (fact): the VSTOXX represents a 30 day implied volatility average from out-of-the money options, i.e. the market consensus with regard to the "to be realized" volatility over the next 30 days
- **non-tradable asset** (fact): the VSTOXX itself is not directly tradable, only derivatives on the VSTOXX can be traded
- **mean-reverting nature** (fact): the VSTOXX index is mean-reverting, it does not show a positive or negative drift over longer periods of time

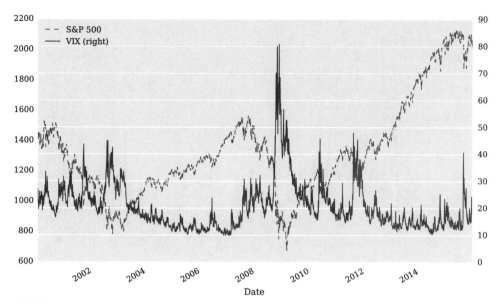

FIGURE 1.5   Different scalings for the S&P 500 and VIX indexes to illustrate the negative correlation. Data source: Yahoo! Finance

- **negative correlation** (stylized fact): the VSTOXX is (on average) negatively correlated with the respective equity index, the EURO STOXX 50
- **positive jumps** (stylized fact): during times of stock market crisis, the VSTOXX can jump to rather high levels; the mean reversion generally happens much more slowly
- **higher than realized volatility** (stylized fact): on average, the VSTOXX index is higher than the realized volatility over the next 30 days.

Figure 1.5 illustrates the negative correlation between the S&P 500 index and the VIX index graphically. Over the period shown, the correlation is about −0.75.

The value of a VSTOXX future represents the (market) expectation with regard to the future value of the VSTOXX at the maturity date of the future. Given this background, typical volatility trading strategies involving futures include the following:

- **long VSTOXX future**: such a position can be used to hedge equity positions (due to the negative correlation with the EURO STOXX 50) or to increase returns of an equity portfolio (e.g. through a constant-proportion investment strategy, see chapter 4, *Data Analysis and Strategies*); it can also be used to hedge a short realized volatility strategy
- **short VSTOXX future**: such a trade can be entered, for example, when the VSTOXX spikes and the expectation is that it will revert (fast enough) to its mean; it might also serve to reduce vega exposure in long vega option portfolios
- **term structure arbitrage**: for example, shorting the front month futures contract and going long the nearby futures contract represents a typical term structure arbitrage strategy when the term structure is in contango; this is due to different carries associated with different futures contracts and maturities, respectively

- **relative value arbitrage**: VSTOXX futures can also be traded against other volatility/-variance sensitive instruments and positions, like OTC variance swaps, equity options portfolios, etc.

Similar and other strategies can be implemented involving VSTOXX options. With regard to exercise they are European in nature and can be delta hedged by using VSTOXX futures which is yet another motive for trading in futures. Typical trading strategies involving VSTOXX options are:

- **long OTM calls**: such a position might protect an equity portfolio from losses due to a market crash (again due to the negative correlation between VSTOXX and EURO STOXX 50)
- **short ATM calls**: writing ATM calls, and pocketing the option premium, might be attractive when the current implied volatility levels are relatively high
- **long ATM straddle**: buying put and call options on the VSTOXX with same (ATM) strike and maturity yields a profit when the VSTOXX moves fast enough in one direction; this is typically to be expected when the volatility of volatility (vol-vol) is high.

For both VSTOXX futures and options many other strategies can be implemented that exploit some special situation (e.g. contango or backwardation in the futures prices) or reflect a certain expectation of the trader (e.g. that realized volatility will be lower/higher than the implied/expected volatility).

1.4.2 Variance Trading

The motives and rationales for trading in EURO STOXX 50 variance futures are not too different from those involving VSTOXX derivatives (see Bossu et al. (2005)). Typical strategies include:

- **long variance future**: this position benefits when the realized variance is higher than the variance strike (implied variance at inception); it might also be used to hedge equity portfolio risks or short vega options positions
- **short variance future**: this position benefits when the realized variance is below the variance strike which tends to be the case on average; it can also hedge a long vega options position
- **forward volatility/variance trading**: since variance is additive over time (which volatility is not), one can get a perfect exposure to forward implied volatility by, for example, shorting the September variance future and going long the October contract; this gives an exposure to the forward implied volatility from September maturity to October maturity
- **correlation trading**: variance futures can be traded to exploit (statistical) arbitrage opportunities between, for example, the (implied) variance of an equity index and its components or the (implied) variance of one equity index versus another one; in both cases, the rationale is generally based on the correlation of the different assets and their variance, respectively.

1.5 PYTHON AS OUR TOOL OF CHOICE

There are some general reasons why Python is a good choice for computational finance and financial data science these days. Among others, these are:

- **open source**: Python is open source and can be used by students and big financial institutions alike for free
- **syntax**: Python's readable and concise syntax make it a good choice for presenting formal concepts, like those in finance
- **ecosystem**: compared to other languages Python has an excellent ecosystem of libraries and packages that are useful for data analytics and scientific computing in general and financial analytics in particular
- **performance**: in recent years, the ecosystem of Python has grown especially in the area of performance libraries, making it much easier to get to computing speeds more than sufficient for the most computationally demanding algorithms, such as Monte Carlo simulation
- **adoption**: at the time of writing, Python has established itself as a core technology at major financial institutions, be it leading investment banks, big hedge funds or more traditional asset management firms
- **career**: given the widespread adoption of Python, learning and mastering the language seems like a good career move for everybody working in the industry or planning to do so.

In view of the scope and style of the book, one special feature is noteworthy:

- **interactivity**: the majority of the code examples presented in this book can be executed in interactive fashion within the Jupyter Notebook environment (see http://jupyter.org); in this regard, Python has a major advantage as an interpreted language compared to a compiled one with its typical edit-compile-run cycle.

Chapter 1 of Hilpisch (2014) provides a more detailed overview of aspects related to Python for Finance. All the code presented in this book is available via resources listed under http://lvvd.tpq.io, especially on the Quant Platform for which you can register under http://lvvd.quant-platform.com.

1.6 QUICK GUIDE THROUGH THE REST OF THE BOOK

The remainder of this introductory part of the book is organized as follows:

- **chapter 2**: this chapter introduces Python as a technology platform for (interactive) financial analytics; a more detailed account of Python for Finance is provided in Hilpisch (2014)
- **chapter 3**: this chapter presents the model-free replication approach for variance; it is important for both volatility indexes and derivatives written on them as well as for variance futures.

The second part of the book is about the VSTOXX and listed volatility derivatives. It comprises the following chapters:

- **chapter 4**: as a starting point, chapter 4 uses Python to analyze historical data for the VSTOXX and EURO STOXX 50 indexes; a focal point is the analysis of some simple trading strategies involving the VSTOXX
- **chapter 5**: using the model-free replication approach for variance, this chapter shows in detail how the VSTOXX index is calculated and how to use Python to (re-)calculate it using raw option data as input
- **chapter 6**: Grünbichler and Longstaff (1996) were among the first to propose a parameterized model to value futures and options on volatility indexes; chapter 6 presents their model which is based on a square-root diffusion process and shows how to simulate and calibrate it to volatility option market quotes
- **chapter 7**: building on chapter 6, chapter 7 presents a more sophisticated framework – a deterministic shift square-root jump diffusion (SRJD) process – to model the VSTOXX index and to better capture the implied volatility smiles and volatility term structure observed in the market; the exposition is slightly more formal compared to the rest of the book
- **chapter 8**: this brief chapter discusses terms of the VSTOXX volatility index as well as the futures and options traded on the VSTOXX.

Part three of the book is about the Eurex Variance Futures contract as listed in September 2014. This part comprises three chapters:

- **chapter 9**: listed variance futures are mainly based on the popular OTC variance swap contracts with some differences introduced by intraday trading; chapter 9 therefore covers variance swaps in some detail and also discusses differences between variance and volatility as an underlying asset
- **chapter 10**: this chapter provides a detailed discussion of all concepts related to the listed Eurex Variance Futures contract and shows how to (re-)calculate its value given historical data; it also features a comparison between the futures contract and a respective OTC variance swap contract
- **chapter 11**: this chapter discusses all those special characteristics of the Eurex Variance Futures when it comes to (intraday) trading and settlement.

Part four of the book focuses on the DX Analytics financial library (see http://dx-analytics.com) to model the VSTOXX index and to calibrate different models to VSTOXX options quotes. It consists of three chapters:

- **chapter 12**: this chapter introduces basic concepts and API elements of the DX Analytics library
- **chapter 13**: using the square-root diffusion model as introduced in chapter 6, this chapter implements a calibration study to a single maturity of VSTOXX options over the first quarter of 2014
- **chapter 14**: chapter 14 replicates the same calibration study but in a more sophisticated fashion; it calibrates the deterministic shift square-root jump diffusion process not only to a single maturity of options but to as many as five simultaneously.

## CHAPTER 2

Introduction to Python

Python has become a powerful programming language and has developed a huge ecosystem of helpful libraries over the last couple of years. This chapter provides a concise overview of Python and two of the major pillars of the the the so-called *scientific stack*:

- NumPy (see http://numpy.scipy.org)
- pandas (see http://pandas.pydata.org)

NumPy provides performant array operations on numerical data while pandas is specifically designed to handle more complex data analytics operations, e.g. on (financial) times series data.

Such an introductory chapter – only addressing selected topics relevant to the contents of this book – can of course not replace a thorough introduction to Python and the libraries covered. However, if you are rather new to Python or programming in general you might get a first overview and a feeling of what Python is all about. If you are already experienced in another language typically used in quantitative finance (e.g. Matlab, R, C++, VBA), you see what typical data structures, programming paradigms and idioms in Python look like.

For a comprehensive overview of Python applied to finance see Hilpisch (2014). Other, more general introductions to the language with a scientific and data analysis focus are Haenel et al. (2013), Langtangen (2009) and McKinney (2012).

This chapter and the rest of the book is based on Python 2.7 although the majority of the code should be easily transformed to Python 3.5 after some minor modifications.

2.1 PYTHON BASICS

This section introduces basic Python data types and structures, control structures and some Python idioms.

2.1.1 Data Types

It is noteworthy that Python is a *dynamically typed system* which means that types of objects are inferred from their contexts. Let us start with numbers.

```
In [1]: a = 3   # defining an integer object

In [2]: type(a)
Out[2]: int

In [3]: a.bit_length()   # number of bits used
Out[3]: 2

In [4]: b = 5.   # defining a float object

In [5]: type(b)
Out[5]: float
```

Python can handle arbitrarily large integers which is quite beneficial for number of theoretical applications, for instance:

```
In [6]: c = 10 ** 100   # googol number

In [7]: type(c)
Out[7]: long

In [8]: c   # long integer object
Out[8]: 100000000000000000000000000000000000000000000000000000000000000000
0000000000000000000000000000000000000000L

In [9]: c.bit_length()   # number of bits used
Out[9]: 333
```

Arithmetic operations on these objects work as expected.

```
In [10]: 3 / 5.   # division
Out[10]: 0.6

In [11]: a * b   # multiplication
Out[11]: 15.0

In [12]: a - b   # difference
Out[12]: -2.0

In [13]: b + a   # addition
Out[13]: 8.0

In [14]: a ** b   # power
Out[14]: 243.0
```

However, be aware of the floor division which is standard in Python 2.7.

```
In [15]: 3 / 5   # int type inferred => floor division
Out[15]: 0
```

Many often used mathematical functions are found in the `math` module which is part of Python's standard library.

```
In [16]: import math   # importing the library into the namespace

In [17]: math.log(a)   # natural logarithm
Out[17]: 1.0986122886681098

In [18]: math.exp(a)   # exponential function
Out[18]: 20.085536923187668

In [19]: math.sin(b)   # sine function
Out[19]: -0.9589242746631385
```

Another important basic data type is string objects.

```
In [20]: s = 'Listed Volatility and Variance Derivatives.'

In [21]: type(s)
Out[21]: str
```

This object type has multiple methods attached.

```
In [22]: s.lower()   # converting to lower case characters
Out[22]: 'listed volatility and variance derivatives.'

In [23]: s.upper()   # converting to upper case characters
Out[23]: 'LISTED VOLATILITY AND VARIANCE DERIVATIVES.'
```

String objects can be easily sliced. Note that Python has in general zero-based numbering and indexing.

```
In [24]: s[0:6]
Out[24]: 'Listed'
```

Such objects can also be combined using the + operator. The index value -1 represents the last character of a string (or last element of a sequence in general).

```
In [25]: st = s[0:6] + s[-13:-1]

In [26]: print st
Listed Derivatives
```

String replacements are often used to parametrize text output.

```
In [27]: repl = "My name is %s, I am %d years old and %4.2f m tall."

# replace %s by a string, %d by an integer and
# %4.2f by a float showing 2 decimal values
In [28]: print repl % ('Peter', 35, 1.88)
My name is Peter, I am 35 years old and 1.88 m tall.
```

A different way to reach the same goal is the following:

```
In [29]: repl = "My name is {:s}, I am {:d} years old and {:4.2f} m tall."

In [30]: print repl.format('Peter', 35, 1.88)
My name is Peter, I am 35 years old and 1.88 m tall.
```

2.1.2 Data Structures

A lightweight data structure is tuples. These are immutable collections of other objects and are constucted by objects separated by commas – with or without parentheses.

```
In [31]: t1 = (a, b, st)

In [32]: t1
Out[32]: (3, 5.0, 'Listed Derivatives')

In [33]: type(t1)
Out[33]: tuple

In [34]: t2 = st, b, a

In [35]: t2
Out[35]: ('Listed Derivatives', 5.0, 3)

In [36]: type(t2)
Out[36]: tuple
```

Nested structures are also possible.

```
In [37]: t = (t1, t2)

In [38]: t
Out[38]: ((3, 5.0, 'Listed Derivatives'), ('Listed Derivatives', 5.0, 3))

In [39]: t[0][2]   # take 3rd element of 1st element
Out[39]: 'Listed Derivatives'
```

List objects are mutable collections of other objects and are generally constructed by providing a comma separated collection of objects in brackets.

```
In [40]: l = [a, b, st]

In [41]: l
Out[41]: [3, 5.0, 'Listed Derivatives']

In [42]: type(l)
Out[42]: list

In [43]: l.append(s.split()[3])   # append 4th word of string

In [44]: l
Out[44]: [3, 5.0, 'Listed Derivatives', 'Variance']
```

Sorting is a typical operation on list objects which can also be constructed using the `list` constructor (here applied to a tuple object).

```
In [45]: l = list(('Z', 'Q', 'D', 'J', 'E', 'H', 5., a))

In [46]: l
Out[46]: ['Z', 'Q', 'D', 'J', 'E', 'H', 5.0, 3]

In [47]: l.sort()   # in-place sorting

In [48]: l
Out[48]: [3, 5.0, 'D', 'E', 'H', 'J', 'Q', 'Z']
```

Dictionary objects are so-called key-value stores and are generally constructed with curly brackets.

```
In [49]: d = {'int_obj': a,
    ....:       'float_obj': b,
    ....:       'string_obj': st}
    ....:

In [50]: type(d)
Out[50]: dict

In [51]: d
Out[51]: {'float_obj': 5.0, 'int_obj': 3, 'string_obj': 'Listed Derivatives'}

In [52]: d['float_obj']   # look-up of value given key
Out[52]: 5.0

In [53]: d['long_obj'] = c / 10 ** 90   # adding new key value pair

In [54]: d
Out[54]:
{'float_obj': 5.0,
 'int_obj': 3,
 'long_obj': 10000000000L,
 'string_obj': 'Listed Derivatives'}
```

Keys and values of a dictionary object can be retrieved as list objects.

```
In [55]: d.keys()
Out[55]: ['long_obj', 'int_obj', 'float_obj', 'string_obj']

In [56]: d.values()
Out[56]: [10000000000L, 3, 5.0, 'Listed Derivatives']
```

2.1.3 Control Structures

Iterations are very important operations in programming in general and financial analytics in particular. Many Python objects are iterable which proves rather convenient in many circumstances. Consider the special list object constructor range.

```
In [57]: range(5)   # all integers from zero to 5 excluded
Out[57]: [0, 1, 2, 3, 4]

In [58]: range(3, 15, 2)   # start at 3, step with 2 until 15 excluded
Out[58]: [3, 5, 7, 9, 11, 13]
```

Such a list object constructor is often used in the context of a `for` loop.

```
In [59]: for i in range(5):
   ....:         print i ** 2,
   ....:
0 1 4 9 16
```

However, you can iterate over any sequence.

```
# iteration over list object
In [60]: for _ in l:
   ....:         print _,
   ....:
3 5.0 D E H J Q Z
```

```
# iteration over string object
In [61]: for c in st:
   ....:         print c + '|',
   ....:
L| i| s| t| e| d| | D| e| r| i| v| a| t| i| v| e| s|
```

`while` loops are similar to their counterparts in other languages.

```
In [62]: i = 0   # initialize counter

In [63]: while i < 5:
   ....:         print i ** 0.5,   # output
   ....:         i += 1   # increase counter by 1
   ....:
0.0 1.0 1.41421356237 1.73205080757 2.0
```

The `if-elif-else` control structure is introduced below in the context of Python function definitions.

2.1.4 Special Python Idioms

Python relies in many places on a number of special idioms. Let us start with a rather popular one, the list comprehension.

```
In [64]: lc = [i ** 2 for i in range(10)]

In [65]: lc
Out[65]: [0, 1, 4, 9, 16, 25, 36, 49, 64, 81]
```

As the name suggests, the result is a list object.

```
In [66]: type(lc)
Out[66]: list
```

So-called lambda or anonymous functions are useful helpers in many places.

```
In [67]: f = lambda x: math.cos(x)   # returns cos of x

In [68]: f(5)
Out[68]: 0.28366218546322625
```

List comprehensions can be combined with lambda functions to achieve concise constructions of list objects.

```
In [69]: lc = [f(x) for x in range(10)]

In [70]: lc
Out[70]:
[1.0,
0.5403023058681398,
-0.4161468365471424,
-0.9899924966004454,
-0.6536436208636119,
0.28366218546322625,
0.960170286650366,
0.7539022543433046,
-0.14550003380861354,
-0.9111302618846769]
```

However, there is an even more concise way of constructing the same list object – using functional programming approaches, in the following case with map.

```
In [71]: map(lambda x: math.cos(x), range(10))
Out[71]:
[1.0,
0.5403023058681398,
-0.4161468365471424,
-0.9899924966004454,
-0.6536436208636119,
0.28366218546322625,
0.960170286650366,
0.7539022543433046,
-0.14550003380861354,
-0.9111302618846769]
```

In general, one works with regular Python functions (as opposed to lambda functions) which are constructed as follows:

```
In [72]: def f(x):
    ....:         return math.exp(x)
    ....:
```

The general construction looks like this:

```
In [73]: def f(*args):   # multiple arguments
    ....:         for arg in args:
    ....:             print arg
    ....:         return None   # return result(s) (not necessary)
    ....:

In [74]: f(1)
[3, 5.0, 'D', 'E', 'H', 'J', 'Q', 'Z']
```

Consider the following function definition which returns different values/strings based on an if-elif-else control structure:

```
In [75]: import random   # import random number library

In [76]: a = random.randint(0, 999)   # draw random number between 0 and 999

In [77]: print "Random number is %d" % a
Random number is 627

In [78]: def number_decide(number):
    ....:         if a < 10:
    ....:             return "Number is single digit."
    ....:         elif 10 <= a < 100:
    ....:             return "Number is double digit."
    ....:         else:
    ....:             return "Number is triple digit."
    ....: number_decide(a)
    ....:
Out[78]: 'Number is triple digit.'
```

A specialty of Python is generator objects. One constructor for such objects that is commonly used is xrange.

```
In [79]: g = xrange(10)

In [80]: type(g)   # object type
Out[80]: xrange

In [81]: g   # object instance
Out[81]: xrange(10)

In [82]: for _ in g:
   ....:         print _,   # integers are "generated" when needed
   ....:
0 1 2 3 4 5 6 7 8 9
```

Generator objects can in many scenarios replace (typical) list objects and have the major advantage that they are in general much more memory efficient. Consider a financial algorithm that requires 10 mn loops. Iterating over a list of integers from 0 to 9,999,999 is not efficient since the algorithm (in general) does not need to have all these numbers available at the same time. But this is what happens when using `range` for such a loop.

Consider the following construction of the respective list object containing all integers:

```
In [83]: %time r = range(10000000)
CPU times: user 87.4 ms, sys: 211 ms, total: 299 ms
Wall time: 299 ms
```

This object consumes 80 MB (!) of RAM (10 mn times 8 bytes).

```
In [84]: import sys

In [85]: sys.getsizeof(r)   # size in bytes of object
Out[85]: 80000072
```

On the other hand, consider the analogous construction based on a generator (`xrange`) object. It is much, much faster since no memory has to be allocated, no list object has to be generated up-front, etc.

```
In [86]: %time xr = xrange(10000000)
CPU times: user 3 us, sys: 1e+03 ns, total: 4 us
Wall time: 5.96 us
```

Memory consumption is also much, much more efficient – 40 bytes compared to 80 MB.

```
In [87]: sys.getsizeof(xr)
Out[87]: 40
```

However, in practical applications the two can be used often interchangeably such that one should always resort to the more efficient alternative when possible. The following examples calculate – using the functional programming operation `reduce` – the sum of all integers from 0 to 9,999,999. Although in this case there is hardly a performance difference, the first operation requires 80 MB of memory while the second might only require less than 100 bytes.

```
In [88]: %time reduce(lambda x, y: x + y, range(1000000))
CPU times: user 131 ms, sys: 15.9 ms, total: 147 ms
Wall time: 147 ms
Out[88]: 499999500000
```

```
In [89]: %time reduce(lambda x, y: x + y, xrange(1000000))
CPU times: user 118 ms, sys: 0 ns, total: 118 ms
Wall time: 117 ms
Out[89]: 499999500000
```

More Pythonic (and faster in general) is to calculate the sum using the built-in `sum` function – in this case a significant performance advantage for the generator approach emerges.

```
In [90]: %timeit sum(range(1000000))
10 loops, best of 3: 26.6 ms per loop
```

```
In [91]: %timeit sum(xrange(1000000))
100 loops, best of 3: 12.9 ms per loop
```

There is also a way of indirectly constructing a generator object, i.e. by the use of parentheses. The following code results in a generator object for the sine values of the numbers from 0 to 99:

```
In [92]: g = (math.sin(x) for x in xrange(100))

In [93]: g
Out[93]: <generator object <genexpr> at 0x2ab247901f50>
```

Such an object stores its internal state and yields the next value when the method `next ()` is called.

```
In [94]: g.next()
Out[94]: 0.0

In [95]: g.next()
Out[95]: 0.8414709848078965
```

Yet another way of constructing a generator object is by a definition style that resembles the standard function definition closely. The difference is that instead of the `return` statement, the `yield` statement is used.

```
In [96]: def g(start, end):
   ....:         while start <= end:
   ....:             yield start   # yield "next" value
   ....:             start += 1    # increase by one
   ....:
```

Usage then might be as follows:

```
In [97]: go = g(15, 20)

In [98]: for _ in go:
   ....:         print _,
   ....:
15 16 17 18 19 20
```

2.2 NumPy

Many operations in computational finance take place over (large) arrays of numerical data. NumPy is a Python library that allows the efficient handling of and operation on such data structures. Although quite a mighty library with a wealth of functionality, it suffices for the purposes of this book to cover the basics of NumPy.

```
In [99]: import numpy as np
```

The workhorse is the NumPy `ndarray` class which provides the data structure for n-dimensional, immutable array objects. You can generate an `ndarray` object e.g. out of a list object.

```
In [100]: a = np.array(range(24))

In [101]: a
Out[101]:
array([ 0,  1,  2,  3,  4,  5,  6,  7, 8, 9, 10, 11, 12, 13, 14, 15, 16,
       17, 18, 19, 20, 21, 22, 23])
```

The power of these objects lies in the management of n-dimensional data structures (e.g. matrices or cubes of data).

```
In [102]: b = a.reshape((4, 6))

In [103]: b
Out[103]:
array([[ 0,  1,  2,  3,  4,  5],
       [ 6,  7,  8,  9, 10, 11],
       [12, 13, 14, 15, 16, 17],
       [18, 19, 20, 21, 22, 23]])

In [104]: c = a.reshape((2, 3, 4))

In [105]: c
Out[105]:
array([[[ 0, 1,  2,  3],
        [ 4, 5,  6,  7],
        [ 8, 9, 10, 11]],

       [[12, 13, 14, 15],
        [16, 17, 18, 19],
        [20, 21, 22, 23]]])
```

So-called *standard arrays* (in contrast to e.g. structured arrays) have a single dtype (i.e. NumPy data type). Consider the following operation which changes the dtype parameter of the b object to float:

```
In [106]: b = np.array(b, dtype=np.float)

In [107]: b
Out[107]:
array([[  0.,  1.,  2.,  3.,  4.,  5.],
       [  6.,  7.,  8.,  9., 10., 11.],
       [ 12., 13., 14., 15., 16., 17.],
       [ 18., 19., 20., 21., 22., 23.]])
```

A major strength of NumPy is *vectorized operations*.

```
In [108]: 2 * b
Out[108]:
array([[  0.,   2.,   4.,   6.,   8.,  10.],
       [ 12.,  14.,  16.,  18.,  20.,  22.],
       [ 24.,  26.,  28.,  30.,  32.,  34.],
       [ 36.,  38.,  40.,  42.,  44.,  46.]])

In [109]: b ** 2
Out[109]:
array([[   0.,    1.,    4.,    9.,   16.,   25.],
       [  36.,   49.,   64.,   81.,  100.,  121.],
       [ 144.,  169.,  196.,  225.,  256.,  289.],
       [ 324.,  361.,  400.,  441.,  484.,  529.]])
```

You can also pass `ndarray` objects to lambda or standard Python functions.

```
In [110]: f = lambda x: x ** 2 - 2 * x + 0.5

In [111]: f(a)
Out[111]:
array([   0.5,   -0.5,    0.5,    3.5,    8.5,   15.5,   24.5,  35.5,
         48.5,   63.5,   80.5,   99.5,  120.5,  143.5,  168.5, 195.5,
        224.5,  255.5,  288.5,  323.5,  360.5,  399.5,  440.5, 483.5])
```

In many scenarios, only a (small) part of the data stored in an `ndarray` object is of interest. NumPy supports basic and advanced slicing and other selection features.

```
In [112]: a[2:6]   # 3rd to 6th element
Out[112]: array([2, 3, 4, 5])

In [113]: b[2, 4]   # 3rd row, final (5th)
Out[113]: 16.0

In [114]: b[1:3, 2:4]   # middle square of numbers
Out[114]:
array([[  8.,   9.],
       [ 14.,  15.]])
```

Boolean operations are also supported in many places.

```
# which numbers are larger than 10?
In [115]: b > 10
Out[115]:
array([[False, False, False, False, False, False],
       [False, False, False, False, False,  True],
       [ True,  True,  True,  True,  True,  True],
       [ True,  True,  True,  True,  True,  True]], dtype=bool)

# only those numbers (flat) that are larger than 10
In [116]: b[b > 10]
Out[116]:
array([ 11., 12., 13., 14., 15., 16., 17., 18., 19., 20., 21.,
        22., 23.])
```

Furthermore, ndarray objects have multiple (convenience) methods already built in.

```
In [117]: a.sum()   # sum of all elements
Out[117]: 276

In [118]: b.mean()   # mean of all elements
Out[118]: 11.5

In [119]: b.mean(axis=0)   # mean along 1st axis
Out[119]: array([ 9., 10., 11., 12., 13., 14.])

In [120]: b.mean(axis=1)   # mean along 2nd axis
Out[120]: array([ 2.5, 8.5, 14.5, 20.5])

In [121]: c.std()   # standard deviation for all elements
Out[121]: 6.9221865524317288
```

Similarly, there is a wealth of so-called *universal functions* that the NumPy library provides. Universal in the sense that they can be applied in general to NumPy ndarray objects and to standard numerical Python data types.

```
In [122]: np.sum(a)   # sum of all elements
Out[122]: 276

In [123]: np.mean(b, axis=0)   # mean along 1st axis
Out[123]: array([ 9., 10., 11., 12., 13., 14.])

In [124]: np.sin(b).round(2)   # sine of all elements (rounded)
Out[124]:
array([[ 0.  , 0.84, 0.91, 0.14, -0.76, -0.96],
       [-0.28, 0.66, 0.99, 0.41, -0.54, -1.  ],
```

```
        [-0.54,  0.42,  0.99,  0.65,  -0.29,  -0.96],
        [-0.75,  0.15,  0.91,  0.84,  -0.01,  -0.85]])

In [125]: np.sin(4.5)   # sine of Python float object
Out[125]: -0.97753011766509701
```

However, you should be aware that applying NumPy universal functions to standard Python data types generally comes with a significant performance burden.

```
In [126]: %time l = [np.sin(x) for x in xrange(100000)]
CPU times: user 188 ms, sys: 3.89 ms, total: 192 ms
Wall time: 192 ms
```

```
In [127]: import math

In [128]: %time l = [math.sin(x) for x in xrange(100000)]
CPU times: user 27.7 ms, sys: 0 ns, total: 27.7 ms
Wall time: 27.7 ms
```

Using the vectorized operations from NumPy is faster than both of the above alternatives which result in list objects.

```
In [129]: %time np.sin(np.arange(100000))
CPU times: user 5.23 ms, sys: 0 ns, total: 5.23 ms
Wall time: 5.24 ms
Out[129]:
array([ 0.        ,  0.84147098,  0.90929743,  ...,  0.10563876,
        0.89383946,  0.86024828])
```

Here, we use the `ndarray` object constructor `arange` which yields an `ndarray` object of integers – below is a simple example:

```
In [130]: ai = np.arange(10)

In [131]: ai
Out[131]: array([0, 1, 2, 3, 4, 5, 6, 7, 8, 9])

In [132]: ai.dtype
Out[132]: dtype('int64')
```

Using this constructor, you can also generate `ndarray` objects with different `dtype` attributes:

```
In [133]: af = np.arange(0.5, 9.5, 0.5)   # start, end, step size

In [134]: af
Out[134]:
array([ 0.5, 1. , 1.5, 2. , 2.5, 3. , 3.5, 4. , 4.5, 5. , 5.5,
        6. , 6.5, 7. , 7.5, 8. , 8.5, 9. ])

In [135]: af.dtype
Out[135]: dtype('float64')
```

In this context the `linspace` operator is also useful, providing an `ndarray` object with evenly spaced numbers.

```
In [136]: np.linspace(0, 10, 12)   # start, end, number of elements
Out[136]:
array([ 0.        , 0.90909091, 1.81818182, 2.72727273,
        3.63636364, 4.54545455, 5.45454545, 6.36363636,
        7.27272727, 8.18181818, 9.09090909, 10.        ])
```

In financial analytics one often needs (pseudo-)random numbers. NumPy provides many functions to sample from different distributions. Those needed in this book are the standard normal distribution and the Poisson distribution. The respective functions are found in the sub-library `numpy.random`.

```
In [137]: np.random.standard_normal(10)
Out[137]:
array([ 1.70352821, -1.30223997, -0.16846238, -0.33605234, 0.84842565,
       -0.7012202 ,  1.31232816,  1.34394536, -0.08358828, 1.53690444])

In [138]: np.random.poisson(0.5, 10)
Out[138]: array([0, 1, 0, 1, 0, 0, 1, 2, 2, 0])
```

Let us generate an `ndarray` object which is a bit more "realistic" and which we work with in what follows:

```
In [139]: np.random.seed(1000)   # fix the rng seed value

In [140]: data = np.random.standard_normal((5, 100))
```

Although this is a slightly larger array one cannot expect that the 500 numbers are indeed standard normally distributed in the sense that the first moment is 0 and the second moment is 1. However, at least this can be easily corrected.

```
In [141]: data.mean()  # should be 0.0
Out[141]: -0.02714981205311327

In [142]: data.std()  # should be 1.0
Out[142]: 1.0016799134894265
```

The correction is called moment matching and can be implemented with NumPy by vectorized operations.

```
In [143]: data = data - data.mean()  # correction for the 1st moment

In [144]: data = data / data.std()  # correction for the 2nd moment

In [145]: data.mean()  # now really close to 0.0
Out[145]: 7.105427357601002e-18

In [146]: data.std()  # now really close to 1.0
Out[146]: 1.0
```

2.3 matplotlib

At this stage, it makes sense to introduce plotting with matplotlib, the plotting work horse in the Python ecosystem. We use matplotlib (see http://matplotlib.org) with the settings of another library throughout, namely seaborn (see http://stanford.edu/~mwaskom/software/seaborn/) – this results in a more modern plotting style.

```
In [147]: import matplotlib.pyplot as plt  # import main plotting library

In [148]: import seaborn as sns; sns.set()  # set seaborn standards

In [149]: import matplotlib

# set font to serif
In [150]: matplotlib.rcParams['font.family'] = 'serif'
```

A standard plot is the *line plot*. The result of the code below is shown as Figure 2.1.

```
In [151]: plt.figure(figsize=(10, 6));  # size of figure

In [152]: plt.plot(data.cumsum());  # cumulative sum over all elements
```

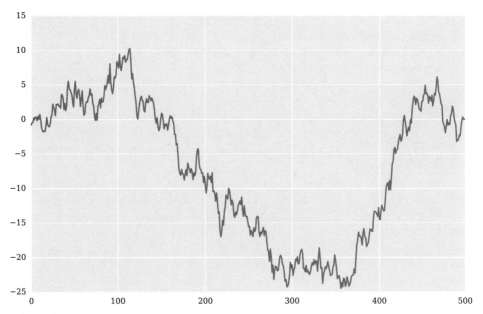

FIGURE 2.1　Standard line plot with matplotlib.

Multiple lines plots are also easy to generate (see Figure 2.2). The operator T stands for the transpose of the ndarray object ("matrix").

```
In [153]: plt.figure(figsize=(10, 6));  # size of figure

# plotting five cumulative sums as lines
In [154]: plt.plot(data.T.cumsum(axis=0), label='line');

In [155]: plt.legend(loc=0);  # legend in best location

In [156]: plt.xlabel('data point');  # x axis label

In [157]: plt.ylabel('value');  # y axis label

In [158]: plt.title('random series');  # figure title
```

Other important plotting types are *histograms* and *bar charts*. A histogram for all 500 values of the data object is shown as Figure 2.3. In the code, the flatten() method is used to generate a one-dimensional array from the two-dimensional one.

```
In [159]: plt.figure(figsize=(10, 6));  # size of figure

In [160]: plt.hist(data.flatten(), bins=30);
```

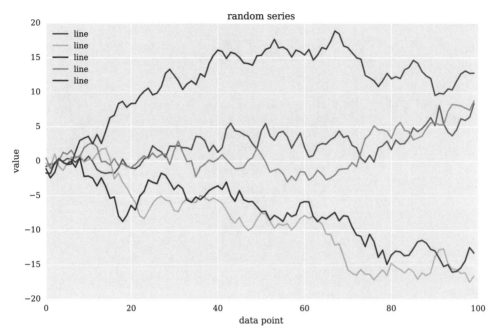

FIGURE 2.2   Multiple lines plot with matplotlib.

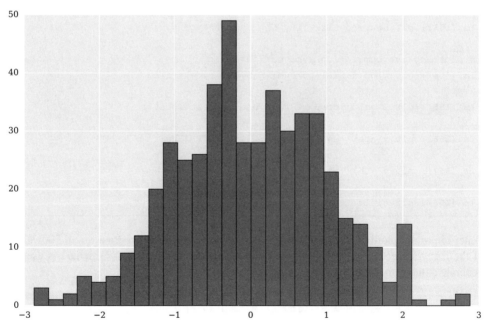

FIGURE 2.3   Histrogram with matplotlib.

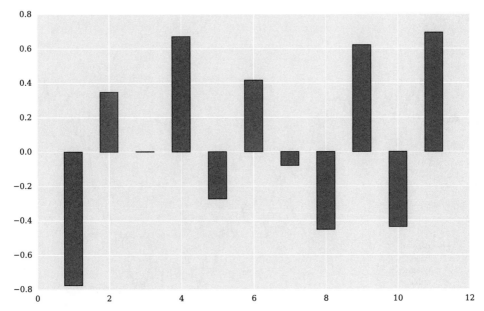

FIGURE 2.4   Bar chart with matplotlib.

Finally, consider the bar chart presented in Figure 2.4.

```
In [161]: plt.figure(figsize=(10, 6));   # size of figure

In [162]: plt.bar(np.arange(1, 12) - 0.25, data[0, :11], width=0.5);
```

To conclude the introduction to matplotlib consider the ordinary least squares (OLS) regression of the sample data displayed in Figure 2.1. NumPy provides with the two functions `polyfit()` and `polyval()` convenience functions to implement OLS based on simple monomials i.e. $x, x^2, x^3, ..., x^n$. For illustration purposes consider linear, quadratic and cubic OLS.

```
In [163]: x = np.arange(len(data.cumsum()))

In [164]: y = data.cumsum()

In [165]: rg1 = np.polyfit(x, y, 1)   # linear OLS

In [166]: rg2 = np.polyfit(x, y, 2)   # quadratic OLS

In [167]: rg3 = np.polyfit(x, y, 3)   # cubic OLS
```

Figure 2.5 illustrates the regression results graphically.

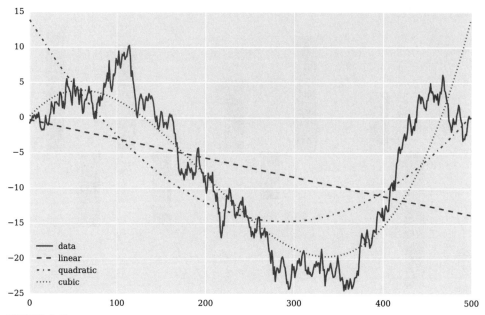

FIGURE 2.5 Linear, quadratic and cubic regression.

```
In [168]: plt.figure(figsize=(10, 6));

In [169]: plt.plot(x, y, 'r', label='data');

In [170]: plt.plot(x, np.polyval(rg1, x), 'b--', label='linear');

In [171]: plt.plot(x, np.polyval(rg2, x), 'b-.', label='quadratic');

In [172]: plt.plot(x, np.polyval(rg3, x), 'b:', label='cubic');

In [173]: plt.legend(loc=0);
```

2.4 pandas

pandas is a library with which you can manage and operate on time series data and other tabular data structures. It allows implementation of even sophisticated data analytics tasks on larger data sets. While the focus lies on in-memory operations, there are also multiple options for out-of-memory (on-disk) operations. Although pandas provides a number of different data structures, embodied by powerful classes, the structure most often used is the DataFrame class which resembles a typical table of a relational (SQL) database and is used to manage, for instance, financial time series data. This is what we focus on in this section.

2.4.1 pandas DataFrame class

In its most basic form, a `DataFrame` object is characterized by an index, column names and tabular data. To make this more specific, consider the following sample data set:

```
In [174]: np.random.seed(1000)

In [175]: a = np.random.standard_normal(( 10, 3)).cumsum(axis=0)
```

Also, consider the following dates which shall be our index:

```
In [176]: index = ['2016-1-31', '2016-2-28', '2016-3-31',
   .....:           '2016-4-30', '2016-5-31', '2016-6-30',
   .....:           '2016-7-31', '2016-8-31', '2016-9-30',
   .....:           '2016-10-31']
   .....:
```

Finally, the column names:

```
In [177]: columns = ['no1', 'no2', 'no3']
```

The instantiation of a `DataFrame` object then looks as follows:

```
In [178]: import pandas as pd

In [179]: df = pd.DataFrame(a, index=index, columns=columns)
```

A look at the new object reveals its resemblance with a typical table from a relational database (or e.g. an Excel spreadsheet).

```
In [180]: df
Out[180]:
                  no1        no2        no3
2016-1-31   -0.804458   0.320932  -0.025483
2016-2-28   -0.160134   0.020135   0.363992
2016-3-31   -0.267572  -0.459848   0.959027
2016-4-30   -0.732239   0.207433   0.152912
2016-5-31   -1.928309  -0.198527  -0.029466
2016-6-30   -1.825116  -0.336949   0.676227
2016-7-31   -0.553321  -1.323696   0.341391
2016-8-31   -0.652803  -0.916504   1.260779
2016-9-30   -0.340685   0.616657   0.710605
2016-10-31  -0.723832  -0.206284   2.310688
```

DataFrame objects have built in a multitude of basic, advanced and convenience methods, a few of which are illustrated without much commentary below.

```
In [181]: df.head()   # first five rows
Out[181]:
                 no1        no2        no3
2016-1-31  -0.804458   0.320932  -0.025483
2016-2-28  -0.160134   0.020135   0.363992
2016-3-31  -0.267572  -0.459848   0.959027
2016-4-30  -0.732239   0.207433   0.152912
2016-5-31  -1.928309  -0.198527  -0.029466


In [182]: df.tail()   # last five rows
Out[182]:
                  no1        no2       no3
2016-6-30   -1.825116  -0.336949  0.676227
2016-7-31   -0.553321  -1.323696  0.341391
2016-8-31   -0.652803  -0.916504  1.260779
2016-9-30   -0.340685   0.616657  0.710605
2016-10-31  -0.723832  -0.206284  2.310688


In [183]: df.index   # index object
Out[183]:
Index([u'2016-1-31', u'2016-2-28', u'2016-3-31', u'2016-4-30', u'2016-5-31',
       u'2016-6-30', u'2016-7-31', u'2016-8-31', u'2016-9-30', u'2016-10-31'],
      dtype='object')


In [184]: df.columns   # column names
Out[184]: Index([u'no1', u'no2', u'no3'], dtype='object')


In [185]: df.info()   # meta information
<class 'pandas.core.frame.DataFrame'>
Index: 10 entries, 2016-1-31 to 2016-10-31
Data columns (total 3 columns):
no1     10 non-null float64
no2     10 non-null float64
no3     10 non-null float64
dtypes: float64(3)
memory usage: 320.0+ bytes


In [186]: df.describe()   # typical statistics
Out[186]:
                 no1         no2         no3
count      10.000000   10.000000   10.000000
mean       -0.798847   -0.227665    0.672067
std         0.607430    0.578071    0.712430
min        -1.928309   -1.323696   -0.029466
```

```
25%            -0.786404    -0.429123    0.200031
50%            -0.688317    -0.202406    0.520109
75%            -0.393844     0.160609    0.896922
max            -0.160134     0.616657    2.310688
```

Numerical operations are in general as easy with DataFrame objects as with NumPy ndar-ray objects. They are also quite close in terms of syntax.

```
In [187]: df * 2   # vectorized multiplication
Out[187]:
                  no1          no2          no3
2016-1-31   -1.608917     0.641863    -0.050966
2016-2-28   -0.320269     0.040270     0.727983
2016-3-31   -0.535144    -0.919696     1.918054
2016-4-30   -1.464479     0.414866     0.305823
2016-5-31   -3.856618    -0.397054    -0.058932
2016-6-30   -3.650232    -0.673898     1.352453
2016-7-31   -1.106642    -2.647393     0.682782
2016-8-31   -1.305605    -1.833009     2.521557
2016-9-30   -0.681369     1.233314     1.421210
2016-10-31  -1.447664    -0.412568     4.621376

In [188]: df.std()   # standard deviation by column
Out[188]:
no1      0.607430
no2      0.578071
no3      0.712430
dtype: float64

In [189]: df.mean(axis=1)   # mean by index value
Out[189]:
2016-1-31    -0.169670
2016-2-28     0.074664
2016-3-31     0.077202
2016-4-30    -0.123965
2016-5-31    -0.718767
2016-6-30    -0.495280
2016-7-31    -0.511875
2016-8-31    -0.102843
2016-9-30     0.328859
2016-10-31    0.460191
dtype: float64

In [190]: np.mean(df)   # mean via universal function
Out[190]:
```

```
no1    -0.798847
no2    -0.227665
no3     0.672067
dtype: float64
```

Pieces of data can be looked up via different mechanisms.

```
In [191]: df['no2']   # 2nd column
Out[191]:
2016-1-31      0.320932
2016-2-28      0.020135
2016-3-31     -0.459848
2016-4-30      0.207433
2016-5-31     -0.198527
2016-6-30     -0.336949
2016-7-31     -1.323696
2016-8-31     -0.916504
2016-9-30      0.616657
2016-10-31    -0.206284
Name: no2, dtype: float64

In [192]: df.iloc[0]   # 1st row
Out[192]:
no1    -0.804458
no2     0.320932
no3    -0.025483
Name: 2016-1-31, dtype: float64

In [193]: df.iloc[2:4]   # 3rd & 4th row
Out[193]:
                 no1        no2       no3
2016-3-31  -0.267572  -0.459848  0.959027
2016-4-30  -0.732239   0.207433  0.152912

In [194]: df.iloc[2:4, 1]   # 3rd & 4th row, 2nd column
Out[194]:
2016-3-31    -0.459848
2016-4-30     0.207433
Name: no2, dtype: float64

In [195]: df.no3.iloc[3:7]   # dot look-up for column name
Out[195]:
2016-4-30     0.152912
2016-5-31    -0.029466
2016-6-30     0.676227
2016-7-31     0.341391
Name: no3, dtype: float64
```

```
In [196]: df.loc['2016-3-31']   # row given index value
Out[196]:
no1    -0.267572
no2    -0.459848
no3     0.959027
Name: 2016-3-31, dtype: float64

In [197]: df.loc['2016-5-31', 'no3']   # single data point
Out[197]: -0.02946577492329111

In [198]: df['no1'] + 3 * df['no3']   # vectorized arithmetic operations
Out[198]:
2016-1-31     -0.880907
2016-2-28      0.931841
2016-3-31      2.609510
2016-4-30     -0.273505
2016-5-31     -2.016706
2016-6-30      0.203564
2016-7-31      0.470852
2016-8-31      3.129533
2016-9-30      1.791130
2016-10-31     6.208233
dtype: float64
```

Data selections based on Boolean operations are also a strength of pandas.

```
In [199]: df['no3'] > 0.5
Out[199]:
2016-1-31      False
2016-2-28      False
2016-3-31       True
2016-4-30      False
2016-5-31      False
2016-6-30       True
2016-7-31      False
2016-8-31       True
2016-9-30       True
2016-10-31      True
Name: no3, dtype: bool

In [200]: df[df['no3'] > 0.5]
Out[200]:
                  no1        no2        no3
2016-3-31   -0.267572  -0.459848   0.959027
2016-6-30   -1.825116  -0.336949   0.676227
```

```
2016-8-31   -0.652803   -0.916504   1.260779
2016-9-30   -0.340685    0.616657   0.710605
2016-10-31  -0.723832   -0.206284   2.310688


In [201]: df[(df.no3 > 0.5) & (df.no2 > 0.25)]
Out[201]:
                   no1          no2          no3
2016-9-30     -0.340685    0.616657    0.710605
2016-10-31    -0.723832   -0.206284    2.310688


In [202]: df[df.index > '2016-4-30']
Out[202]:
                 no1          no2          no3
2016-5-31  -1.928309   -0.198527   -0.029466
2016-6-30  -1.825116   -0.336949    0.676227
2016-7-31  -0.553321   -1.323696    0.341391
2016-8-31  -0.652803   -0.916504    1.260779
2016-9-30  -0.340685    0.616657    0.710605
```

pandas is well integrated with the matplotlib library which makes it really convenient to plot data stored in `DataFrame` objects. In general, a single method call does the trick (see Figure 2.6).

```
In [203]: df.plot(figsize=(10, 6));
```

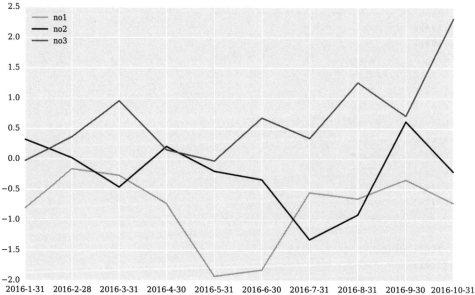

FIGURE 2.6   Line plot from pandas DataFrame.

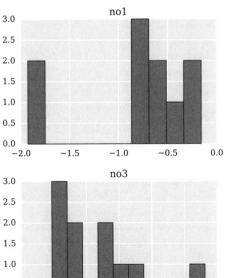
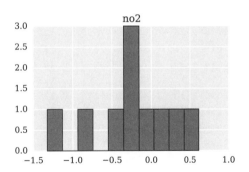

FIGURE 2.7   Histograms from pandas DataFrame.

Histograms are also generated this way (see Figure 2.7). In both cases, pandas takes care of the handling of the single columns and automatically generates single lines (with respective legend entries) and generates respective sub-plots with three different histograms.

```
In [204]: df.hist(figsize=(10, 6));
```

2.4.2 Input-Output Operations

Another strength of pandas is the exporting and importing of data to and from diverse data storage formats. Consider the case of comma separated value (CSV) files.

```
In [205]: df.to_csv('data.csv')   # exports to CSV file
```

Let us have a look at the file just saved with basic Python functionality.

```
In [206]: with open('data.csv') as f:  # open file
     .....:     for l in f.readlines():  # iterate over all lines
     .....:         print l,  # print line
     .....:
,no1,no2,no3
```

```
2016-1-31,-0.804458303525,0.32093154709,-0.0254828804721
2016-2-28,-0.160134475098,0.0201348743028,0.363991673815
2016-3-31,-0.267571776789,-0.459848201058,0.959027175892
2016-4-30,-0.732239302984,0.20743310593,0.152911565449
2016-5-31,-1.92830913682,-0.19852705543,-0.0294657749233
2016-6-30,-1.82511624278,-0.336949044016,0.676226600036
2016-7-31,-0.553320966375,-1.32369637281,0.341391146824
2016-8-31,-0.652802664384,-0.916504272472,1.26077868603
2016-9-30,-0.340684654318,0.616656792886,0.710604821
2016-10-31,-0.723832065202,-0.206284170553,2.31068818906
```

Reading data from such files is also straightforward.

```
In [207]: from_csv = pd.read_csv('data.csv',  # filename
     .....:                          index_col=0,   # index column
     .....:                          parse_dates=True)   # date index
     .....:


In [208]: from_csv.head()
Out[208]:
                   no1        no2        no3
2016-01-31 -0.804458   0.320932 -0.025483
2016-02-28 -0.160134   0.020135  0.363992
2016-03-31 -0.267572 -0.459848  0.959027
2016-04-30 -0.732239   0.207433  0.152912
2016-05-31 -1.928309 -0.198527 -0.029466
```

However, in general you would store DataFrame objects on disk in more efficient binary formats like HDF5 (see http://hdfgroup.org). pandas in this case wraps the functionality of the PyTables library (see http://pytables.org). The constructor function to be used is HDFStore().

```
In [209]: h5 = pd.HDFStore('data.h5', 'w')  # open for writing


In [210]: h5['df'] = df  # write object to database


In [211]: h5
Out[211]:
<class 'pandas.io.pytables.HDFStore'>
File path: data.h5
/df                  frame          (shape->[10,3])
```

Data retrieval is as simple as writing.

```
In [212]: from_h5 = h5['df']   # reading from database

In [213]: h5.close()   # closing the database

In [214]: from_h5.tail()
Out[214]:
                    no1         no2         no3
2016-6-30   -1.825116  -0.336949   0.676227
2016-7-31   -0.553321  -1.323696   0.341391
2016-8-31   -0.652803  -0.916504   1.260779
2016-9-30   -0.340685   0.616657   0.710605
2016-10-31  -0.723832  -0.206284   2.310688


In [215]: !rm data.csv data.h5   # remove the objects from disk
```

2.4.3 Financial Analytics Examples

When it comes to financial data, there are useful data retrieval functions available that wrap both the Yahoo! Finance and Google Finance financial data APIs. The following code reads historical daily data for the S&P 500 index and the VIX volatility index:

```
In [216]: from pandas_datareader import data as web

In [217]: spx = web.DataReader('^GSPC', data_source='yahoo',
                                                end='2015-12-31')

In [218]: vix = web.DataReader('^VIX', data_source='yahoo',
                                                end='2015-12-31')

In [219]: spx.info()
<class 'pandas.core.frame.DataFrame'>
DatetimeIndex: 1510 entries, 2010-01-04 to 2015-12-31
Data columns (total 6 columns):
Open          1510 non-null float64
High          1510 non-null float64
Low           1510 non-null float64
Close         1510 non-null float64
Volume        1510 non-null int64
Adj Close     1510 non-null float64
dtypes: float64(5), int64(1)
memory usage: 82.6 KB

In [220]: vix.info()
<class 'pandas.core.frame.DataFrame'>
DatetimeIndex: 1510 entries, 2010-01-04 to 2015-12-31
```

```
Data columns (total 6 columns):
Open          1510 non-null float64
High          1510 non-null float64
Low           1510 non-null float64
Close         1510 non-null float64
Volume        1510 non-null int64
Adj Close     1510 non-null float64
dtypes: float64(5), int64(1)
memory usage: 82.6 KB
```

Let us combine the respective `Close` columns into a single `DataFrame` object. There are multiple ways to accomplish this goal.

```
# construction via join
In [221]: spxvix = pd.DataFrame(spx['Close']).join(vix['Close'] ,
     .....:                             lsuffix='SPX', rsuffix='VIX')
     .....:

In [222]: spxvix.info()
<class 'pandas.core.frame.DataFrame'>
DatetimeIndex: 1510 entries, 2010-01-04 to 2015-12-31
Data columns (total 2 columns):
CloseSPX    1510 non-null float64
CloseVIX    1510 non-null float64
dtypes: float64(2)
memory usage: 35.4 KB


# construction via merge
In [223]: spxvix = pd.merge(pd.DataFrame(spx['Close']),
     .....:                 pd.DataFrame(vix['Close']),
     .....:                 left_index=True,   # merge on left index
     .....:                 right_index=True,  # merge on right index
     .....:                 suffixes=['SPX', 'VIX'])
     .....:

In [224]: spxvix.info()
<class 'pandas.core.frame.DataFrame'>
DatetimeIndex: 1510 entries, 2010-01-04 to 2015-12-31
Data columns (total 2 columns):
CloseSPX    1510 non-null float64
CloseVIX    1510 non-null float64
dtypes: float64(2)
memory usage: 35.4 KB
```

In a case like this, the approach via `dictionary` objects might be the best and most intuitive way.

```
# construction via dictionary object
In [225]: spxvix = pd.DataFrame({'SPX': spx['Close'] ,
     .....:                      'VIX': vix['Close'] } ,
     .....:                      index=spx.index)
     .....:

In [226]: spxvix.info()
<class 'pandas.core.frame.DataFrame'>
DatetimeIndex: 1510 entries, 2010-01-04 to 2015-12-31
Data columns (total 2 columns):
SPX    1510 non-null float64
VIX    1510 non-null float64
dtypes: float64(2)
memory usage: 35.4 KB
```

Having available the merged data in a single object makes visual analysis straightforward (see Figure 2.8).

```
In [227]: spxvix.plot(figsize=(10, 6), subplots=True, color='b');
```

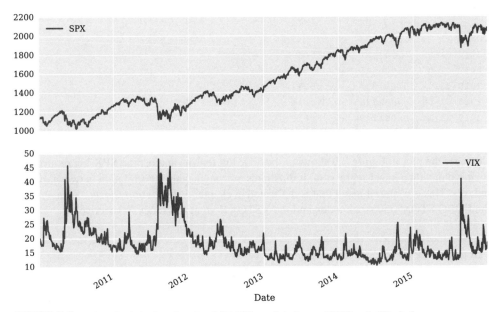

FIGURE 2.8 Historical closing data for S&P 500 stock index and VIX volatility index.

pandas also allows vectorized operations on whole `DataFrame` objects. The following code calculates the log returns over the two columns of the `spxvix` object simultaneously in vectorized fashion. The `shift()` method shifts the data set by the number of index values as provided (in this particular case by one trading day).

```
In [228]: rets = np.log(spxvix / spxvix.shift(1))

In [229]: rets.head()
Out[229]:
                  SPX          VIX
Date
2010-01-04        NaN          NaN
2010-01-05   0.003111    -0.035038
2010-01-06   0.000545    -0.009868
2010-01-07   0.003993    -0.005233
2010-01-08   0.002878    -0.050024
```

There is one row of log returns missing at the very beginning. This row can be deleted via the `dropna()` method.

```
In [230]: rets = rets.dropna()

In [231]: rets.head()
Out[231]:
                  SPX          VIX
Date
2010-01-05   0.003111    -0.035038
2010-01-06   0.000545    -0.009868
2010-01-07   0.003993    -0.005233
2010-01-08   0.002878    -0.050024
2010-01-11   0.001745    -0.032514
```

Consider the plot in Figure 2.9 showing the VIX log returns against the SPX log returns in a scatter plot with a linear regression. It illustrates a strong negative correlation between the two indexes. This is a central result that is replicated in chapter 4, *Data Analysis and Strategies* for the EURO STOXX 50 stock index and the VSTOXX volatility index, respectively.

```
In [232]: rets.plot(kind='scatter', x='SPX', y='VIX',
     .....:                 style='.', figsize=(10, 6));
     .....:
In [233]: rg = np.polyfit(rets['SPX'], rets['VIX'], 1)
In [234]: plt.plot(rets['SPX'], np.polyval(rg, rets['SPX']), 'r.-');
```

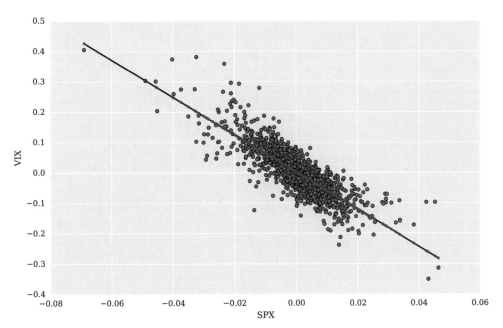

FIGURE 2.9   Daily log returns for S&P 500 stock index and VIX volatility index and regression line.

Having financial time series data stored in a pandas `DataFrame` object makes the calculation of typical statistics straightforward.

```
In [235]: ret = rets.mean() * 252   # annualized return

In [236]: ret
Out[236]:
SPX     0.098532
VIX    -0.015992
dtype: float64

In [237]: vol = rets.std() * math.sqrt(252)   # annualized volatility

In [238]: vol
Out[238]:
SPX     0.159335
VIX     1.185408
dtype: float64

In [239]: (ret - 0.01) / vol   # Sharpe ratio with rf = 0.01
Out[239]:
SPX     0.555635
VIX    -0.021926
dtype:  float64
```

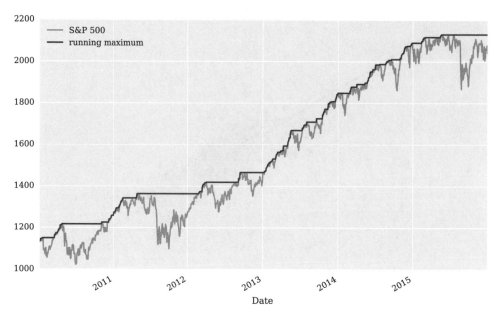

FIGURE 2.10   S&P 500 stock index and running maximum value.

The *maximum drawdown*, which we only calculate for the S&P 500 index, is a bit more involved. For its calculation, we use the cummax() method which records the running, historical maximum of the time series up to a certain date. Consider the plot in Figure 2.10 which shows the S&P 500 index and the running maximum.

```
In [240]: plt.figure(figsize=(10, 6));

In [241]: spxvix['SPX'].plot(label='S&P 500');

In [242]: spxvix['SPX'].cummax().plot(label='running maximum');

In [243]: plt.legend(loc=0);
```

The maximum drawdown is the largest difference between the running maximum and the current index level – in our particular case it is 264.

```
In [244]: adrawdown = spxvix['SPX'].cummax() - spxvix['SPX']

In [245]: adrawdown.max()
Out[245]: 264.38000499999998
```

The relative maximum drawdown might sometimes be slightly more meaningful. Here it is a drawdown of about 20%.

```
In [246]: rdrawdown = (spxvix['SPX'].cummax() - spxvix['SPX']) /
                                        spxvix['SPX'].cummax()

In [247]: rdrawdown.max()
Out[247]: 0.19388242085950988
```

The longest drawdown period is calculated as follows. The code below selects all those data points where the drawdown is zero. It then calculates the difference between two consecutive index values (i.e. trading dates) for which the drawdown is zero and takes the maximum value. Given the data set we are analyzing, the longest drawdown period is 301 days.

```
In [248]: temp = adrawdown[adrawdown == 0]

In [249]: periods_spx = (temp.index[1:].to_pydatetime()
     .....:                 - temp.index[:-1].to_pydatetime())
     .....:

In [250]: periods_spx[50:60]   # some selected data points
Out[250]:
array([datetime.timedelta(67), datetime.timedelta(1),
       datetime.timedelta(1), datetime.timedelta(1),
       datetime.timedelta(301), datetime.timedelta(3),
       datetime.timedelta(1), datetime.timedelta(2),
       datetime.timedelta(12), datetime.timedelta(2)], dtype=object)

In [251]: max(periods_spx)
Out[251]: datetime.timedelta(301)
```

See Appendix C of Hilpisch (2014) for the handling of date-time information with Python, NumPy and pandas.

2.5 CONCLUSIONS

This chapter introduces basic data types and structures as well as certain Python idioms needed for analyses in later chapters of the book. In addition, NumPy and the `ndarray` class are introduced which allow the efficient handling of and operating on (numerical) data stored as arrays. Some basic visualization techniques using the matplotlib library are also introduced. However, working with pandas and its powerful `DataFrame` class for tabular and time series data makes plotting a bit more convenient – in general only a single method call is needed. Using pandas and the capabilities of the `DataFrame` class, the chapter also illustrates by means of some basic financial examples how to implement typical interactive financial analytics tasks.

## CHAPTER 3

Model-Free Replication of Variance

3.1 INTRODUCTION

Although volatility derivatives, variance swaps and futures are considered second generation derivatives (since they are defined on volatility and variance directly), some of the most elegant and robust results of quantitative finance apply to these kinds of derivatives. In particular, it is possible to statically replicate realized variance without using any kind of specific model. This, for example, does not apply to most other important concepts in option pricing and trading, such as implied volatility or delta hedging of options.

This chapter mainly covers the following topics:

- **spanning with options**: Breeden and Litzenberger (1978) showed in the 1970s how to replicate state-contingent payoffs (satisfying certain conditions) by using positions in options
- **log contracts**: an important piece in the replication of (realized) variance and the valuation of variance swaps is the so-called log contract
- **static replication of variance**: this relates to the central result of replicating realized variance by a log contract as well as static positions in options
- **derivatives with constant dollar gamma**: in the replication and valuation of variance swaps, constant dollar gamma positions play a central role
- **practical replication of variance swaps**: using the theoretical insights and results, the chapter also illustrates the generation of constant dollar gamma positions and thus the practical replication of variance swaps based on numerical examples
- **VSTOXX as volatility index**: using the central result, the final section in this chapter explains and justifies the definition of the VSTOXX volatility index (and the VIX index to this end).

The theoretical parts of this chapter roughly follow the lines of chapter 11 of Gatheral (2006). Since they are of importance for both volatility and variance derivatives we have placed them up front and present them in a connected fashion.

3.2 SPANNING WITH OPTIONS

Breeden and Litzenberger (1978) use option prices to derive prices for *elementary securities*, i.e. securities that pay exactly 1 unit of currency at a certain future date given a certain state of the economy. In economics, *Arrow-Debreu security* is also a common term. The prices of elementary securities are generally called *state prices*. Having state prices available, every other contingent claim can be priced by multiplying the contingent claim's state-dependent payoff by the respective state prices.

Let $t \geq 0$ denote the current date and $T > t$ the future date of interest (e.g. maturity of a derivative instrument). For simplicity, states of the economy should be distinguished by the level of a stock index S only. Let $p(S_T, T; S_t, t)$ denote the *state price* given a stock index level of S_t at t for a stock index level S_T at T, then:

$$p(S_T, T; S_t, t) = \left.\frac{\partial^2 P(S_t, K, T)}{\partial K^2}\right|_{S_T=K} = \left.\frac{\partial^2 C(S_t, K, T)}{\partial K^2}\right|_{S_T=K}$$

Here, P and C represent prices (given by some pricing formula) of European put and call options, respectively. Therefore, a state price can be derived by taking the second partial derivative of option pricing formula with respect to the strike of the option. Equipped with these state prices, the value of a state-contingent claim with payoff function $g(S_T)$ is

$$\mathbf{E}_t(g(S_T)|S_t) = \int_0^\infty g(K)p(K, T; S_t, t)dK$$

$$= \int_0^F g(K)\frac{\partial^2 P(S_t, K, T)}{\partial K^2}dK + \int_F^\infty g(K)\frac{\partial^2 C(S_t, K, T)}{\partial K^2}dK$$

with F being the T-forward price of the index at t (see Breeden and Litzenberger (1978)).

We now apply integration by parts. With $u = u(x), v = v(x), du = u'(x)dx, dv = v'(x)dx$, integration by parts states that

$$\int u(x)v'(x)dx = u(x)v(x) - \int u'(x)v(x)dx$$

Therefore, we get

$$\mathbf{E}_t(g(S_T)|S_t) = g(K)\frac{\partial P(S_t, K, T)}{\partial K}\bigg|_0^F - \int_0^F g'(K)\frac{\partial P(S_t, K, T)}{\partial K}dK$$

$$+ g(K)\frac{\partial C(S_t, K, T)}{\partial K}\bigg|_F^\infty - \int_F^\infty g'(K)\frac{\partial C(S_t, K, T)}{\partial K}dK$$

$$= g(F) - \int_0^F g'(K)\frac{\partial P(S_t, K, T)}{\partial K}dK - \int_F^\infty g'(K)\frac{\partial C(S_t, K, T)}{\partial K}dK$$

Applying integration by parts once again yields

$$\begin{aligned}
\mathbf{E}_t(g(S_T)|S_t) &= g(F) - g'(K)P(S_t, K, T)\big|_0^F + \int_0^F g''(K)P(S_t, K, T)dK \\
&\quad - g'(K)C(S_t, K, T)\big|_F^\infty + \int_F^\infty g''(K)C(S_t, K, T)dK \\
&= g(F) + \int_0^F g''(K)P(S_t, K, T)dK + \int_F^\infty g''(K)C(S_t, K, T)dK
\end{aligned}$$

As is evident from this last equation, in this setting any twice continuously differentiable payoff g due at T can be replicated by infinite strips of European put and call options maturing at T. In other words, these options span the space of twice continuously differentiable payoffs.

3.3 LOG CONTRACTS

So-called *log contracts* are a kind of derivative instrument that plays an important role in the valuation of variance swaps. Recall that a long position in a variance contract pays at maturity the difference between the realized variance over the life time of the swap and an up-front fixed variance strike.

Consider the payoff $g(S_T) = \log \frac{S_T}{F} = \log S_T - \log F$. Then

$$g'(S_T) = \frac{1}{S_T}$$
$$g''(S_T) = -\frac{1}{S_T^2}$$

Valuing this contract by making use of the option spanning approach yields

$$\begin{aligned}
\mathbf{E}\left(\log \frac{S_T}{F}\bigg|S_t\right) &= \log \frac{F}{F} + \int_0^F -\frac{1}{K^2}P(S_t, K, T)dK + \int_F^\infty -\frac{1}{K^2}C(S_t, K, T)dK \\
&= -\int_0^F P(S_t, K, T)\frac{dK}{K^2} - \int_F^\infty C(S_t, K, T)\frac{dK}{K^2}
\end{aligned}$$

As a consequence, the log contract can be replicated by (infinite strips of) European put and call options on the underlying. Every option is weighted by the square of the strike.

3.4 STATIC REPLICATION OF REALIZED VARIANCE AND VARIANCE SWAPS

Assume for simplicity zero short rates such that $F = S_t$. For $t = 0$, one has

$$\begin{aligned}
\log \frac{S_T}{F} &= \log \frac{S_T}{S_0} \\
&= \int_0^T d\log(S_t) \\
&= \int_0^T \frac{dS_t}{S_t} - \int_0^T \frac{\sigma^2(S_t)}{2}dt
\end{aligned}$$

Compare this result with equation 1.1. Such a comparison further illustrates the connection between the (discrete) delta hedging of an option and (the valuation of) variance swaps. Above, we use the fact that the *total return* over the interval $[0, T]$ equals the integral over the marginal returns of S for the same time interval. The second term in the last equation results from the application of Itô's lemma. This term is equal to half of the total variance of S over the time interval $[0, T]$. Taking the risk-neutral expectation of that expression gives

$$\mathbf{E}\left(\int_0^T \sigma^2(S_t)dt \right) = -2\mathbf{E}\left(\log \frac{S_T}{F} \right)$$

Combining the results with regard to the log contract replication and valuation with this last insight shows that realized variance is given in a model-free manner through the prices of European put and call options. This is due to the fact that realized variance can be replicated by the use of a log contract.

3.5 CONSTANT DOLLAR GAMMA DERIVATIVES AND PORTFOLIOS

Above, we establish the replication of realized variance by the log contract. The log contract has, as a defining characteristic, a *constant dollar gamma*. The *gamma* of a derivative defined on some underlying S with value $f_t(S_t)$ is defined as

$$\Gamma_t = \frac{\partial^2 f_t}{\partial S_t^2}$$

i.e. the second partial derivative of the pricing function with respect to the value of the underlying (assuming that the pricing function is indeed twice continuously differentiable).

Its *dollar gamma* is then defined by the product of the gamma and the square of the value of the underlying (sometimes the factor 0.5 is added):

$$\Gamma_t^{\$} \equiv \Gamma_t \cdot S_t^2$$

Omitting the time index, a constant dollar gamma implies, for some fixed value a, a gamma of

$$\Gamma^{\$} = \Gamma \cdot S^2 \equiv a$$
$$\Leftrightarrow \Gamma = \frac{a}{S^2}$$

We therefore have

$$\frac{\partial^2 f}{\partial S^2} = \frac{a}{S^2}$$

This partial differential equation has a solution of the form

$$f(S) = a \log(S) + bS + c$$

Indeed, the log contract fits trivially into the general solution by setting $a = 1, b = 0, c = 0$, i.e.

$$f(S) = \log(S)$$

illustrating its importance.

With $\hat{\sigma}^2$ being the realized variance and σ_K^2 being the fixed variance strike, a long position in a *variance swap* (with notional of 1 currency unit), pays at expiry

$$\hat{\sigma}^2 - \sigma_K^2$$

With this payoff, we get a replicating portfolio of

$$f_t(S_t) = 2\log(S_t) + e^{-r(T-t)}\sigma_K^2$$

i.e. $a = 2, b = 0, c = e^{-r(T-t)}\sigma_K^2$. A variance swap therefore also has a constant dollar gamma. This insight is used in the next section.

3.6 PRACTICAL REPLICATION OF REALIZED VARIANCE

Consider the Black-Scholes-Merton (1973) model economy (no dividends) with the present value of a European call option given by

$$C(S, K, t, T, r, \sigma) = S_t \cdot N(d_1) - e^{-r(T-t)} \cdot K \cdot N(d_2)$$

$$N(d) = \frac{1}{\sqrt{2\pi}} \int_{-\infty}^{d} e^{-\frac{1}{2}x^2} dx$$

$$d_1 = \frac{\log\frac{S_t}{K} + \left(r + \frac{\sigma^2}{2}\right)(T-t)}{\sigma\sqrt{T-t}}$$

$$d_2 = \frac{\log\frac{S_t}{K} + \left(r - \frac{\sigma^2}{2}\right)(T-t)}{\sigma\sqrt{T-t}}$$

Here, S_t is the index level at date t, K is the option strike, T date of maturity (in year fractions), r the constant, risk-less short rate and σ the instantaneous volatility.

The *gamma* of an option in this model is given as follows

$$\Gamma_t = \frac{\partial^2 C_t}{\partial S_t^2} = \frac{N'(d_1)}{S_t\sigma\sqrt{T-t}}$$

with

$$N'(d) = \frac{1}{\sqrt{2\pi}}e^{-\frac{1}{2}x^2}$$

Our aim in this section is to build a portfolio of European call options with a constant dollar gamma, i.e. $\Gamma^{Portfolio} \cdot S_t^2 \equiv a$ for some fixed value a.

The Python function `dollar_gamma` implements the dollar gamma formula for the European call option.

```
In [1]: import math

In [2]: import numpy as np

In [3]: import scipy.stats as scs

In [4]: def dollar_gamma(St, K, t, T, r, sigma):
   ...:     ''' Returns European call option dollar gamma. '''
   ...:     d1 = ((np.log(St / K) + (r + 0.5 * sigma ** 2) * (T - t))
   ...:           / sigma * math.sqrt(T- t))
   ...:     gamma = scs.norm.pdf(d1) / (St * sigma * math.sqrt(T - t))
   ...:     return gamma * St ** 2
   ...:
```

Let us parametrize the financial model for $t = 0$, leaving the values for the initial index level S_0 and for the option strike K undefined for the moment.

```
In [5]: t  =  0.0  # current date in year fractions

In [6]: T  =  1.0  # maturity in year fractions

In [7]: r  =  0.01  # constant risk-less short rate

In [8]: sigma  =  0.2  # instantanous volatility
```

Next, we can calculate the dollar gamma values for different strikes of the European call options over a range, respectively, of initial values for the index level.

```
In [9]: import pandas as pd

In [10]: import matplotlib.pyplot as plt

In [11]: import seaborn as sns; sns.set()

In [12]: import matplotlib

In [13]: matplotlib.rcParams['font.family'] = 'serif'
```

```
In [14]: gammas = pd.DataFrame()

# 300 data points over the range form 0 to 300
In [15]: s_range = np.linspace(0.0001, 300, 300)

In [16]: strike_range = range(25, 226, 25)

In [17]: for K in strike_range:
   ....:         gammas['K=%d' % K] = dollar_gamma(s_range, K, t, T, r, sigma)
   ....:
```

For every strike level gamma values for 300 different initial values of the stock index have been calculated and collected.

```
In [18]: gammas.info()
<class 'pandas.core.frame.DataFrame'>
RangeIndex: 300 entries, 0 to 299
Data columns (total 9 columns):
K=25      300 non-null float64
K=50      300 non-null float64
K=75      300 non-null float64
K=100     300 non-null float64
K=125     300 non-null float64
K=150     300 non-null float64
K=175     300 non-null float64
K=200     300 non-null float64
K=225     300 non-null float64
dtypes: float64(9)
memory usage: 21.2 KB
```

Having the data stored in a pandas `DataFrame` object, the results are easily visualized. From Figure 3.1, you can see that dollar gamma is more pronounced the higher the strike of the option. A doubling of the strike leads to a doubling of the maximum dollar gamma value which is always achieved at the ATM level (see strikes 25, 50, 100, 200).

```
In [19]: gammas.plot(figsize=(10, 5));

In [20]: plt.xlabel('index level');

In [21]: plt.ylabel('dollar gamma');
```

Let us check what happens when we add all dollar gamma values up by simply composing a portfolio in which every option has weight 1 or equal weight.

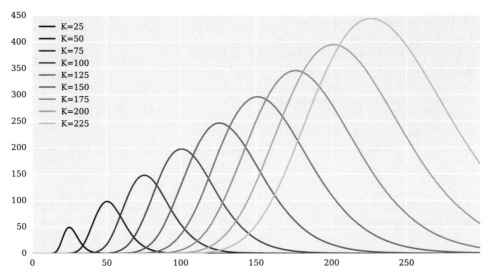

FIGURE 3.1   Dollar gamma values different strikes and 300 different initial stock index values.

```
In [22]: gammas['sum'] = gammas.sum(axis=1)

In [23]: gammas.plot(figsize=(10, 5));

In [24]: plt.xlabel('index level');

In [25]: plt.ylabel('dollar gamma');
```

Obviously, given Figure 3.2 the dollar gamma of the portfolio of equally weighted options is all but constant. Let us try a different weighting scheme that attaches a higher weight to smaller strikes and a lower weight to higher strikes. To this end, we divide all dollar gamma values by the strike K. This brings all maximum dollar gamma values in line (to two in this case).

```
In [26]: gammas_k = pd.DataFrame()

In [27]: for K in strike_range:
    ....:     gammas_k['K=%d' % K] = dollar_gamma(s_range, K, t, T, r, sigma) / K
    ....:

In [28]: gammas_k['sum'] = gammas_k.sum(axis=1)

In [29]: gammas_k.plot(figsize=(10, 5));

In [30]: plt.xlabel('index level');

In [31]: plt.ylabel('$K$ weighted dollar gamma');
```

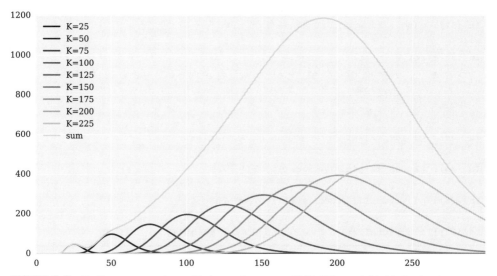

FIGURE 3.2 Dollar gamma values added over the range of 300 different initial index levels.

According to Figure 3.3 this seems to be slightly better in the sense that although we still do not have a constant dollar gamma we do at least have a range where dollar gamma is linear (mainly between strikes of 75 and 150). Therefore, let us weight the dollar gammas by the square of the strike (something we have already seen in the replication result for log contract). In this case the highest dollar gamma values are observed for the lowest strikes and vice versa.

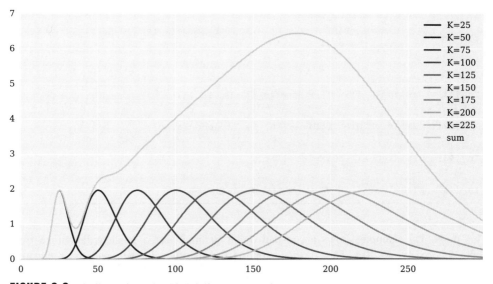

FIGURE 3.3 Strike-weighted, added dollar gamma values.

```
In [32]: gammas_k2 = pd.DataFrame()

In [33]: for K in strike_range:
    ....:      gammas_k2['K=%d' % K] = dollar_gamma(s_range, K, t, T, r,
                  sigma) / K ** 2
    ....:

In [34]: gammas_k2['sum'] = gammas_k2.sum(axis=1)

In [35]: gammas_k2.plot(figsize=(10, 5));

In [36]: plt.xlabel('index level');

In [37]: plt.ylabel('$K^2$ weighted dollar gamma');
```

As Figure 3.4 shows, this approach finally yields a constant dollar gamma value between strikes of 75 and 150 at least. Let us have a final look at a more dense grid of option strikes since the theoretical result is based on infinite strips of options. The graphical output is shown in Figure 3.5.

```
# more dense strike range
In [38]: strike_range = range(10, 350, 5)

In [39]: gammas_k2 = pd.DataFrame()

In [40]: for K in strike_range:
    ....:      gammas_k2['K=%d' % K] = dollar_gamma(s_range, K, t, T, r,
                  sigma) / K ** 2
    ....:

In [41]: gammas_k2 ['sum'] = gammas_k2.sum(axis=1)

In [42]: gammas_k2.plot(figsize=(10, 5), legend=False);

In [43]: plt.xlabel('index level');

In [44]: plt.ylabel('$K^2$ weighted dollar gamma');
```

This numerical example shows a constant dollar gamma over a much wider range from about 25 to beyond 200. This further supports the theoretical result and the replication approach.

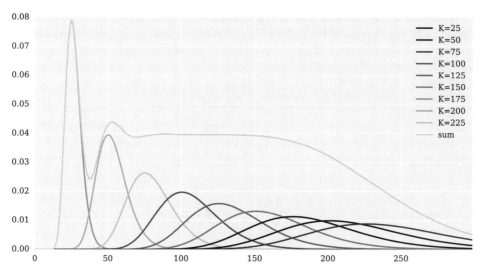

FIGURE 3.4   Squared strike-weighted, added dollar gamma values.

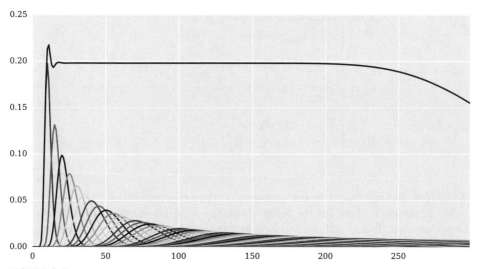

FIGURE 3.5   Strike-weighted, added dollar gamma values.

3.7 VSTOXX AS VOLATILITY INDEX

The VSTOXX volatility index measures the implied total variance across all options written on the EURO STOXX 50 stock index for a given time-to-maturity. Another interpretation is that the VSTOXX gives the fair variance swap rate for a variance swap with the respective maturity. The major index with symbol V2TX has a fixed time-to-maturity of 30 days and is calculated by the interpolation of two sub-indexes. Sub-indexes are calculated for a number of fixed maturity dates.

Assume now the following setting. The discounted, i.e. time t, prices $C_i, i = 0, ..., n$, of a series of European call options on the EURO STOXX 50 stock index are given, with fixed time-to-maturity T and strike prices $K_i, i = 0, ..., n$, as well as the discounted prices $P_i, i = 0, ..., n$, of a series of European put options with the same time-to-maturity and strike prices. Let us further hold $K_i < K_{i+1}$ for all $i \in \{0, ..., n-1\}$.

The value of the VSTOXX (sub-)index V at $t = 0$ is defined by

$$V \equiv 100 \cdot \sqrt{\hat{\sigma}^2}$$

where

$$\hat{\sigma}^2 \equiv \frac{2}{T} \sum_{i=0}^{n} \frac{\Delta K_i}{K_i^2} e^{rT} M_i - \frac{1}{T} \left(\frac{F}{K_*} - 1 \right)^2$$

with

$$\Delta K_i = \begin{cases} K_1 - K_0, & \text{for } i = 0 \\ \frac{K_{i+1} - K_{i-1}}{2}, & \text{for } i = 1, ..., n-1 \\ K_n - K_{n-1}, & \text{for } i = n \end{cases}$$

$$F = K_j + e^{rT} |C_j - P_j|, \text{ where } j = \min_{i \in \{0,...,n\}} \{|C_i - P_i|\}$$

$$K_* = \max_{K_i, i \in \{0,...,n\}} \{K_i < F\}$$

$$M_i = \begin{cases} P_i, & \text{for } K_i < K_* \\ \frac{P_i - C_i}{2}, & \text{for } K_i = K_* \\ C_i, & \text{for } K_i > K_* \end{cases}$$

and r the constant risk-free short rate appropriate for time-to-maturity T.

We are aiming to show that the defining equation for $\hat{\sigma}^2$ is indeed a valid approximation for total variance. To this end, we combine the above equations for the log contract and the total variance to obtain

$$\hat{\sigma}^2 = -2 \cdot \left(-\int_0^F P(S_t, K, T) \frac{dK}{K^2} - \int_F^\infty C(S_t, K, T) \frac{dK}{K^2} \right) \cdot e^{rT}$$

$$\Leftrightarrow \frac{\hat{\sigma}^2 T}{2e^{rT}} = \int_0^F P(S_t, K, T) \frac{dK}{K^2} + \int_F^\infty C(S_t, K, T) \frac{dK}{K^2}$$

$$= \int_0^{K_*} P(S_t, K, T) \frac{dK}{K^2} + \int_{K_*}^\infty C(S_t, K, T) \frac{dK}{K^2}$$

$$+ \int_{K_*}^F [P(S_t, K, T) - C(S_t, K, T)] \frac{dK}{K^2}$$

$$= \int_0^\infty M(S_t, K, T) \frac{dK}{K^2} + \int_{K_*}^F e^{-rT} [K - F] \frac{dK}{K^2}$$

The last term follows from the observation that only the call option is in-the-money, i.e. $e^{-rT}[F - K] > 0$, given the integration boundaries. Then

$$\hat{\sigma}^2 = \frac{2}{T} \int_0^\infty e^{rT} M(S_t, K, T) \frac{dK}{K^2} + \frac{2}{T} \frac{1}{K_*^2} \int_{K_*}^F [K - F] \, dK$$

$$= \frac{2}{T} \int_0^\infty e^{rT} M(S_t, K, T) \frac{dK}{K^2} - \frac{1}{T} \frac{(K_* - F)^2}{K_*^2}$$

Note that

$$\frac{(K_* - F)^2}{K_*^2} = \frac{K_*^2 - 2K_* F + F^2}{K_*^2}$$

$$= \frac{F^2}{K_*^2} - \frac{2F}{K_*} + 1$$

$$= \left(\frac{F}{K_*} - 1 \right)^2$$

A possible discretization for the integral then is

$$\hat{\sigma}^2 \approx \frac{2}{T} \sum_{i=0}^n \frac{\Delta K_i}{K_i^2} e^{rT} M_i - \frac{1}{T} \left(\frac{F}{K_*} - 1 \right)^2$$

giving the defining equation for $\hat{\sigma}^2$.

The calculation of implied volatilities, or variances, naturally relies on some option pricing model, like that one of Black-Scholes-Merton (1973). By contrast, the VSTOXX and VIX volatility index calculation only takes as input market-observed options prices. This is possible since realized variance at a given future date can be replicated by strips of European call and put prices maturing at the same date. The realized volatility can then be extracted by taking the square root of the realized variance. The calculation of the VSTOXX and VIX avoids a "model-bias" and uses standard market practice for the valuation of important variance related instruments, like variance swaps.

3.8 CONCLUSIONS

This chapter introduces the elegant theory of the model-free replication of realized variance and variance swaps which dates back at least to Breeden and Litzenberger (1978). The role of log contracts and constant dollar gamma positions is discussed. Numerical examples also illustrate how to construct constant dollar gamma options positions in practice. Finally, based on this theory the definition of the VSTOXX and VIX volatility indexes is presented and justified. Subsequent chapters draw in different ways on these cornerstones in the theory of volatility and variance modeling, measuring and trading.

Listed Volatility Derivatives

CHAPTER 4

Data Analysis and Strategies

4.1 INTRODUCTION

This chapter is about the analysis of data and investment strategies related to the EURO STOXX 50 and VSTOXX indexes. It uses public data sources ("open data") and draws heavily on the capabilities of the Python library pandas for data analytics.

The chapter has two major goals. First, it reproduces the stylized fact that stock indexes and volatility indexes in general are *negatively correlated*. This suggests that (products based on) volatility indexes are a means to hedge market risk resulting from stock indexes. The question, however, is how to best exploit the negative correlation in asset allocation terms. Therefore, the second goal is to illustrate the benefits for equity investors resulting from *constant proportion investment strategies* involving a volatility index like the VSTOXX. For simplicity, the respective analysis assumes that a direct investment in the VSTOXX is possible. This replicates results as found, for example, in the study by Guobuzaite and Martellini (2012).

4.2 RETRIEVING BASE DATA

This section shows how to retrieve and store historical daily closing data for the EURO STOXX 50 index and the VSTOXX volatility index. We mainly work with pandas in the following:

```
In [1]: import numpy as np

In [2]: import pandas as pd

In [3]: path = './source/data/'   # path to data folder
```

4.2.1 EURO STOXX 50 Data

On the website http://stoxx.com of the index provider STOXX Limited, you find text files containing historical closing data for the EURO STOXX 50 index and others. Such data files are found in this folder:

```
In [4]: source = 'https://www.stoxx.com/document/Indices/Current/HistoricalData/'
```

The respective file for the EURO STOXX 50 index has the following name and is updated daily after closing.

```
In [5]: es_url = source + 'hbrbcpe.txt'
```

Let us inspect the first few rows of the data file directly, i.e. without pandas. We use the requests library to read the file from the web source and to print the first 1,000 characters of the string object returned.

```
In [6]: import requests

In [7]: print requests.get(es_url).text[:1000].replace(' ', ' ')
PriceIndices-EUROCurrency
Date;Blue-Chip;Blue-Chip;Broad;Broad;ExUK;ExEuroZone;Blue-Chip;Broad
;Europe;Euro-Zone;Europe;Euro-Zone;;;Nordic;Nordic
;SX5P;SX5E;SXXP;SXXE;SXXF;SXXA;DK5F;DKXF
31.12.1986;775.00;900.82;82.76;98.58;98.06;69.06;645.26;65.56
01.01.1987;775.00;900.82;82.76;98.58;98.06;69.06;645.26;65.56
02.01.1987;770.89;891.78;82.57;97.80;97.43;69.37;647.62;65.81
05.01.1987;771.89;898.33;82.82;98.60;98.19;69.16;649.94;65.82
06.01.1987;775.92;902.32;83.28;99.19;98.83;69.50;652.49;66.06
07.01.1987;781.21;899.15;83.78;98.96;98.62;70.59;651.97;66.20
08.01.1987;777.62;887.37;83.52;97.87;97.68;71.01;645.57;65.62
09.01.1987;769.80;868.31;83.03;96.31;96.22;71.40;638.03;65.14
```

The file changes the format in which data rows are presented (at least at the time of writing) such that we need to use a little trick to import the data correctly with pandas. Namely, we have to add an additional column which we call DEL.

```
# new column names (without white space)
# adding column 'DEL' -- to be deleted after parsing
In [8]: columns = ['Date', 'SX5P', 'SX5E', 'SXXP', 'SXXE',
   ...:            'SXXF', 'SXXA', 'DK5F', 'DKXF', 'DEL']
   ...:
```

We also skip the first four rows which we do not need and set a few other parameters for the importing procedure with pandas.

```
In [9]: es = pd.read_csv(es_url,  # url/filename
   ...:                  index_col=0,  # index column (dates)
   ...:                  parse_dates=True,  # parse date information
   ...:                  dayfirst=True,  # day before month
   ...:                  header=None,  # ignore header information
```

```
...:                        skiprows=4,  # ignore first 4 rows
...:                        names=columns,  # use custom column names
...:                        sep=';')  # separator character
...:
```

The additional helper column can be deleted after the import because it is no longer needed (and empty in any case).

```
In [10]: del es['DEL']  # deletes helper column
```

Let us inspect the first few rows of the DataFrame object. Given the raw data from above, we seem to have done everything right.

```
In [11]: es = es[es.index <= '2015-12-31']  # data until the end of 2015

In [12]: es.tail()
Out[12]:
                SX5P     SX5E    SXXP    SXXE    SXXF    SXXA     DK5F    DKXF
Date
2015-12-24 3108.11 3284.47 366.28 346.05 433.43 375.39  9931.72 614.38
2015-12-28 3093.61 3256.49 364.49 343.54 431.26 374.32  9873.94 611.58
2015-12-29 3139.28 3314.28 369.68 349.29 438.43 378.86 10023.66 620.66
2015-12-30 3118.07 3287.98 367.70 347.02 435.82 377.20  9956.22 617.48
2015-12-31 3100.26 3267.52 365.81 345.16 433.81 375.34  9978.59 618.73
```

The single time series starts at the end of 1986 and goes to the last available trading day or in our case the final trading day of 2015.

```
In [13]: es.info()
<class 'pandas.core.frame.DataFrame'>
DatetimeIndex: 7476 entries, 1986-12-31 to 2015-12-31
Data columns (total 8 columns):
SX5P    7476 non-null float64
SX5E    7476 non-null float64
SXXP    7476 non-null float64
SXXE    7476 non-null float64
SXXF    7476 non-null float64
SXXA    7476 non-null float64
DK5F    7476 non-null float64
DKXF    7476 non-null float64
dtypes: float64(8)
memory usage: 525.7 KB
```

FIGURE 4.1   Historical EURO STOXX 50 index levels.

Before going on to the corresponding procedure for the VSTOXX data, the following visualizes the historical closing values for the EURO STOXX 50 index, i.e. for symbol SX5E (see Figure 4.1):

```
In [14]: import seaborn as sns; sns.set()

In [15]: import matplotlib

In [16]: matplotlib.rcParams['font.family'] = 'serif'  # set serif font

In [17]: es['SX5E'].plot(grid=True, figsize=(10, 6));
```

4.2.2 VSTOXX Data

Reading the data from the same source for the VSTOXX index is slightly more straightforward since the respective data file does not change its format.

```
In [18]: vs_url = source + 'h_vstoxx.txt'

In [19]: print(requests.get(vs_url).text[160:1040])
Date,V2TX,V6I1,V6I2,V6I3,V6I4,V6I5,V6I6,V6I7,V6I8
04.01.1999,18.2033,21.2458,17.5555,31.2179,33.3124,33.7327,33.2232,31.8535,23.8209
05.01.1999,29.6912,36.6400,28.4274,32.6922,33.7326,33.1724,32.8457,32.2904,25.0532
06.01.1999,25.1670,25.4107,25.1351,32.2186,32.6459,31.9673,32.9260,33.2871,26.0107
```

```
07.01.1999,32.5205,35.4410,32.2004,36.1265,34.5150,33.1095,33.2843,33.7269,26.2205
08.01.1999,33.2296,35.8846,33.0020,36.0813,36.3964,33.4658,33.4837,33.9227,26.3672
11.01.1999,36.8411,46.9742,36.4643,39.9139,38.0755,34.6165,34.4576,34.6615,26.6732
12.01.1999,37.5664,48.6277,37.2998,40.5525,38.7981,35.0575,37.5290,36.5965,28.0273
13.01.1999,39.7373,55.2934,39.5218,43.0083,40.1301,36.0443,38.3889,37.2219,28.1443
14.01.1999,39.1373,NA,39.9544,41.7597,40.5913,36.3330,38.6781,37.4249,28.1515
15.01.1999,38.6741,NA,39.0602,40.1232,39.2451,35.9745,37.7796,36.7660,28.0793
```

The parametrization for pandas to import the data to a `DataFrame` object is as follows:

```
In [20]: vs = pd.read_csv(vs_url,   # url/filename
    ....:                 index_col=0,   # index column (dates)
    ....:                 parse_dates=True,   # parse date information
    ....:                 dayfirst=True,   # day before month
    ....:                 header=2)   # header/column names
    ....:
```

In this case, data is available from the beginning of 1999 until the last available trading day. However, we again select only data until the last trading day of 2015.

```
In [21]: vs = vs[vs.index <= '2015-12-31']

In [22]: vs.info()
<class 'pandas.core.frame.DataFrame'>
DatetimeIndex: 4327 entries, 1999-01-04 to 2015-12-30
Data columns (total 9 columns):
V2TX    4327 non-null float64
V6I1    3878 non-null float64
V6I2    4327 non-null float64
V6I3    4267 non-null float64
V6I4    4327 non-null float64
V6I5    4327 non-null float64
V6I6    4310 non-null float64
V6I7    4327 non-null float64
V6I8    4313 non-null float64
dtypes: float64(9)
memory usage: 338.0 KB
```

Figure 4.2 visualizes the times series data for the main volatility index with symbol V2TX. Inspection of the figure reveals that the volatility index increases and even spikes when there are crises in the markets – which is best seen towards the end of 2008.

```
In [23]: vs['V2TX'].plot(grid=True, figsize=(10, 6));
```

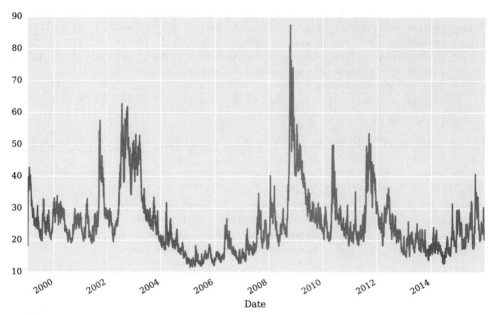

FIGURE 4.2   Historical VSTOXX index levels.

4.2.3 Combining the Data Sets

For what follows, we only need the time series data for the major indexes with symbols SX5E and V2TX and only for those dates where data is available for both time series. To this end, the following code generates a new `DataFrame` object out of the two original ones:

```
In [24]: import datetime as dt

In [25]: data = pd.DataFrame({'EUROSTOXX':
    ....:                 es['SX5E'][es.index > dt.datetime(1999, 1, 1)],
    ....:                 'VSTOXX':
    ....:                 vs['V2TX'][vs.index > dt.datetime(1999, 1, 1)]})
    ....:

In [26]: data = data.dropna()  # deletes those rows with NaN values
```

The code below provides an overview of the new data set and excerpts from all three `DataFrame` objects:

```
In [27]: data.info()
<class 'pandas.core.frame.DataFrame'>
DatetimeIndex: 4326 entries, 1999-01-04 to 2015-12-30
Data columns (total 2 columns):
EUROSTOXX    4326 non-null float64
VSTOXX       4326 non-null float64
```

```
dtypes: float64(2)
memory usage: 101.4 KB


In [28]: es.iloc[-10:]
Out[28]:
                  SX5P     SX5E    SXXP    SXXE    SXXF    SXXA     DK5F    DKXF
Date
2015-12-17  3095.83  3306.47  364.90  347.46  433.96  371.43   9857.04  610.15
2015-12-18  3065.07  3260.72  361.23  343.23  429.32  368.38   9722.97  602.49
2015-12-21  3022.51  3213.01  357.15  338.55  424.21  364.99   9707.52  601.18
2015-12-22  3019.26  3214.32  356.87  338.77  423.95  364.23   9691.72  599.53
2015-12-23  3109.23  3286.68  366.39  346.14  433.58  375.53   9927.33  614.12
2015-12-24  3108.11  3284.47  366.28  346.05  433.43  375.39   9931.72  614.38
2015-12-28  3093.61  3256.49  364.49  343.54  431.26  374.32   9873.94  611.58
2015-12-29  3139.28  3314.28  369.68  349.29  438.43  378.86  10023.66  620.66
2015-12-30  3118.07  3287.98  367.70  347.02  435.82  377.20   9956.22  617.48
2015-12-31  3100.26  3267.52  365.81  345.16  433.81  375.34   9978.59  618.73


In [29]: np.round(vs, 2).iloc[-10:]
Out[29]:
              V2TX   V6I1   V6I2   V6I3   V6I4   V6I5   V6I6   V6I7   V6I8
Date
2015-12-15  27.46  41.71  27.41  26.63  26.72  26.66  26.41  26.36  27.44
2015-12-16  25.44  49.12  25.44  25.21  25.34  25.57  25.54  25.77  26.65
2015-12-17  22.58    NaN  22.50  23.47  23.94  24.80  25.01  25.34  26.24
2015-12-18  23.90    NaN  23.76  24.78  25.06  25.80  25.75  25.91  26.54
2015-12-21  23.88  23.56  24.62  24.99  25.80  25.87  26.04  26.64    NaN
2015-12-22  22.54  21.92  23.64  24.14  25.25  25.31  25.64  26.04  26.05
2015-12-23  20.25  19.42  21.45  22.24  24.01  24.46  24.84  25.65  25.44
2015-12-28  22.45  21.43  23.08  23.65  24.70  24.91  25.25  25.46  25.34
2015-12-29  21.61  20.56  22.14  22.87  24.31  24.59  25.06  25.65  25.26
2015-12-30  22.17  21.13  22.64  23.33  24.64  24.72  25.15  25.48  25.16


In [30]: data.iloc[-10:]
Out[30]:
            EUROSTOXX   VSTOXX
Date
2015-12-15     3241.51  27.4591
2015-12-16     3246.78  25.4362
2015-12-17     3306.47  22.5761
2015-12-18     3260.72  23.8989
2015-12-21     3213.01  23.8836
2015-12-22     3214.32  22.5361
2015-12-23     3286.68  20.2504
2015-12-28     3256.49  22.4544
2015-12-29     3314.28  21.6067
2015-12-30     3287.98  22.1745
```

4.2.4 Saving the Data

Finally, the DataFrame objects are saved to a HDFStore object on disk for later use. Something not really needed when an internet connection is available, but helpful when it is not.

```
In [31]: h5 = pd.HDFStore(path + 'es_vs_data.h5', 'w')

In [32]: h5['es'] = es

In [33]: h5['vs'] = vs

In [34]: h5['data'] = data

In [35]: h5
Out[35]:
<class 'pandas.io.pytables.HDFStore'>
File path: ./source/data/es_vs_data.h5
/data              frame        (shape->[4326,2])
/es                frame        (shape->[7476,8])
/vs                frame        (shape->[4327,9])

In [36]: h5.close()
```

4.3 BASIC DATA ANALYSIS

To illustrate how to read the data from the HDFStore object, consider the following code which is almost "symmetric" to the code that writes the data to disk:

```
In [37]: h5 = pd. HDFStore(path + 'es_vs_data.h5', 'r')

In [38]: h5
Out[38]:
<class 'pandas.io.pytables.HDFStore'>
File path: ./source/data/es_vs_data.h5
/data              frame        (shape->[4326,2])
/es                frame        (shape->[7476,8])
/vs                frame        (shape->[4327,9])

In [39]: es = h5['es']

In [40]: vs = h5['vs']

In [41]: data = h5['data']

In [42]: h5.close()
```

As seen in chapter 2, *Introduction to Python*, pandas provides a wealth of options to analyze data stored in `DataFrame` objects. A method which is sometimes helpful is `describe()` which provides selected meta statistics for the single data sub-sets stored in `DataFrame` columns.

```
In [43]: data.describe()
Out[43]:
          EUROSTOXX       VSTOXX
count   4326.000000   4326.000000
mean    3265.935767     25.209891
std      770.513845      9.670981
min     1809.980000     11.596600
25%     2692.385000     18.670200
50%     3089.965000     23.162700
75%     3725.357500     28.310725
max     5464.430000     87.512700
```

Sub-plots of multiple data sub-sets are easily generated with pandas. The result of the following plotting code is found as Figure 4.3:

```
In [44]: data.plot(subplots=True,   # generate sub-plots per column
   ....:                 figsize=(10, 6),   # sizing of the figure
   ....:                 color='blue');   # color to plot the data
   ....:
```

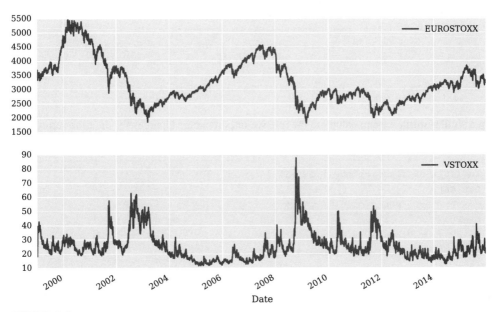

FIGURE 4.3   Historical EURO STOXX 50 and VSTOXX index levels.

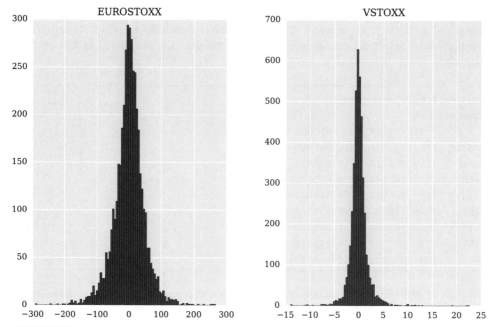

FIGURE 4.4 Histograms of historical absolute daily differences of EURO STOXX 50 and VSTOXX.

Similarly, you can visualize the absolute differences (over time) by using the `diff` method and plotting them as a histogram (see Figure 4.4).

```
In [45]: data.diff().hist(figsize=(10, 6),   # figure sizing
   ....:                    color='blue',   # color for the plotted data
   ....:                    bins=100);  # number of bins to be used
   ....:
```

In a similar spirit, we can calculate the relative or percentage changes for the time series data.

```
In [46]: data.pct_change().ix[-10:]
Out[46]:
               EUROSTOXX     VSTOXX
Date
2015-12-15   0.032578  -0.097067
2015-12-16   0.001626  -0.073670
2015-12-17   0.018384  -0.112442
2015-12-18  -0.013837   0.058593
2015-12-21  -0.014632  -0.000640
2015-12-22   0.000408  -0.056419
```

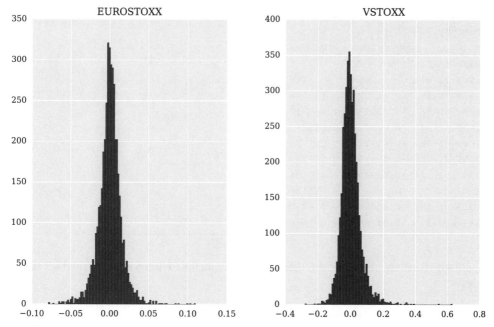

FIGURE 4.5 Histograms of historical percentage changes of EURO STOXX 50 and VSTOXX.

```
2015-12-23    0.022512  -0.101424
2015-12-28   -0.009186   0.108837
2015-12-29    0.017746  -0.037752
2015-12-30   -0.007935   0.026279
```

The code to visualize this kind of result is the same as before (see Figure 4.5).

```
In [47]: data.pct_change().hist(figsize=(10, 6),
    ....:                        color='blue',
    ....:                        bins=100);
    ....:
```

The majority of statistical analysis approaches rely on (log) returns and not on absolute time series data. The next few lines of code calculate the log returns for the two time series and store them in yet another `DataFrame` object, called `log_rets`.

```
In [48]: import numpy as np

# fully vectorized calculation of log returns
In [49]: log_rets = np.log(data / data.shift(1))
```

```
In [50]: log_rets.ix[:10]
Out[50]:
              EUROSTOXX      VSTOXX
Date
1999-01-04         NaN         NaN
1999-01-05    0.017228    0.489248
1999-01-06    0.022138   -0.165317
1999-01-07   -0.015723    0.256337
1999-01-08   -0.003120    0.021570
1999-01-11   -0.019593    0.103173
1999-01-12   -0.012490    0.019496
1999-01-13   -0.048535    0.056180
1999-01-14    0.008648   -0.015214
1999-01-15    0.017855   -0.011906
```

Figure 4.6 visualizes the log returns times series for both the EURO STOXX 50 and VSTOXX indexes.

```
In [51]: log_rets.plot(subplots=True,
    ....:              figsize=(10, 6),
    ....:              color='blue',
    ....:              grid=True);
    ....:
```

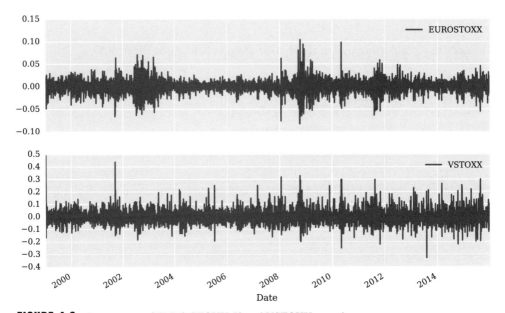

FIGURE 4.6   Log returns of EURO STOXX 50 and VSTOXX over time.

4.4 CORRELATION ANALYSIS

Equipped with the log returns, a thorough investigation of the correlation between the EURO STOXX 50 and VSTOXX indexes is straightforward. For example, pandas provides the `corr()` method to calculate correlations between time series data stored in different `DataFrame` columns.

```
In [52]: log_rets.corr()
Out[52]:
             EUROSTOXX      VSTOXX
EUROSTOXX   1.000000  -0.735032
VSTOXX      -0.735032   1.000000
```

Similar results are obtained by calculating the correlation of the data stored in one pandas `Series` object with another data set in another `Series` object.

```
In [53]: log_rets['EUROSTOXX'].corr(log_rets['VSTOXX'])
Out[53]: 0.73503163966378138
```

The `plot` method of pandas `DataFrame` objects allows for different types of plots. For example, scatter plots are helpful to visualize return data of two different time series (see Figure 4.7).

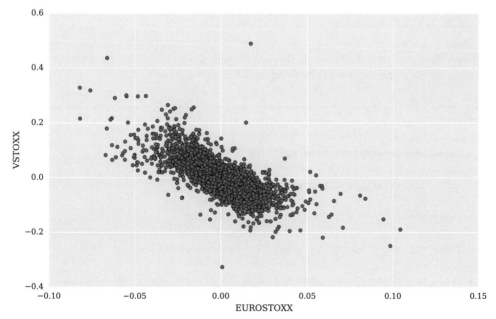

FIGURE 4.7   Scatter plot of log returns of EURO STOXX 50 and VSTOXX.

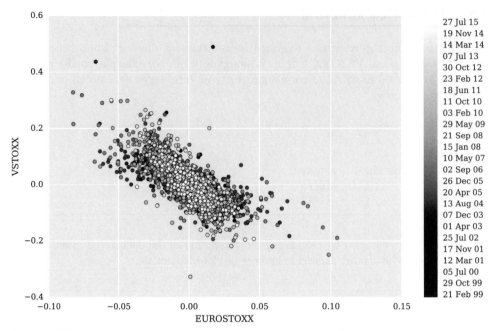

FIGURE 4.8   Scatter plot of log returns of EURO STOXX 50 and VSTOXX with dates.

```
# plot log returns as scatter plot
In [54]: log_rets.plot(x=' EUROSTOXX', y=' VSTOXX',
    ....:                   kind=' scatter', figsize=(10, 6));
    ....:
```

Figure 4.8 adds the time dimension to the data through shades of gray to illustrate the relation between the two time series over time (during different "regimes").

```
In [55]: log_rets = log_rets.dropna()   # delete NaN values

In [56]: import matplotlib as mpl

In [57]: import matplotlib.pyplot as plt

In [58]: plt.ioff()   # turn off interactive mode

In [59]: plt.set_cmap(mpl.cm.gray);   # set color map

In [60]: mpl_dates = mpl.dates.date2num(log_rets.index.to_pydatetime())
            # conversion

In [61]: plt.figure(figsize=(10, 6));
```

```
In [62]: plt.scatter(log_rets['EUROSTOXX'], log_rets['VSTOXX'],
    ....:             c=mpl_dates, marker='o');  # the actual plot
    ....:

In [63]: plt.xlabel('EUROSTOXX');

In [64]: plt.ylabel('VSTOXX');

In [65]: plt.colorbar(ticks=mpl.dates.DayLocator(interval=250),
    ....:         format=mpl.dates.DateFormatter('%d %b %y'));  # adding bar
    ....:
```

Although the negative correlation between the two indexes is almost evident from Figures 4.7 and 4.8, let us formally calculate and represent the negative correlation by a linear regression line. Figure 4.9 adds such a regression line to the raw log returns in the scatter plot. Negative correlation translates into a negative slope of the regression line.

```
# conduct linear regression
In [66]: p = np.polyfit(log_rets['EUROSTOXX'].values,
    ....:             log_rets['VSTOXX'].values,
    ....:             deg=1)  # the regression
    ....:
```

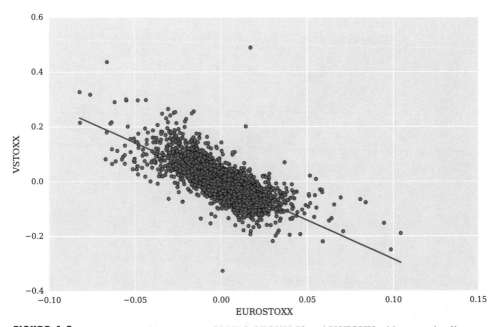

FIGURE 4.9 Scatter plot of log returns of EURO STOXX 50 and VSTOXX with regression line.

```
In [67]: log_rets.plot(x='EUROSTOXX', y='VSTOXX',
   ....:                    kind='scatter', figsize=(10, 6));  # the actual plotting
   ....:

# plot the regression line
In [68]: plt.plot(log_rets['EUROSTOXX'], np.polyval(p, log_rets['EUROSTOXX']),
   ....:              'r');  # adding the regression line
   ....:
```

The seaborn plotting library is specifically developed with statistical applications in mind. It therefore provides multiple useful, high level plotting capabilities. One of these is the jointplot() function. The result of applying this function to the log return data is displayed as Figure 4.10. This is definitely the richest and most insightful presentation so far for our purposes.

```
In [69]: sns.jointplot(x=log_rets['EUROSTOXX'], y=log_rets['VSTOXX'],
   ....:                    kind='reg', size=7);
   ....:
```

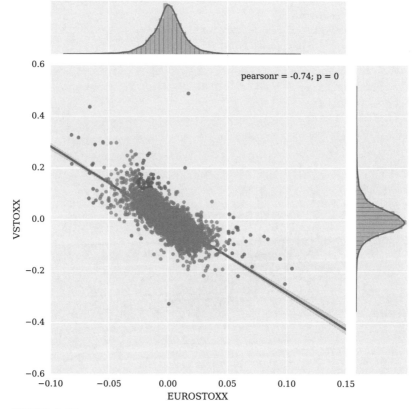

FIGURE 4.10 Scatter plot of log returns of EURO STOXX 50 and VSTOXX with regression line and histograms.

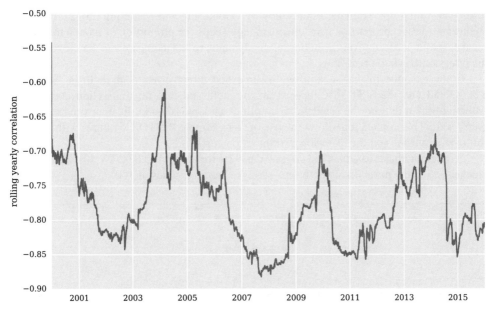

FIGURE 4.11   Rolling yearly correlation of EURO STOXX 50 and VSTOXX.

The final analysis in this section considers correlation *over time*. To this end, pandas provides the rolling() method which allows, among others, the vectorized calculation of correlation for moving time windows via corr(). We chose a window size of 252 trading days which represents roughly one year.

```
In [70]: data['CORR'] = log_rets['EUROSTOXX'].rolling(
    ....:                       window=252).corr(log_rets['VSTOXX'])
    ....:
```

Figure 4.11 plots the rolling correlation data and illustrates well that correlation fluctuates for different yearly windows but that it is negative for any chosen yearly window.

```
In [71]: to_plot = data.dropna()   # drop NaN values

In [72]: plt.figure(figsize=(10, 6));

In [73]: plt.plot(data.index, data.CORR);

In [74]: plt.ylabel('rolling yearly correlation');
```

4.5 CONSTANT PROPORTION INVESTMENT STRATEGIES

One way to make use of the fact that the VSTOXX index is negatively correlated with the EURO STOXX 50 index is to implement a *constant proportion investment strategy*. Respective results are found, for example, in the study by Guobuzaite and Martellini (2012). Basically, a constant (dollar) proportion investment strategy keeps the proportion of money invested in securities of a portfolio over time constant by dynamic re-balancings given the movements in the prices of the single securities.

In the example in this section, we assume that direct investments both in the EURO STOXX 50 and the VSTOXX indexes are possible and that no transaction costs apply. Although this might not be realistic, it simplifies the anaylsis and illustrates the basic idea pretty well. This application allows the use of, for example, VSTOXX futures with different roll-over strategies and the inclusion of transaction costs.

To begin with, let us adjust the original data sets for the EURO STOXX 50 and VSTOXX indexes by mainly normalizing both time series to starting values of 100.

```
In [75]: del data['CORR']   # delete correlation data

In [76]: data = data.dropna()   # drop NaN values

In [77]: data = data / data.iloc[0] * 100   # normalization
```

```
In [78]: data.head()
Out[78]:
                EUROSTOXX       VSTOXX
Date
1999-01-04  100.000000  100.000000
1999-01-05  101.737744  163.108887
1999-01-06  104.015128  138.255152
1999-01-07  102.392538  178.651673
1999-01-08  102.073608  182.547121
```

First, we analyze a typical *passive investment strategy* allocating 30% of a portfolio to the VSTOXX index and the remaining 70% to the EURO STOXX 50.

```
In [79]: invest = 100   # initial investment

In [80]: cratio = 0.3   # VSTOXX ratio in the beginning

# number of EURO STOXX (fictional) securities
In [81]: data['Equity'] = (1 - cratio) * invest / data['EUROSTOXX'][0]

# number of VSTOXX (fictional) securities
In [82]: data['Volatility'] = cratio * invest / data['VSTOXX'][0]
```

In vectorized fashion, we calculate next the absolute values of such a portfolio over time, i.e. as a time series.

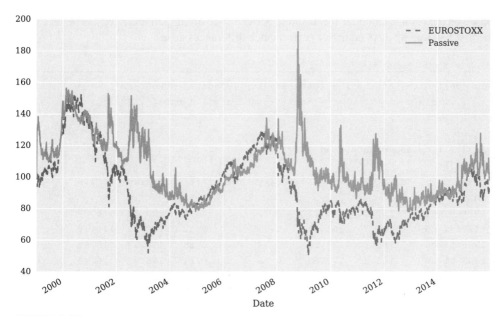

FIGURE 4.12   Passive investment strategy (hypothetical) with EURO STOXX 50 and VSTOXX.

```
In [83]: data['Passive'] = (data['Equity'] * data['EUROSTOXX']
    ....:                    + data['Volatility'] * data['VSTOXX'])
    ....:
```

Figure 4.12 illustrates the performance of this particular passive investment strategy in comparison to a passive strategy purely investing in the EURO STOXX 50 index. In times of crisis, for example at the end of 2008, the strategy peforms better. However, over the whole period there is hardly any difference in the end result.

```
In [84]: data[['EUROSTOXX', 'Passive']].plot(figsize=(10, 6), style=['--', '-']);
```

Second, the *active constant proportion investment strategy*, which keeps the dollar proportion invested in the VSTOXX index constant at 30% over time through daily re-balancings of the portfolio. In this case, the single calculations are done step-by-step through looping over the single historical trading dates.

```
In [85]: for i in range(1, len(data)):  # daily re-balancing
    ....:     evalue = data['Equity'][i - 1] * data['EUROSTOXX'][i]
    ....:     vvalue = data['Volatility'][i - 1] * data['VSTOXX'][i]
    ....:     tvalue = evalue + vvalue  # total wealth
    ....:     data['Equity'][i] = (1 - cratio) * tvalue / data['EUROSTOXX'][i]
    ....:     data['Volatility'][i] = cratio * tvalue / data['VSTOXX'][i]
    ....:
```

Based on the results, calculate the absolute performance of this active strategy as before. Over the first few trading days no major performance differences arise.

```
In [86]: data['Active'] = (data['Equity'] * data['EUROSTOXX']
   ....:                     + data['Volatility'] * data['VSTOXX'])
   ....:

In [87]: np.round(data.head(), 2)
Out[87]:
             EUROSTOXX  VSTOXX  Equity  Volatility  Passive  Active
Date
1999-01-04      100.00  100.00    0.70        0.30   100.00  100.00
1999-01-05      101.74  163.11    0.83        0.22   120.15  120.15
1999-01-06      104.02  138.26    0.78        0.25   114.29  116.54
1999-01-07      102.39  178.65    0.86        0.21   125.27  125.48
1999-01-08      102.07  182.55    0.86        0.21   126.22  126.03
```

Over the whole time period, however, the active strategy – showing a 800+% gain – significantly outperforms the passive one.

```
In [88]: np.round(data.tail(), 2)
Out[88]:
             EUROSTOXX  VSTOXX  Equity  Volatility  Passive  Active
Date
2015-12-22       90.72  123.80    7.22        2.27   100.65  936.01
2015-12-23       92.76  111.25    6.96        2.49    98.31  922.28
2015-12-28       91.91  123.35    7.21        2.30   101.34  946.46
2015-12-29       93.54  118.70    7.09        2.39   101.09  947.50
2015-12-30       92.80  121.82    7.16        2.34   101.50  949.71
```

Let us briefly verify whether the above implementation indeed yields constant proportions for the two (fictional) securities in the portfolio.

```
In [89]: (data['Volatility'] * data['VSTOXX'] / data['Active'])[:5]
Out[89]:
Date
1999-01-04    0.3
1999-01-05    0.3
1999-01-06    0.3
1999-01-07    0.3
1999-01-08    0.3
dtype: float64
```

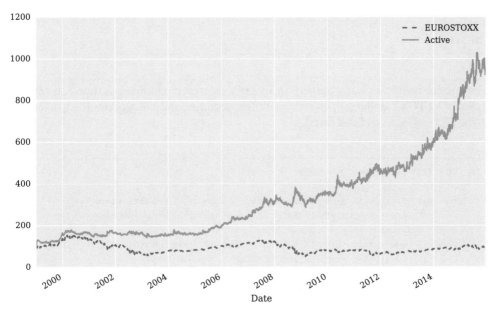

FIGURE 4.13 Active, constant proportion investment strategy (hypothetical) with EURO STOXX 50 and VSTOXX.

```
In [90]: (data['Equity'] * data['EUROSTOXX'] / data['Active'])[:5]
Out[90]:
Date
1999-01-04    0.7
1999-01-05    0.7
1999-01-06    0.7
1999-01-07    0.7
1999-01-08    0.7
dtype: float64
```

Being assured that we have indeed implemented a constant proportion trading strategy, have a look at Figure 4.13 which impressively illustrates the outperformance of the active approach over a passive investment in the stock index itself. However, bear in mind that all this rests on a number of simplifying assumptions.

```
In [91]: data[['EUROSTOXX', 'Active']].plot(figsize=(10, 6), style=['--', '-']);
```

The assumption of 30% invested in the VSTOXX index might seem a bit ad hoc. Therefore, the following derives the optimal allocation for the given time period and data sets by a brute force approach. First, we clean up the `DataFrame` object to reduce it again to the original time series data for the two indexes.

```
# re-initialize DataFrame
In [92]: data = data[['EUROSTOXX', 'VSTOXX']]
```

The function below calculates the performance of a constant proportion investment strategy for different VSTOXX dollar proportions and different starting and ending dates (both defaulting to the data sets' start and end dates).

```
In [93]: from copy import deepcopy

In [94]: def vstoxx_strategy(cratio, start=data.index[0], end=data.index[-1]):
    ....:     base = deepcopy(data[(data.index >= start) & (data.index <= end)])
    ....:     invest = 100  # initial invest
    ....:     base['Equity'] = (1 - cratio) * invest / base['EUROSTOXX'][0]
    ....:     base['Volatility'] = cratio * invest / base['VSTOXX'][0]
    ....:     for i in range(1, len(base)):  # daily re-balancing
    ....:         evalue = base['Equity'][i - 1] * base['EUROSTOXX'][i]
    ....:         vvalue = base['Volatility'][i - 1] * base['VSTOXX'][i]
    ....:         tvalue = evalue + vvalue
    ....:         base['Equity'][i] = (1 - cratio) * tvalue / base['EUROSTOXX'][i]
    ....:         base['Volatility'][i] = cratio * tvalue / base['VSTOXX'][i]
    ....:     base['Active'] = (base['Equity'] * base['EUROSTOXX']
    ....:                      + base['Volatility'] * base['VSTOXX'])  # wealth position
    ....:     print("A con. VSTOXX ratio of %.2f yields a net perform. of %6.1f %%.") \
    ....:         % (cratio, (base['Active'][-1] / base['Active'][0] - 1) * 100)
    ....:
```

Equipped with this function, let us calculate the net perfomance for a VSTOXX dollar ratio of 30% as before.

```
In [95]: vstoxx_strategy(0.3)
A con. VSTOXX ratio of 0.30 yields a net perform.of 849.7%.
```

We do the same for 40% which obviously yields an even better result.

```
In [96]: vstoxx_strategy(0.4)
A con. VSTOXX ratio of 0.40 yields a net perform.of 1231.9%.
```

Applying an approach which is slightly more systematic, we get the following results for different constant dollar proportion assumptions. Over the whole period for which data is available a 50:50 investment strategy seems to be optimal with a net performance of more than 1,400%.

```
In [97]: for cratio in np.arange(0, 1.01, 0.1):
   ....:         vstoxx_strategy(cratio)
   ....:
A con. VSTOXX ratio of 0.00 yields a net perform.of   -7.2%.
A con. VSTOXX ratio of 0.10 yields a net perform.of  151.5%.
A con. VSTOXX ratio of 0.20 yields a net perform.of  445.4%.
A con. VSTOXX ratio of 0.30 yields a net perform.of  849.7%.
A con. VSTOXX ratio of 0.40 yields a net perform.of 1231.9%.
A con. VSTOXX ratio of 0.50 yields a net perform.of 1408.7%.
A con. VSTOXX ratio of 0.60 yields a net perform.of 1283.2%.
A con. VSTOXX ratio of 0.70 yields a net perform.of  928.4%.
A con. VSTOXX ratio of 0.80 yields a net perform.of  521.0%.
A con. VSTOXX ratio of 0.90 yields a net perform.of  204.9%.
A con. VSTOXX ratio of 1.00 yields a net perform.of   21.8%.
```

Let us implement the same analysis for the time period beginning in January 2013 and ending with the last quarter of 2015. In this case, a constant dollar proportion invested in the VSTOXX of again about 50% seems optimal and yields a net performance of close to 110%.

```
In [98]: for cratio in np.arange(0, 1.01, 0.1):
   ....:         vstoxx_strategy(cratio, start='2013-1-1', end=' 2015-12-31')
   ....:
A con. VSTOXX ratio of 0.00 yields a net perform.of   21.3%.
A con. VSTOXX ratio of 0.10 yields a net perform.of   47.9%.
A con. VSTOXX ratio of 0.20 yields a net perform.of   72.4%.
A con. VSTOXX ratio of 0.30 yields a net perform.of   92.2%.
A con. VSTOXX ratio of 0.40 yields a net perform.of  105.0%.
A con. VSTOXX ratio of 0.50 yields a net perform.of  109.2%.
A con. VSTOXX ratio of 0.60 yields a net perform.of  104.3%.
A con. VSTOXX ratio of 0.70 yields a net perform.of   91.1%.
A con. VSTOXX ratio of 0.80 yields a net perform.of   71.2%.
A con. VSTOXX ratio of 0.90 yields a net perform.of   46.9%.
A con. VSTOXX ratio of 1.00 yields a net perform.of   20.8%.
```

4.6 CONCLUSIONS

This chapter is about the retrieval and analysis of EURO STOXX 50 and VSTOXX historical data. It shows how to use Python and pandas to retrieve and clean up historical data sets from the index provider's website http://stoxx.com with pandas. It also shows how to implement Python code to replicate central stylized facts about stock and volatility indexes, namely their highly negative correlation and the benefits of constant (dollar) proportion investment strategies involving (products based on) equity and volatility indexes.

## CHAPTER 5

VSTOXX Index

5.1 INTRODUCTION

This chapter is about the (re-)calculation of the VSTOXX index, the volatility index based on EURO STOXX 50 index options. The goal is to achieve a good understanding of the processes and underlying mechanics of calculating the VSTOXX index. You will find all the background information as well as Python code that will enable you to recalculate both historical VSTOXX index values and current ones in (almost) real-time. Chapter 3, *Model-Free Replication of Variance* provides the theoretical background for the concepts presented in this chapter.

   The (main) VSTOXX index itself is based on two sub-indexes, which themselves are derived from Eurex option series for both European puts and calls on the EURO STOXX 50 index. The algorithm, and therefore this chapter as well, are comprised of three main parts:

- collect and clean-up the data of the necessary option series
- compute the sub-indexes from the option data
- compute the VSTOXX index from the relevant sub-indexes.

A few remarks about the option series and sub-indexes used and their expiry dates and time horizons, respectively, seem in order. There are eight sub-indexes of the VSTOXX which each measure the implied volatility of an option series with fixed expiry. For example, the VSTOXX 1M sub-index starts with the option series that has one month expiry and is calculated up to two days prior to the fixed maturity date of the relevant option series. The VSTOXX index measures the implied volatility of an "imaginary" options series with a fixed time to expiry of 30 days. This is achieved through linear interpolation of the two nearest sub-indexes, generally VSTOXX 1M and VSTOXX 2M. On the two days before VSTOXX 1M expiry, the VSTOXX 2M and VSTOXX 3M are used instead and an extrapolation takes place.

   Table 5.1 lists all the sub-indexes and provides additional information.

5.2 COLLECTING OPTION DATA

As already pointed out, the VSTOXX is based on two sub-indexes, generally the VSTOXX 1M and VSTOXX 2M, sometimes the VSTOXX 2M and VSTOXX 3M. The sub-indexes

TABLE 5.1   The VSTOXX sub-indexes.

Sub-index	Code	ISIN	Settlement date of the option series used
VSTOXX 1M	V6I1	DE000A0G87B2	The last available within 1 month
VSTOXX 2M	V6I2	DE000A0G87C0	The last available within 2 months
VSTOXX 3M	V6I3	DE000A0G87D8	The last available within 3 months
VSTOXX 6M	V6I4	DE000A0G87E6	The last available within 6 months
VSTOXX 9M	V6I5	DE000A0G87F3	The last available within 9 months
VSTOXX 12M	V6I6	DE000A0G87G1	The last available within 12 months
VSTOXX 18M	V6I7	DE000A0G87H9	The last available within 18 months
VSTOXX 24M	V6I8	DE000A0G87J5	The last available within 24 months

themselves are based on the option series on the EURO STOXX 50 index with respective time to expiry. We therefore need the prices of all options with maturities up to 3 months. We use historical data as provided by Eurex itself as the data source. See the website http://bit.ly/1GY5KCI.

The code to collect the data can be found in the module `index_collect_option_ data.py` (see sub-section 5.6.1, *index_collect_option_data.py* for the complete script). As usual, the module starts with some imports and parameter definitions.

```
import requests
import datetime as dt
import pandas as pd
import numpy as np
from StringIO import *
from index_date_functions import *


#
# The URL template
#
url1 = 'http://www.eurexchange.com/action/exchange-en/'
url2 = '180106-180102/180102/onlineStats.do?productGroupId=846'
url3 = '&productId=19068&viewType=3&cp=%s&month=%s&year=%s&busDate=%s'
URL = url1 + url2 + url3
```

In addition, the module contains six functions. The first is `collect_option_series()`:

```
def collect_option_series(month, year, start):
    ''' Collects daily option data from web source.

    Parameters
    ==========
    month: int
        maturity month
    year: int
        maturity year
```

```
    start: datetime object
        starting date

    Returns
    =======
    dataset: pandas DataFrame object
        object containing the collected data
    '''
    end = dt.datetime.today()
    delta = (end - start).days

    dataset = pd.DataFrame()
    for t in range(0, delta):   # runs from start to today
        date = start + dt.timedelta(t)
        dummy = get_data(month, year, date)   # get data for one day
        if len(dummy) != 0:
            if len(dataset) == 0:
                dataset = dummy
            else:
                dataset = pd.concat((dataset, dummy))   # add data
    return dataset
```

This function collects the data of the option series with maturity in the month month and year year. It is called by the function start_collecting() and calls the function get_data() for every single day from the date start to today. It returns a complete set of prices (both puts and calls) for that series.

The second function is get_data().

```
def get_data(month, year, date):
    ''' Get the data for an option series.

    Parameters
    ==========
    month: int
        maturity month
    year: int
        maturity year
    date: datetime object
        the date for which the data is collected

    Returns
    =======
    dataset: pandas DataFrame object
        object containing call & put option data
    '''
```

```
    date_string = date.strftime('%Y%m%d')
    # loads the call data from the web
    data = get_data_from_www('Call', month, year, date_string)
    calls = parse_data(data, date)   # parse the raw data
    calls = calls.rename(columns={'Daily settlem.price': 'Call_Price'})

    calls = pd.DataFrame(calls.pop('Call_Price').astype(float))
    # the same for puts
    data = get_data_from_www('Put', month, year, date_string)
    puts = parse_data(data, date)
    puts = puts.rename(columns={'Daily settlem.price': 'Put_Price'})
    puts = pd.DataFrame(puts.pop('Put_Price').astype(float))

    dataset = merge_and_filter(puts, calls)   # merges the two time series

    return dataset
```

This one is called by the function collect_option_series() and calls itself the
functions get_data_from_www(), parse_data(data, date) and merge_and_
filter(). It returns the prices of the option series with expiry date in month month and year
year for the day date.

The third function is get_data_from_www().

```
def get_data_from_www(oType, matMonth, matYear, date):
    ''' Retrieves the raw data of an option series from the web.

    Parameters
    ==========
    oType: string
        either 'Put' or 'Call'
    matMonth: int
        maturity month
    matYear: int
        maturity year
    date: string
        expiry in the format 'YYYYMMDD'

    Returns
    =======
    a: string
        raw text with option data
    '''
    url = URL % (oType, matMonth, matYear, date)   # parametrizes the URL
    a = requests.get(url).text
    return a
```

The function collects the prices of an option series for a single day (defined by `date`) from the web. The option series is defined by the date of its expiry, given by `matMonth` and `matYear`; the type of the options is given by `oType` which can be either `Put` or `Call`. It returns a complete HTML file.

`merge_and_filter()` is the fourth function.

```
def merge_and_filter(puts, calls):
    ''' Gets two pandas time series for the puts and calls
    (from the same option series), merges them, filters out
    all options with prices smaller than 0.5 and
    returns the resulting DataFrame object.

    Parameters
    ==========
    puts: pandas DataFrame object
        put option data
    calls: pandas DataFrame object
        call option data

    Returns
    =======
    df: pandas DataFrame object
        merged & filtered options data
    '''

    df = calls.join(puts, how='inner')  # merges the two time series
    # filters all prices which are too small
    df = df[(df.Put_Price >= 0.5) & (df.Call_Price >= 0.5)]

    return df
```

This one gets two time series `puts` and `calls` (typically of the same option series), merges them, filters out all options with prices below 0.5 and returns the resulting pandas `DataFrame` object.

`parse_data()` is the fifth function.

```
def parse_data(data, date):
    ''' Parses the HTML table and transforms it into a CSV compatible
    format. The result can be directly imported into a pandas DataFrame.

    Parameters
    ==========
    data: string
        document containing the Web content
    date: datetime object
        date for which the data is parsed
```

```
    Returns
    =======
    dataset: pandas DataFrame object
        transformed option raw data
    '''
    parts = data.split('<table')
    parts2 = parts[1].split('</table')
    dummy = parts2[0].replace(' class="odd"','')
    dummy = dummy.replace(' class="even"','')
    parts3 = dummy.split('<tr><td><b>Total</b>')
    table = parts3[0]  # the html table containing the data
    table = table.replace('class="dataTable"><thead>', 'Pricing day')

    # replace tags by commas and newlines
    table = table.replace('</tr>', '\n')
    table = table.replace(',', '')
    table = table.replace('<td>', ',')
    table = table.replace('</td>', '')
    table = table.replace('<th>', ',')
    table = table.replace('</th>', '')
    table = table.replace('</thead><tbody>', '\n')

    # the resulting string looks like a CSV file
    date_string = date.strftime('%d.%m.%Y')
    table = table.replace('<tr>', date_string)

    string = StringIO(table)  # mask the string as file
    dataset = pd.read_csv(string, parse_dates=[0], index_col=(0, 1),
                dayfirst=True)  # read the 'file' as pandas DataFrame object

    return dataset
```

It gets the string data which contains the HTML text delivered by function
get_data_from_www(), parses that string to a pandas DataFrame object with
double index date and strike price and returns that object.

The sixth and final function is data_collection().

```
def data_collection(path):
    ''' Main function which saves data into the HDF5 file
    'index_option_series.h5' for later use.

    Parameters
    ==========
    path: string
        path to store the data
```

```
    '''
    # file to store data
    store = pd.HDFStore(path + 'index_option_series.h5', 'a')
    today = dt.datetime.today()
    start = today - dt.timedelta(31)  # the last 31 days

    day = start.day
    month = start.month
    year = start.year

    for i in range(4):  # iterates over the next 4 months
        dummy_month = month + i
        dummy_year = year
        if dummy_month > 12:
            dummy_month -= 12
            dummy_year += 1

        # collect daily data beginning 31 days ago (start) for
        # option series with expiry dummy_month, dummy_year
        dataset = collect_option_series(dummy_month, dummy_year, start)

        dummy_date = dt.datetime(dummy_year, dummy_month, day)

        # abbreviation for expiry date (for example Oct14)
        series_name = dummy_date.strftime('%b%y')

        if series_name in store.keys():  # if data for that series exists
            index_old = store[series_name].index
            index_new = dataset.index

            if len(index_new - index_old) > 0:
                dummy = pd.concat((store[series_name],
                    dataset.ix[index_new - index_old]))  # add the new data

                store[series_name] = dummy
        else:
            if len(dataset) > 0:
            # if series is new, write whole data set into data store
                store[series_name] = dataset
    store.close()
```

This function is to initiate and finalize the collection of all relevant option series data sets. It saves the resulting data in a file named index_option_series.h5.

```
In [1]: path = './source/data/'
```

Let us collect option data since all other steps depend on this data. We import the module as `icod`.

```
In [2]: import numpy as np

In [3]: import pandas as pd

In [4]: import datetime as dt

In [5]: import index_collect_option_data as icod
```

Next, fix a target day relative to today such that you hit a business day for which closing data is available.

```
In [6]: today = dt.datetime.now()

# make sure to hit a business day
In [7]: target_day = today - dt.timedelta(days=1)

In [8]: ds = target_day.strftime('%Y%m%d')

In [9]: ds
Out[9]: '20160201'
```

Then, for example, collect option data for puts and calls with a maturity defined by the parameters as follows:

```
# adjust maturity parameters if necessary
In [10]: call_data = icod.get_data_from_www(oType='Call', matMonth=3,
....:                                       matYear=2016, date=ds)
....:


In [11]: put_data = icod.get_data_from_www(oType='Put', matMonth=3,
....:                                      matYear=2016, date=ds)
....:
```

The return objects need to be parsed.

```
# parse the raw data
In [12]: calls = icod.parse_data(call_data, target_day)

In [13]: puts = icod.parse_data(put_data, target_day)
```

Let us have a look at some meta information about the call options data.

```
In [14]: calls.info()
<class 'pandas.core.frame.DataFrame'>
MultiIndex: 114 entries, (2016-02-01 00:00:00, 600.0) to
(2016-02-01 00:00:00, 6000.0)
Data columns (total 8 columns):
Version number             114 non-null float64
Opening price              114 non-null float64
Daily high                 114 non-null float64
Daily low                  114 non-null float64
Underlying closing price   114 non-null float64
Daily settlem. price       114 non-null float64
Traded contracts           114 non-null int64
Open interest (adj.)*      114 non-null int64
dtypes: float64(6), int64(2)
memory usage: 8.0+ KB
```

And about the put options data.

```
In [15]: puts.info()
<class 'pandas.core.frame.DataFrame'>
MultiIndex: 114 entries, (2016-02-01 00:00:00, 600.0) to
(2016-02-01 00:00:00, 6000.0)
Data columns (total 8 columns):
Version number             114 non-null float64
Opening price              114 non-null float64
Daily high                 114 non-null float64
Daily low                  114 non-null float64
Underlying closing price   114 non-null float64
Daily settlem. price       114 non-null float64
Traded contracts           114 non-null int64
Open interest (adj.)*      114 non-null int64
dtypes: float64(6), int64(2)
memory usage: 8.0+ KB
```

In a next step, we take out the daily settlement prices for both the puts and calls and define two new DataFrame objects.

```
In [16]: calls = pd.DataFrame(calls.rename(
    ....:           columns={'Daily settlem. price': 'Call_Price'}
    ....:                          ).pop('Call_Price').astype(float))
    ....:
```

```
In [17]: puts = pd.DataFrame(puts.rename(
    ....:             columns={'Daily settlem. price':  'Put_Price'}
    ....:                             ).pop('Put_Price').astype(float))
    ....:
```

These two are then merged via the function `merge_and_filter()` into another new `DataFrame` object.

```
In [18]: dataset = icod.merge_and_filter(puts, calls)

In [19]: dataset.info()
<class 'pandas.core.frame.DataFrame'>
MultiIndex: 67 entries, (2016-02-01 00:00:00, 1900.0) to
(2016-02-01 00:00:00, 3625.0)
Data columns (total 2 columns):
Call_Price     67 non-null float64
Put_Price      67 non-null float64
dtypes: float64(2)
memory usage: 1.6+ KB
```

This whole procedure is implemented in the function `collect_option_series()` which yields the same result.

```
In [20]: os = icod.collect_option_series(3, 2016, target_day)

In [21]: os.info()
<class 'pandas.core.frame.DataFrame'>
MultiIndex: 67 entries, (2016-02-01 00:00:00, 1900.0) to
(2016-02-01 00:00:00, 3625.0)
Data columns (total 2 columns):
Call_Price     67 non-null float64
Put_Price      67 non-null float64
dtypes: float64(2)
memory usage: 1.6+ KB
```

The function `data_collection()` repeats this procedure for all those dates for which option data is available and writes (appends) the results in a HDF5 database file.

```
# uncomment to initiate the process (takes a while)
# %time icod.data_collection(path)
```

For the further analyses, we open this HDF5 database file.

```
In [22]: store = pd.HDFStore(path + 'index_option_series.h5', 'r')

In [23]: store
```

```
Out[23]:
<class 'pandas.io.pytables.HDFStore'>
File path: ./source/data/index_option_series.h5
/Feb16               frame          (shape->[1398,2])
/Jan16               frame          (shape->[638,2])
/Mar16               frame          (shape->[1385,2])
```

The collected option series data is easily read from the HDF5 database file in monthly chunks.

```
In [24]: Mar16 = store['Mar16']

In [25]: Mar16.info()
<class 'pandas.core.frame.DataFrame'>
MultiIndex: 1385 entries, (2015-12-18 00:00:00, 1500.0) to (2016-01-15
   00:00:00, 3650.0)
Data columns (total 2 columns):
Call_Price     1385 non-null float64
Put_Price      1385 non-null float64
dtypes: float64(2)
memory usage: 32.5+ KB

In [26]: store.close()
```

Some selected option prices from the large data set:

```
In [27]: Mar16.ix[25:35]
Out[27]:
                            Call_Price Put_Price
  Pricing day Strike price
2015-12-18    2675.0               600.4      21.9
              2700.0               577.3      23.8
              2725.0               554.3      25.9
              2750.0               531.6      28.1
              2775.0               509.0      30.6
              2800.0               486.6      33.2
              2825.0               464.5      36.1
              2850.0               442.6      39.3
              2875.0               421.0      42.6
              2900.0               399.6      46.3
```

5.3 CALCULATING THE SUB-INDEXES

In this section, we use the data file created in the previous one. For all dates of the data file, the Python module index_subindex_calculation.py (see *index_subindex_calculation.py* for the complete script) used in this section decides whether the VSTOXX 1M sub-index is defined or not (remember that the sub-index is not defined at the final settlement day and one day before). If it is defined, the script computes the value of the sub-indexes VSTOXX 1M and VSTOXX 2M; if not, it computes the values of the sub-indexes VSTOXX 2M and VSTOXX 3M, respectively. Finally, it returns a pandas `DataFrame` object with the three time series.

5.3.1 The Algorithm

First, we focus on the computation of the value of a single sub-index for a given date. The prices $C_i, i \in \{0, ..., n\}$, of a series of European call options on the EURO STOXX 50 with fixed maturity date T and exercise prices $K_i, i \in \{0, ..., n\}$ are given, as well as the prices $P_i, i \in \{0, ..., n\}$, of a series of European put options on EURO STOXX 50 with the same maturity date T and exercise prices K_i. Let us further hold that $K_i < K_{i+1}$ for all $i \in \{0, ..., n-1\}$.

Then, the value of the relevant sub-index V is as follows (see chapter 3, *Model-Free Replication of Variance*):

$$V = 100 \cdot \sqrt{\hat{\sigma}^2}$$

with

$$\hat{\sigma}^2 = \frac{2}{T} \sum_{i=0}^{n} \frac{\Delta K_i}{K_i^2} e^{rT} M_i - \frac{1}{T} \left(\frac{F}{K_*} - 1 \right)^2$$

where

$$\Delta K_i = \begin{cases} K_1 - K_0 & \text{for } i = 0 \\ \dfrac{K_{i+1} - K_{i-1}}{2} & \text{for } i = 1, ..., n-1 \\ K_n - K_{n-1} & \text{for } i = n \end{cases}$$

r = constant risk-free short rate appropriate for maturity T

F $= K_j + e^{rT}|C_j - P_j|$, where $j = \min\limits_{i \in \{0,...,n\}} \{|C_i - P_i|\}$

K_* $= \max\limits_{K_i | i \in \{0,...,n\}} \{K_i < F\}$,

$$M_i = \begin{cases} P_i & \text{for } K_i < K_* \\ \dfrac{P_i - C_i}{2} & \text{for } K_i = K_* \\ C_i & \text{for } K_i > K_* \end{cases}$$

We implement a function to compute one value of a single sub-index. Thereafter, we extend that function to compute time series for both VSTOXX 1M and VSTOXX 2M indexes as well as parts of the VSTOXX 3M index. Imports again make up the beginning of the script.

```
import math
import numpy as np
import pandas as pd
import datetime as dt
import index_date_functions as idf
```

A core function of the script is `compute_subindex()`.

```python
def compute_subindex(data, delta_T, R):
    ''' Computes a sub-index for given option series data.

    Parameters
    ==========
    data: pandas.DataFrame object
        contains the option data
    delta_T: float
        time interval
    R: float
        discount factor

    Returns
    =======
    subVSTOXX: float
        sub-index value
    '''
    # difference between put and call option with same strike
    data['Diff_Put_Call']  = np.abs(data.Put_Price - data.Call_Price)
    # converts the strike price which serves as index so far
    # to a regular data column
    data = data.reset_index()
    data['delta_K'] = None
    # differences between the different strikes of the series
    data['delta_K'].iloc[1:-1] = [(data['Strike price'][i + 1]
            - data['Strike price'][i - 1]) / 2  for i in data.index[1:-1]]
            # where possible, for the i-th entry it is
            # half of the difference between the (i-1)-th
            # and (i+1)-th price
  # for i=0 it is just the difference to the next strike
    data['delta_K'].iloc[0] = data['Strike price'][1] - data['Strike price'][0]

    data['delta_K'].iloc[data.index[-1:]] = float(data['Strike price'][-1:]) \
            - float(data['Strike price'][-2:-1])
            # for the last entry, it is just the difference
            # between the second but last strike and the last strike price

    # find the smallest difference between put and call price
    min_index = data. Diff_Put_Call.argmin()
```

```
# the forward price of that option
forward_price = data['Strike price'][min_index] \
                    + R * data.Diff_Put_Call[min_index]

K_0 = data['Strike price'][forward_price -
                                data['Strike price'] > 0].max()
# the index of the ATM strike
K_0_index = data.index[data['Strike price'] == K_0][0]

# selects the OTM options
data['M'] = pd.concat((data.Put_Price[0:K_0_index],
                       data.Call_Price[K_0_index:]))

# ATM we take the average of put and call price
data['M'].iloc[K_0_index] = (data['Call_Price'][K_0_index]
                        + data['Put_Price'][K_0_index]) / 2
# the single OTM values
data['MFactor'] = (R * (data['delta_K'] * data['M'])
                   / (data['Strike price']) ** 2)

# the forward term
fterm = 1. / delta_T *(forward_price / K_0 - 1) ** 2
# summing up
sigma = 2 / delta_T * np.sum(data.MFactor) - fterm
subVSTOXX = 100 * math.sqrt(sigma)
return subVSTOXX
```

This script calculates a single index value. It implements mainly the following steps:

- the calculation of ΔK_i
- the computation of the forward price and the index of K_*
- the selection of the at-the-money option and the out-of-the-money options
- the combination of the results of the other three steps.

The next step is the derivation of time series data for the VSTOXX 1M and VSTOXX 2M as well as parts of the VSTOXX 3M indexes and storage of the results in a pandas DataFrame object. As data source we use the file created in the last section. Remember that this file contains a dictionary-like HDFStore object with one entry for every options series. The keys for the entries are three letter abbreviations of the respective month's name plus the actual year represented by two numbers, for example Mar16, Jun16 and so on. The value of an entry is a pandas DataFrame object with a pandas MultiIndex (date, strike price) and prices for the put and call options for the dates and strike prices.

All this is implemented as function make_subindex().

```
def make_subindex(path):
    ''' Depending on the content of the file 'index_option_series.h5',
    the function computes the sub-indexes V6I1, V6I2 and parts
    of V6I3 and returns a pandas DataFrame object with the results.
```

```
    Parameters
    ==========
    path: string
        string with path of data file

    Returns
    =======
    df: pandas DataFrame object
        sub-index data as computed by the function
    '''

    # the data source, created with index_collect_option_data.py
    datastore = pd.HDFStore(path + 'index_option_series.h5', 'r')

    max_date = dt.datetime.today()  # find the latest date in the source
    for series in datastore.keys():
        dummy_date = datastore[series].index.get_level_values(0)[0]
        dummy_date = dummy_date.to_pydatetime()
        if dummy_date > max_date:
            max_date = dummy_date

    start_date = dt.datetime.today()  # find the earliest date in the source
    for series in datastore.keys():
        dummy_date = datastore[series].index.get_level_values(0)[0]
        dummy_data = dummy_date.to_pydatetime()
        if dummy_date < start_date:
            start_date = dummy_date

    V1 = dict()   # dicts to store the values, V stands for the sub-indices,
                  # T for their expiry
    V2 = dict()
    V3 = dict()
    T1 = dict()
    T2 = dict()
    T3 = dict()

    # from start_date to max_date, but only weekdays
    for day in pd.bdate_range(start=start_date.date(), end=max_date.date()):
        # is V6I1 defined?
        is_V1_defined = idf.not_a_day_before_expiry(day)
        # the settlement date
        settlement_date = idf.first_settlement_day(day)
        # abbreviation for the expiry date, like Oct14
        key = settlement_date.strftime('%b%y')
        # days until maturity
        delta_T = idf.compute_delta(day, settlement_date)
        try:
            # data of the option series for that date
            data = datastore[key].ix[day]
        except:
            continue
```

```
    if  is_V1_defined:  # if V6I1 is defined
        # compute its value
        V1[day] = compute_subindex(data, delta_T,
                                   math.exp(0.0015 * delta_T))
        T1[day] = settlement_date
    else:
        # compute the value of V6I2 instead
        V2[day] = compute_subindex(data,  delta_T,
                                   math.exp(0.0015 * delta_T))
        T2[day] = settlement_date

    settlement_date_2 = idf.second_settlement_day(day)

    # the same for the next index
    key_2 = settlement_date_2.strftime('%b%y')
    delta_T_2 = idf.compute_delta(day, settlement_date_2)
    data_2 = datastore[key_2].ix[day]

    if is_V1_defined:
        V2[day] = compute_subindex(data_2, delta_T_2,
                                   math.exp(0.001 * delta_T_2))
        T2[day] = settlement_date_2
    else:
        V3[day] = compute_subindex(data_2, delta_T_2,
                                   math.exp(0.001 * delta_T_2))
        T3[day] =  settlement_date_2

    datastore.close()
    # create the pandas DataFrame object and return it
    df = pd.DataFrame(data={'V6I1': V1, 'Expiry V6I1': T1, 'V6I2': V2,
                     'Expiry V6I2': T2, 'V6I3': V3, 'Expiry V6I3': T3})
    return df
```

This function uses the collected option series data and selects those data sub-sets needed for the calculation at hand. It generates sub-index values for all those days for which option data is available. The result is a pandas `DataFrame` object.

Let us see how it works. To this end, we first import the module as `isc`.

```
In [28]: import index_subindex_calculation as isc

In [29]: si = isc.make_subindex(path)

In [30]: si
Out[30]:
           Expiry V6I1 Expiry V6I2  Expiry V6I3        V6I1        V6I2 \
2015-12-18         NaT  2016-01-15   2016-02-19         NaN   23.757165
2015-12-21  2016-01-15  2016-02-19                     NaT   23.616427  24.665801
2015-12-22  2016-01-15  2016-02-19                     NaT   21.908727  23.629867
2015-12-23  2016-01-15  2016-02-19                     NaT   19.398907  21.488879
```

```
2015-12-24  2016-01-15 2016-02-19           NaT  19.839390  21.677283
2015-12-28  2016-01-15 2016-02-19           NaT  21.493148  23.080926
2015-12-29  2016-01-15 2016-02-19           NaT  20.611811  22.199482
2015-12-30  2016-01-15 2016-02-19           NaT  21.522201  22.788559
2015-12-31  2016-01-15 2016-02-19           NaT  22.238762  23.016324
2016-01-04  2016-01-15 2016-02-19           NaT  28.926899  26.646698
2016-01-05  2016-01-15 2016-02-19           NaT  27.510874  25.983436
2016-01-06  2016-01-15 2016-02-19           NaT  27.451164  26.101145
2016-01-07  2016-01-15 2016-02-19           NaT  33.536380  29.502767
2016-01-08  2016-01-15 2016-02-19           NaT  33.400592  30.060601
2016-01-11  2016-01-15 2016-02-19           NaT  35.084411  30.005212
2016-01-12  2016-01-15 2016-02-19           NaT  33.266282  28.420558
2016-01-13  2016-01-15 2016-02-19           NaT  34.566710  28.058019
2016-01-14         NaT 2016-02-19    2016-03-18          NaN  29.864680
2016-01-15         NaT 2016-02-19    2016-03-18          NaN  34.195075


                  V6I3
2015-12-18   24.740060
2015-12-21        NaN
2015-12-22        NaN
2015-12-23        NaN
2015-12-24        NaN
2015-12-28        NaN
2015-12-29        NaN
2015-12-30        NaN
2015-12-31        NaN
2016-01-04        NaN
2016-01-05        NaN
2016-01-06        NaN
2016-01-07        NaN
2016-01-08        NaN
2016-01-11        NaN
2016-01-12        NaN
2016-01-13        NaN
2016-01-14   29.495976
2016-01-15   32.797564
```

For comparison, we retrieve the "real" historical VSTOXX (sub-)index values from the official website.

```
In [31]: vs_url = 'https://www.stoxx.com/document/'

In [32]: vs_url += 'Indices/Current/HistoricalData/h_vstoxx.txt'

In [33]: vs = pd.read_csv(vs_url,    # filename
   ....:                  index_col=0,   # index column (dates)
   ....:                  parse_dates=True,  # parse date information
```

```
    ....:                dayfirst=True,   # day before month
    ....:                header=2)   # header/column names
    ....:

In [34]: vs.to_csv(path + 'vs.csv')   # write as CSV file

In [35]: vs = vs[vs.index <= '2015-12-31']

In [36]: vs.info()
<class 'pandas.core.frame.DataFrame'>
DatetimeIndex: 4327 entries, 1999-01-04 to 2015-12-30
Data columns (total 9 columns):
V2TX    4327 non-null float64
V6I1    3878 non-null float64
V6I2    4327 non-null float64
V6I3    4267 non-null float64
V6I4    4327 non-null float64
V6I5    4327 non-null float64
V6I6    4310 non-null float64
V6I7    4327 non-null float64
V6I8    4313 non-null float64
dtypes: float64(9)
memory usage: 338.0 KB
```

Next, combine the re-calculated VSTOXX 2M values with the historical ones into a new
`DataFrame` object and add a new column with the absolute differences.

```
In [37]: comp = pd.concat((si['V6I2'], vs['V6I2']),
    ....:            axis=1, join='inner')
    ....:

In [38]: comp.index = comp.index.normalize()

In [39]: comp.columns = ['CALC', 'REAL']

In [40]: comp['DIFF'] = comp['CALC'] - comp['REAL']

In [41]: comp
Out[41]:
                    CALC      REAL       DIFF
2015-12-18    23.757165   23.7604   -0.003235
2015-12-21    24.665801   24.6237    0.042101
2015-12-22    23.629867   23.6439   -0.014033
2015-12-23    21.488879   21.4523    0.036579
2015-12-28    23.080926   23.0757    0.005226
2015-12-29    22.199482   22.1429    0.056582
2015-12-30    22.788559   22.6419    0.146659
```

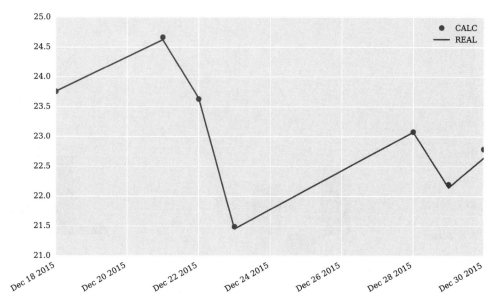

FIGURE 5.1 Calculated VSTOXX 2M sub-index values vs. real ones.

Figure 5.1 shows the two time series in direct comparison.

```
In [42]: import seaborn as sns; sns.set()

In [43]: import matplotlib

In [44]: matplotlib.rcParams['font.family'] = 'serif'  # set serif font

In [45]: comp[['CALC', 'REAL']].plot(style=['ro', 'b'], figsize=(10, 6));
```

Figure 5.2 shows the point-wise differences between the two time series.

```
In [46]: import matplotlib.pyplot as plt

In [47]: plt.figure(figsize=(10, 6));

In [48]: plt.bar(comp.index, comp['DIFF']);

In [49]: plt.gcf().autofmt_xdate();
```

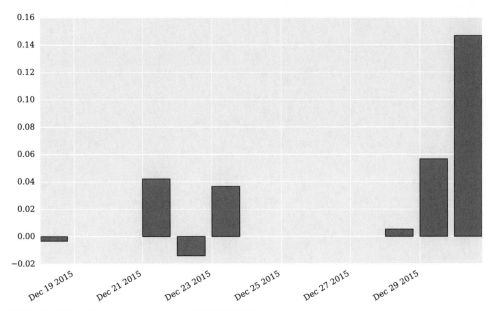

FIGURE 5.2   Differences of calculated VSTOXX 2M index values and real ones.

5.4 CALCULATING THE VSTOXX INDEX

If the values for the sub-indexes VSTOXX 1M and VSTOXX 2M, V_1 and V_2 say, are given, then the value for the VSTOXX index itself, V say, is calculated by the linear interpolation of V_1 and V_2:

$$V = \sqrt{\left(T_1 \cdot V_1^2 \cdot \left(\frac{N_{T_2} - N_{30}}{N_{T_2} - N_{T_1}} \right) + T_2 \cdot V_2^2 \cdot \left(\frac{N_{30} - N_{T_1}}{N_{T_2} - N_{T_1}} \right) \right) \cdot \frac{N_{365}}{N_{30}}}$$

where

- N_{T_1} = time to expiry of V_1's options series in seconds
- N_{T_2} = time to expiry of V_2's options series in seconds
- N_{30} = 30 days in seconds
- N_{365} = time for a standard year in seconds
- $T_1 = N_{T_1}/N_{365}$
- $T_2 = N_{T_2}/N_{365}$.

Recall that the sub-index VSTOXX 1M is not defined on the final settlement day of the underlying option series and the day before. For these dates, we use VSTOXX 2M and VSTOXX 3M as V_1 and V_2, respectively.

The Python module index_vstoxx_calculation.py (see sub-section 5.6.3, *index_vstoxx_calculation.py* for the module in its entirety) implements the VSTOXX index calculation routine – given the respective sub-index time series data sets. The module starts as usual with some imports.

```
import pandas as pd
import numpy as np
import matplotlib.pyplot as plt
from index_date_functions import *
```

The function `calculate_vstoxx()` is the core of the module.

```
def calculate_vstoxx(path):
    ''' Function to calculate the VSTOXX volatility index given time series
    of the relevant sub-indexes.

    Parameters
    ==========
    path: string
        string with path of data files

    Returns
    =======
    data: pandas DataFrame object
        results of index calculation
    '''
    # constant parameters
    seconds_year = 365 * 24 * 3600.
    seconds_30_days = 30 * 24 * 3600.

    # import historical VSTOXX data
    data = pd.read_csv(path + 'vs.csv', index_col=0, parse_dates=True)
    # determine the settlement dates for the two underlying option series
    data['Settlement date 1'] = [first_settlement_day(a) for a in data.index]
    data['Settlement date 2'] = [second_settlement_day(a) for a in data.index]

    # deduce the life time (in seconds) from current date to
    # final settlement Date
    data['Life time 1'] = [(data['Settlement date 1'][i] - i).days
                            * 24 * 60 * 60 for i in data.index]
    data['Life time 2'] = [(data['Settlement date 2'][i] - i).days
                            * 24 * 60 * 60 for i in data.index]

    data['Use V6I2'] = data['V6I1'].notnull()  # where V6I1 is not defined
    data['Subindex to use 1'] = [data['V6I1'][i]  if data['Use V6I2'][i]
                        else data['V6I2'][i] for i in data.index]
                        # if V6I1 is defined, use V6I1 and V6I2 as data set
    data['Subindex to use 2'] = [data['V6I2'][i]  if data['Use V6I2'][i]
                        else data['V6I3'][i] for i in data.index]
                        # else use V6I2 and V6I3

    # the linear interpolation of the VSTOXX value
    # from the two relevant sub-indexes
```

```
data['Part 1'] = data['Life time 1'] / seconds_year \
                   * data['Subindex to use 1'] ** 2 \
                   * ((data['Life time 2'] - seconds_30_days)
                   / (data['Life time 2'] - data['Life time 1']))

data['Part 2'] = data['Life time 2'] / seconds_year \
                   * data['Subindex to use 2'] ** 2 \
                   * ((seconds_30_days - data['Life time 1'])
                   / (data['Life time 2'] - data['Life time 1']))

data['VSTOXX'] = np.sqrt((data['Part 1'] + data['Part 2'])  *
                   seconds_year / seconds_30_days)

# difference between original VSTOXX data and re-calculated values
data['Difference'] = data['V2TX'] - data['VSTOXX']

return data
```

As its single argument, the function takes the path to a CSV file containing historical VSTOXX data for the index itself and the sub-indexes. The re-calculation of it then is as straightforward as follows:

```
In [50]: import index_vstoxx_calculation as ivc

In [51]: %time data = ivc.calculate_vstoxx(path)
CPU times: user 1.19 s, sys: 38 us, total: 1.19 s
Wall time: 1.2 s
```

Let us inspect the pandas DataFrame which now contains the results of the previous code execution:

```
In [52]: data.info()
<class 'pandas.core.frame.DataFrame'>
DatetimeIndex: 4357 entries, 1999-01-04 to 2016-02-12
Data columns (total 20 columns):
V2TX                4357 non-null float64
V6I1                3906 non-null float64
V6I2                4357 non-null float64
V6I3                4296 non-null float64
V6I4                4357 non-null float64
V6I5                4357 non-null float64
V6I6                4340 non-null float64
V6I7                4357 non-null float64
V6I8                4343 non-null float64
Settlement date 1   4357 non-null datetime64[ns]
Settlement date 2   4357 non-null datetime64[ns]
Life time 1         4357 non-null int64
```

```
Life time 2              4357 non-null int64
Use V6I2                 4357 non-null bool
Subindex to use 1        4357 non-null float64
Subindex to use 2        4357 non-null float64
Part 1                   4357 non-null float64
Part 2                   4357 non-null float64
VSTOXX                   4357 non-null float64
Difference               4357 non-null float64
dtypes: bool(1), datetime64[ns](2), float64(15), int64(2)
memory usage: 685.0 KB
```

A brief look at the absolute average error of the re-calculation reveals that the implementation yields quite accurate results.

```
# output: average error of re-calculation
In [53]: data['Difference'].mean()
Out[53]: 0.0012799470095575995
```

Figure 5.3 compares the original V2TX time series with the re-calculated values.

```
# original vs. re-calculated VSTOXX index
In [54]: data[['V2TX', 'VSTOXX']].plot(subplots=True, figsize=(10, 6),
    ....:                               style="blue", grid=True);
    ....:
```

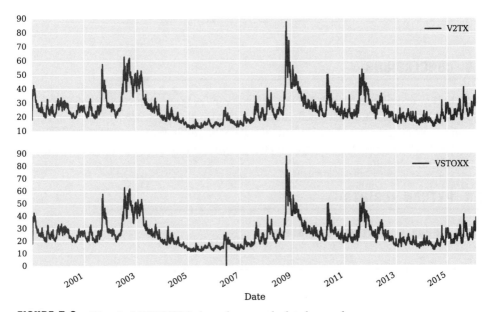

FIGURE 5.3   Historical VSTOXX index values re-calculated vs. real ones.

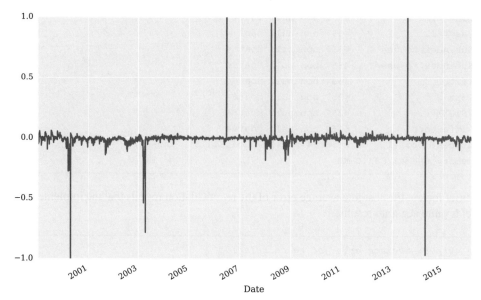

FIGURE 5.4   Differences of historical VSTOXX index values re-calculated vs. real ones.

Finally, Figure 5.4 presents the absolute differences. The figure shows that the differences are in general marginal with a few outliers observed here and there.

```
# differences between single values
In [55]: data['Difference'].plot(figsize=(10, 6), style="r", grid=True,
    ....:                         ylim=(-1, 1));
    ....:
```

5.5 CONCLUSIONS

This chapter (re-)calculates the VSTOXX volatility index based on historical sub-index values and based on the volatility index definition as derived in chapter 3, *Model-Free Replication of Variance*. The chapter also shows how to calculate the sub-index values themselves based on EURO STOXX 50 options data. Python code is provided to automatically collect such data from the Eurex website.

5.6 PYTHON SCRIPTS

5.6.1 index_collect_option_data.py

```
#
# Module to collect option series data
# from the web
```

```python
# Source: www.eurexchange.com
# Data is needed to calculate the VSTOXX
# and its sub-indexes
#
# (c) Dr. Yves J. Hilpisch
# Listed Volatility and Variance Derivatives
#
import requests
import datetime as dt
import pandas as pd
import numpy as np
from StringIO import *
from index_date_functions import *


#
# The URL template
#
url1 = 'http://www.eurexchange.com/action/exchange-en/'
url2 = '180106-180102/180102/onlineStats.do?productGroupId=846'
url3 = '&productId=19068&viewType=3&cp=%s &month=%s &year=%s &busDate=%s'
URL = url1 + url2 + url3


def collect_option_series(month, year, start):
    ''' Collects daily option data from web source.

    Parameters
    ==========
    month: int
        maturity month
    year: int
        maturity year
    start: datetime object
        starting date

    Returns
    =======
    dataset: pandas DataFrame object
        object containing the collected data
    '''
    end = dt.datetime.today()
    delta = (end - start).days

    dataset = pd.DataFrame()
    for t in range(0, delta):  # runs from start to today
        date = start + dt.timedelta(t)
        dummy = get_data(month, year, date)  # get data for one day
        if len(dummy) != 0:
```

```
            if len(dataset) == 0:
                dataset = dummy
            else:
                dataset = pd.concat((dataset, dummy))  # add data
    return dataset

def get_data(month, year, date):
    ''' Get the data for an option series.

    Parameters
    ==========
    month: int
        maturity month
    year: int
        maturity year
    date: datetime object
        the date for which the data is collected

    Returns
    =======
    dataset: pandas DataFrame object
        object containing call & put option data
    '''

    date_string = date.strftime('%Y%m%d')
    # loads the call data from the web
    data = get_data_from_www('Call', month,  year, date_string)
    calls = parse_data(data,  date)  # parse the raw data
    calls = calls.rename(columns={'Daily settlem.price': 'Call_Price'})

    calls = pd.DataFrame(calls.pop('Call_Price').astype(float))
    # the same for puts
    data = get_data_from_www('Put',  month,  year, date_string)
    puts = parse_data(data,  date)
    puts = puts.rename(columns={'Daily settlem.price': 'Put_Price'})
    puts = pd.DataFrame(puts.pop('Put_Price').astype(float))

    dataset = merge_and_filter(puts, calls)  # merges the two time series

    return dataset

def get_data_from_www(oType, matMonth, matYear, date):
    ''' Retrieves the raw data of an option series from the web.

    Parameters
    ==========
    oType: string
        either 'Put' or 'Call'
```

```
        matMonth: int
            maturity month
        matYear: int
            maturity year
        date: string
            expiry in the format 'YYYYMMDD'

        Returns
        =======
        a: string
            raw text with option data
        '''

        url = URL % (oType, matMonth, matYear, date)   # parametrizes the URL
        a = requests.get(url).text
        return a

def merge_and_filter(puts, calls):
        ''' Gets two pandas time series for the puts and calls
        (from the same option series), merges them, filters out
        all options with prices smaller than 0.5 and
        returns the resulting DataFrame object.

        Parameters
        ==========
        puts: pandas DataFrame object
            put option data
        calls: pandas DataFrame object
            call option data

        Returns
        =======
        df: pandas DataFrame object
            merged & filtered options data
        '''

        df = calls.join(puts,  how=' inner')   # merges the two time series
        # filters all prices which are too small
        df = df[(df. Put_Price  >= 0.5)  & (df.Call_Price  >=  0.5)]

        return df

def parse_data(data, date):
        ''' Parses the HTML table and transforms it into a CSV compatible
        format. The result can be directly imported into a pandas DataFrame.

        Parameters
        ==========
```

```
    data: string
        document containing the Web content
    date: datetime object
        date for which the data is parsed

    Returns
    =======
    dataset: pandas DataFrame object
        transformed option raw data
    '''
    parts = data.split('<table')
    parts2  =  parts[1].split('</table')
    dummy = parts2[0].replace('class="odd"','')
    dummy = dummy.replace('class="even"','')
    parts3  =  dummy.split('<tr><td><b>Total</b>')
    table = parts3[0]  # the html table containing the data
    table = table.replace('class="dataTable"><thead>', 'Pricing day')

    # replace tags by commas and newlines
    table = table.replace('</tr>', '\n')
    table = table.replace(',', '')
    table = table.replace('<td>', ',')
    table = table.replace('</td>', '')
    table = table.replace('<th>', ',')
    table = table.replace('</th>', '')
    table = table.replace('</thead><tbody>', '\n')

    # the resulting string looks like a CSV file
    date_string = date.strftime('%d .%m.%Y')
    table = table.replace('<tr>',  date_string)

    string = StringIO(table)  # mask the string as file
    dataset = pd.read_csv(string, parse_dates=[0], index_col=(0, 1),
                dayfirst=True)  # read the 'file' as pandas DataFrame object

    return dataset

def data_collection(path):
    ''' Main function which saves data into the HDF5 file
    'index_option_series.h5' for later use.

    Parameters
    ==========
    path: string
        path to store the data
    '''
    # file to store data
    store = pd.HDFStore(path + 'index_option_series.h5', 'a')
```

```python
    today = dt.datetime.today()
    start = today - dt.timedelta(31)  # the last 31 days

    day = start.day
    month = start.month
    year = start.year

    for i in range(4):  # iterates over the next 4 months
        dummy_month = month + i
        dummy_year = year
        if dummy_month > 12:
            dummy_month -= 12
            dummy_year += 1

        # collect daily data beginning 31 days ago (start) for
        # option series with expiry dummy_month, dummy_year
        dataset = collect_option_series(dummy_month, dummy_year, start)

        dummy_date = dt.datetime(dummy_year, dummy_month, day)

        # abbreviation for expiry date (for example Oct14)
        series_name = dummy_date.strftime('%b%y')

        if series_name in store.keys():  # if data for that series exists
            index_old = store[series_name].index
            index_new = dataset.index

            if len(index_new - index_old) > 0:
                dummy = pd.concat((store[series_name],
                    dataset.ix[index_new - index_old]))  # add the new data

                store[series_name] = dummy
        else:
            if len(dataset) > 0:
            # if series is new, write whole data set into data store
                store[series_name]  =  dataset

    store.close()
```

5.6.2 index_subindex_calculation.py

```python
#
# Module with functions to compute VSTOXX sub-indexes
#
# Data as generated by the script index_collect_option_data.py
# is needed for the calculations in this module
#
# (c) Dr. Yves J. Hilpisch
```

```python
# Listed Volatility and Variance Derivatives
#
import math
import numpy as np
import pandas as pd
import datetime as dt
import index_date_functions as idf


def compute_subindex(data, delta_T, R):
    ''' Computes a sub-index for given option series data.

    Parameters
    ==========
    data: pandas.DataFrame object
        contains the option data
    delta_T: float
        time interval
    R: float
        discount factor

    Returns
    =======
    subVSTOXX: float
        sub-index value
    '''
    # difference between put and call option with same strike
    data['Diff_Put_Call'] = np.abs(data. Put_Price - data.Call_Price)
    # converts the strike price which serves as index so far
    # to a regular data column
    data = data.reset_index()
    data['delta_K'] = None
    # differences between the different strikes of the series
    data['delta_K'].iloc[1:-1] = [(data['Strike price'][i + 1]
            - data['Strike price'][i - 1]) / 2 for i in data.index[1:-1]]
            # where possible, for the i-th entry it is
            # half of the difference between the (i-1)-th
            # and (i+1)-th price
    # for i=0 it is just the difference to the next strike
    data['delta_K'].iloc[0] = data['Strike price'][1] - data['Strike price'][0]

    data['delta_K'].iloc[data.index[-1:]] = float(data['Strike price'][-1:]) \
            - float(data['Strike price'][-2: -1])
            # for the last entry, it is just the difference
            # between the second but last strike and the last strike price

    # find the smallest difference between put and call price
    min_index = data. Diff_Put_Call.argmin()

    # the forward price of that option
    forward_price = data['Strike price'][min_index] \
                    + R * data.Diff_Put_Call[min_index]
```

```
    K_0 = data['Strike price'][forward_price -
                               data['Strike price'] > 0].max()
    # the index of the ATM strike
    K_0_index = data.index[data['Strike price'] == K_0][0]

    # selects the OTM options
    data['M'] = pd.concat((data.Put_Price[0:K_0_index],
                           data.Call_Price[K_0_index:]))

    # ATM we take the average of put and call price
    data['M'].iloc[K_0_index] = (data['Call_Price'][K_0_index]
                        + data['Put_Price'][K_0_index]) / 2
    # the single OTM values
    data['MFactor'] = (R * (data['delta_K'] * data['M'])
                        / (data['Strike price']) ** 2)

    # the forward term
    fterm = 1. / delta_T * (forward_price / K_0 - 1) ** 2
    # summing up
    sigma = 2 / delta_T * np.sum(data.MFactor) - fterm
    subVSTOXX = 100 * math.sqrt(sigma)
    return subVSTOXX

def make_subindex(path):
    ''' Depending on the content of the file 'index_option_series.h5',
    the function computes the sub-indexes V6I1, V6I2 and parts
    of V6I3 and returns a pandas DataFrame object with the results.

    Parameters
    ==========
    path: string
        string with path of data file

    Returns
    =======
    df: pandas DataFrame object
        sub-index data as computed by the function
    '''

    # the data source, created with index_collect_option_data.py
    datastore = pd.HDFStore(path + 'index_option_series.h5', 'r')

    max_date = dt.datetime.today()  # find the latest date in the source
    for series in datastore.keys():
        dummy_date = datastore[series].index.get_level_values(0)[0]
        dummy_date = dummy_date.to_pydatetime()
        if dummy_date > max_date:
            max_date = dummy_date

    start_date = dt.datetime.today()  # find the earliest date in the source
    for series in datastore.keys():
```

```python
        dummy_date = datastore[series].index.get_level_values(0)[0]
        dummy_data = dummy_date.to_pydatetime()
        if dummy_date < start_date:
            start_date = dummy_date

    V1 = dict()  # dicts to store the values, V stands for the sub-indices,
                 # T for their expiry
    V2 = dict()
    V3 = dict()
    T1 = dict()
    T2 = dict()
    T3 = dict()

    # from start_date to max_date, but only weekdays
    for day in pd.bdate_range(start=start_date.date(), end=max_date.date()):
        # is V6I1 defined?
        is_V1_defined = idf.not_a_day_before_expiry(day)
        # the settlement date
        settlement_date = idf.first_settlement_day(day)
        # abbreviation for the expiry date, like Oct14
        key = settlement_date.strftime('%b%y')
        # days until maturity
        delta_T = idf.compute_delta(day, settlement_date)
        try:
            # data of the option series for that date
            data = datastore[key].ix[day]
        except:
            continue

        if is_V1_defined:  # if V6I1 is defined
            # compute its value
            V1[day] = compute_subindex(data, delta_T,
                                       math.exp(0.0015 * delta_T))
            T1[day] = settlement_date
        else:
            # compute the value of V6I2 instead
            V2[day] = compute_subindex(data, delta_T,
                                       math.exp(0.0015 * delta_T))
            T2[day] = settlement_date
        settlement_date_2 = idf.second_settlement_day(day)

        # the same for the next index
        key_2 = settlement_date_2.strftime('%b%y')
        delta_T_2 = idf.compute_delta(day, settlement_date_2)
        data_2 = datastore[key_2].ix[day]

        if is_V1_defined:
            V2[day] = compute_subindex(data_2, delta_T_2,
                                       math.exp(0.001 * delta_T_2))
            T2[day] = settlement_date_2
```

```
        else:
            V3[day] = compute_subindex(data_2, delta_T_2,
                                    math.exp(0.001 * delta_T_2))
            T3[day] = settlement_date_2

    datastore.close()
    # create the pandas DataFrame object and return it
    df = pd.DataFrame(data={'V6I1': V1, 'Expiry V6I1': T1, 'V6I2': V2,
                'Expiry V6I2': T2, 'V6I3': V3, 'Expiry V6I3': T3})
    return df
```

5.6.3 index_vstoxx_calculation.py

```
#
# Module to compute VSTOXX index values
# given the values for the relevant sub-indexes
# as generated by the module index_subindex_calculation.py
#
# (c) Dr. Yves J. Hilpisch
# Listed Volatility and Variance Derivatives
#
import pandas as pd
import numpy as np
import matplotlib.pyplot as plt
from index_date_functions import *


def calculate_vstoxx(path):
    ''' Function to calculate the VSTOXX volatility index given time series
    of the relevant sub-indexes.

    Parameters
    ==========
    path: string
        string with path of data files

    Returns
    =======
    data: pandas DataFrame object
        results of index calculation
    '''
    # constant parameters
    seconds_year = 365 * 24 * 3600.
    seconds_30_days = 30 * 24 * 3600.

    # import historical VSTOXX data
    data = pd.read_csv(path + 'vs.csv', index_col=0, parse_dates=True)
```

```python
    # determine the settlement dates for the two underlying option series
    data['Settlement date 1'] = [first_settlement_day(a) for a in data.index]
    data['Settlement date 2'] = [second_settlement_day(a) for a in data.index]

    # deduce the life time (in seconds) from current date to
    # final settlement Date
    data['Life time 1'] = [(data['Settlement date 1'][i] - i).days
                            * 24 * 60 * 60 for i in data.index]
    data['Life time 2'] = [(data['Settlement date 2'][i] - i).days
                            * 24 * 60 * 60 for i in data.index]

    data['Use V6I2'] = data['V6I1'].notnull()  # where V6I1 is not defined
    data['Subindex to use 1'] = [data['V6I1'][i] if data['Use V6I2'][i]
                        else data['V6I2'][i] for i in data.index]
                        # if V6I1 is defined, use V6I1 and V6I2 as data set
    data['Subindex to use 2'] = [data['V6I2'][i] if data['Use V6I2'][i]
                        else data['V6I3'][i] for i in data.index]
                        # else use V6I2 and V6I3

    # the linear interpolation of the VSTOXX value
    # from the two relevant sub-indexes
    data['Part 1'] = data['Life time 1'] / seconds_year \
                    * data['Subindex to use 1'] ** 2 \
                    * ((data['Life time 2'] - seconds_30_days)
                    / (data['Life time 2'] - data['Life time 1']))

    data['Part 2'] = data['Life time 2'] / seconds_year \
                    * data['Subindex to use 2'] ** 2 \
                    * ((seconds_30_days - data['Life time 1'])
                    / (data['Life time 2'] - data['Life time 1'])) \

    data['VSTOXX'] = np.sqrt((data['Part 1'] + data['Part 2']) *
                    seconds_year / seconds_30_days)

    # difference between original VSTOXX data and re-calculated values
    data['Difference'] = data['V2TX'] - data['VSTOXX']

    return data
```

CHAPTER 6

Valuing Volatility Derivatives

6.1 INTRODUCTION

This chapter illustrates the valuation of volatility futures and options according to Grünbichler and Longstaff (1996), abbreviated in the following by GL96. They derive a semi-analytical ("closed") pricing formula for European volatility call options which is as easy to use as the famous Black-Scholes-Merton formula for equity options pricing. They model volatility directly and make the assumption that volatility follows a square-root diffusion process. The model is quite simple and parsimonious, such that it lends itself pretty well to serve as a starting point.

This chapter introduces the financial model, the futures and option pricing formulas of Grünbichler and Longstaff as well as a discretization of the model for Monte Carlo simulation purposes. For both the formulas and the Monte Carlo simulation approach, Python implementations are presented. Finally, the chapter shows in detail how to calibrate the GL96 model to market quotes for European call options on the VSTOXX volatility index.

6.2 THE VALUATION FRAMEWORK

Grünbichler and Longstaff (1996) model the volatility process (e.g. the process of a volatility index) in direct fashion by a square-root diffusion or CIR process – named after the authors John C. Cox, Jonathan E. Ingersoll and Stephen A. Ross, who first introduced this type of stochastic process to finance; see Cox et al. (1985). The stochastic differential equation describing the evolution of the volatility over time takes the form

$$dv_t = \kappa(\theta - v_t)dt + \sigma\sqrt{v}dZ_t$$

where

- v_t is the time t value of the volatility index, for example the VSTOXX
- θ is the long-run mean of the volatility index
- κ is the rate at which v_t reverts to θ
- σ is the volatility of the volatility ("vol-vol")
- θ, κ, σ are assumed to be constant and positive
- Z_t is a standard Brownian motion.

This process is known to exhibit convenient and realistic features for volatility modeling, such as positivity and mean-reversion.

For the numerical examples in this chapter we use a parametrization as follows:

```
In [1]: import math

# model parameters
In [2]: v0 = 17.5  # initial level of volatility index

In [3]: kappa = 0.1  # speed of mean reversion

In [4]: theta = 20.0  # long-term index level

In [5]: sigma = 2.0  # volatility of volatility

In [6]: zeta = 0.0  # factor of the expected volatility risk premium

In [7]: r = 0.01  # risk-free short rate

# option parameters
In [8]: K = 20.0  # strike

In [9]: T = 1.0  # time horizon in year fractions
```

6.3 THE FUTURES PRICING FORMULA

Denote by $F(v, T)$ the futures price of a futures contract on the volatility index v with maturity T. The pricing of such a contract is done by taking expectations of the index's value at maturity $F(v, T) = E(v_T)$. One obtains the following formula for the futures price:

$$F(v_0, T) = (1 - e^{-\kappa T}) \cdot \theta + e^{-\kappa T} \cdot v_0$$

It is an exponentially weighted average of the long-run mean and the current value of the volatility index. The function `futures_price` implements this formula in Python, in this instance for a general volatility risk premium $\zeta \geq 0$.

```
def futures_price(v0, kappa, theta, zeta, T):
    ''' Futures pricing formula in GL96 model.

    Parameters
    ==========
    v0: float (positive)
        current volatility level
```

```
    kappa: float (positive)
        mean-reversion factor
    theta: float (positive)
        long-run mean of volatility
    zeta: float (positive)
        volatility risk premium
    T: float (positive)
        time-to-maturity

    Returns
    =======
    future: float
        price of a future
    '''
    alpha = kappa * theta
    beta = kappa + zeta
    future =(alpha / beta * (1 - math.exp(-beta * T))
                        +  math.exp(-beta * T) * v0)

    return future
```

Application of the formula and function is straightforward. However, we have to first import the function from the module in which it is stored.

```
In [10]: from srd_functions import *

In [11]: futures_price(v0, kappa, theta, zeta, T)
Out[11]: 17.7379064549101
```

We obtain a futures term structure by calculating the futures prices for different maturities (see Figure 6.1).

```
In [12]: import numpy as np

In [13]: import seaborn as sns; sns.set()

In [14]: import matplotlib

In [15]: matplotlib.rcParams['font.family'] = 'serif'

In [16]: import matplotlib.pyplot as plt

In [17]: maturities = np.linspace(0, 2, 24)
```

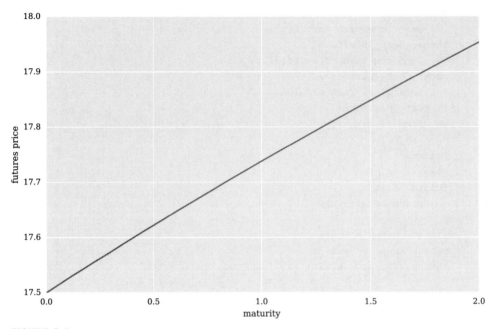

FIGURE 6.1   Futures prices from today to a maturity of 24 months.

```
In [18]: futures_prices = [futures_price(v0, kappa, theta, zeta, T)
    ....:                   for T in maturities]
    ....:

In [19]: plt.figure(figsize=(10, 6));

In [20]: plt.plot(maturities, futures_prices);

In [21]: plt.xlabel('maturity');

In [22]: plt.ylabel('futures price');
```

6.4 THE OPTION PRICING FORMULA

A European call option on the underlying V has a payoff function $\max(V_T - K, 0)$ at maturity T where K is the strike price of the option. Grünbichler and Longstaff (1996) derive the following pricing formula for such a call option:

$$C(v_0, K, T) = e^{-rT} \cdot e^{-\beta T} \cdot V_0 \cdot \mathbf{Q}\,(\gamma \cdot K; v + 4, \lambda)$$
$$+ e^{-rT} \cdot \left(\frac{\alpha}{\beta}\right) \cdot \left(1 - e^{-\beta T}\right) \cdot \mathbf{Q}\,(\gamma \cdot K; v + 2, \lambda)$$
$$- e^{-rT} \cdot K \cdot \mathbf{Q}\,(\gamma \cdot K; v, \lambda)$$

where

$$\alpha = \kappa\theta$$
$$\beta = \kappa + \zeta$$
$$\gamma = \frac{4\beta}{\sigma^2(1 - e^{-\beta T})}$$
$$v = \frac{4\alpha}{\sigma^2}$$
$$\lambda = \gamma \cdot e^{-\beta T} \cdot v_0$$

and e^{-rT} as the discount factor for a fixed short rate r. The parameter ζ denotes as before the expected premium for volatility risk. In the following, we assume $\zeta = 0$.

$\mathbf{Q}(\cdot; v, \lambda)$ is the complementary non-central χ^2 distribution with v degrees of freedom and non-centrality parameter λ.

In our Python implementation `srd_functions.py` (see sub-section 6.9.1, *srd_functions.py* for the complete module), we use the function `ncx2.cdf()` from the `scipy.stats` sub-library for the non-central χ^2 distribution. We implement two different functions, a helper function and the pricing function itself:

- `cx()`: this function returns values for the complementary distribution of the non-central chi-squared density
- `call_price()`: the implementation of the valuation formula for European calls on the volatility index.

The function `cx()` is as follows:

```
def cx(K, gamma, nu, lamb):
    ''' Complementary distribution function of non-central chi-squared density.

    Parameters
    ==========
    K: float (positive)
        strike price
    gamma: float (positive)
        as defined in the GL96 model
    nu: float (positive)
        degrees of freedom
    lamb: float (positive)
        non-centrality parameter

    Returns
    =======
    complementary distribution of nc cs density
    '''
    return 1 - scs.ncx2.cdf(gamma * K, nu, lamb)
```

The function cx() is used in the valuation function call_price().

```
def call_price(v0, kappa, theta, sigma, zeta, T, r, K):
    ''' Call option pricing formula in GL96 Model

    Parameters
    ==========
    v0: float (positive)
        current volatility level
    kappa: float (positive)
        mean-reversion factor
    theta: float (positive)
        long-run mean of volatility
    sigma: float (positive)
        volatility of volatility
    zeta: float (positive)
        volatility risk premium
    T: float (positive)
        time-to-maturity
    r: float (positive)
        risk-free short rate
    K: float (positive)
        strike price of the option

    Returns
    =======
    call: float
        present value of European call option
    '''
    D = math.exp(-r * T)   # discount factor

    alpha = kappa * theta
    beta = kappa + zeta
    gamma = 4 * beta / (sigma ** 2 * (1 - math.exp(-beta * T)))
    nu = 4 * alpha / sigma ** 2
    lamb = gamma * math.exp(-beta * T) * v0
    # the pricing formula
    call = (D * math.exp(-beta * T) * v0 * cx(K, gamma, nu + 4, lamb)
        + D * (alpha / beta) * (1 - math.exp(-beta * T))
        * cx(K, gamma, nu + 2, lamb)
        - D * K * cx(K, gamma, nu, lamb))
    return call
```

As before, being equipped with such a Python function makes applying the pricing formula straightforward.

```
In [23]: call_price(v0, kappa, theta, sigma, zeta, T, r, K)
Out[23]: 3.3682878822902369
```

Let us calculate European call option prices over a wider range of strikes.

```
In [24]: import numpy as np

In [25]: import pandas as pd

In [26]: option_values = []

In [27]: strikes = np.linspace(15, 25)

In [28]: option_values = [call_price(v0, kappa, theta, sigma, zeta, T, r, k)
   ....:                  for k in strikes]
   ....:

In [29]: data = pd.DataFrame(option_values, index=strikes,
   ....:                     columns=['call values', ])
   ....:

In [30]: data.index.name = 'strike'
```

As Figure 6.2 shows, the European call option prices behave comparably to equity options: the higher the strike price the lower the option present value *ceteris paribus*.

```
In [31]: data.plot(figsize=(10, 6));
```

6.5 MONTE CARLO SIMULATION

In this section, we solve the pricing problem for a European call option via Monte Carlo simulation, i.e. based on a large number of simulated volatility index paths. To this end, we have to discretize the stochastic differential equation to obtain a difference equation which we can evaluate numerically.

We use the same numerical parameters as before, but we have to define some additional parameters which will determine the discretization interval and the number of simulated paths:

```
# simulation parameters
In [32]: M = 50  # time steps

In [33]: I = 20000  # number of MCS paths
```

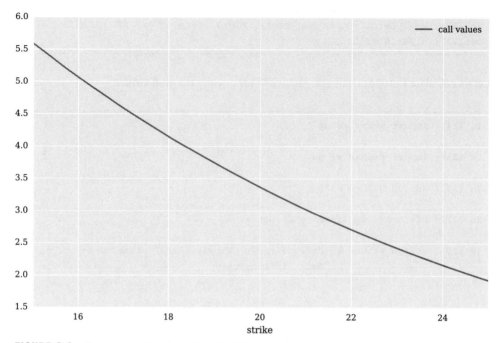

FIGURE 6.2   European call option prices for different volatility strikes in the GL96 model.

There is a large literature available about the discretization of the square-root diffusion (see Hilpisch (2015), ch. 10). In the following, we will implement an exact discretization scheme.

First, we divide the time interval $[0, T]$ into M time intervals with $M + 1$ discrete points in time: $t \in \{0, \Delta t, 2\Delta t, \dots, T\}$. We have:

$$v_t = \frac{\sigma^2(1 - e^{-\kappa \Delta t})}{4\kappa} \tilde{\chi}^2_{\nu,\lambda} \frac{4^{-\kappa \Delta t}}{\sigma^2(1 - e^{-\kappa \Delta t})} \cdot v_s$$

with $s = t - \Delta t$.

$\tilde{\chi}^2_{\nu,\lambda}$ denotes a non-central chi-squared distributed random variable with

$$\nu = \frac{4\theta\kappa}{\sigma^2}$$

degrees of freedom and non-centrality parameter

$$\lambda = \frac{4\kappa e^{-\kappa \Delta t}}{\sigma^2(1 - e^{-\kappa \Delta t})} \cdot v_s$$

As it may be more convenient to sample a chi-squared random variable instead of non-central chi-squared one, we use the following equations:

$$\nu > 1 : \tilde{\chi}^2_{\nu,\lambda} = (z + \sqrt{\lambda})^2 + \chi^2_{\nu-1}$$
$$\nu \leq 1 : \tilde{\chi}^2_{\nu,\lambda} = \chi^2_{\nu+2P}$$

where z is an independent standard normally distributed random variable and P is a Poisson distributed random variable with intensity $\frac{\lambda}{2}$.

We again divide the implementation in Python into two functions:

- `generate_paths()` generates simulated volatility level paths
- `call_estimator()` simulates the volatility process and calculates the Monte Carlo estimator for the European call option value.

The function to generate simulated volatility paths takes on a form as follows:

```python
def generate_paths(x0, kappa, theta, sigma, T, M, I):
    ''' Simulation of square-root diffusion with exact discretization

    Parameters
    ==========
    x0: float (positive)
        starting value
    kappa: float (positive)
        mean-reversion factor
    theta: float (positive)
        long-run mean
    sigma: float (positive)
        volatility (of volatility)
    T: float (positive)
        time-to-maturity
    M: int
        number of time intervals
    I: int
        number of simulation paths

    Returns
    =======
    x: NumPy ndarray object
        simulated paths
    '''
    dt = float(T) / M
    x = np.zeros((M + 1, I), dtype=np.float)
    x[0, :] = x0
    # matrix filled with standard normal distributed rv
    ran = np.random.standard_normal((M + 1, I))
    d = 4 * kappa * theta / sigma ** 2
     # constant factor in the integrated process of x
    c = (sigma ** 2 * (1 - math.exp(-kappa * dt))) / (4 * kappa)
    if d > 1:
        for t in range(1, M + 1):
            # non-centrality parameter
            l = x[t - 1, :] * math.exp(-kappa * dt) / c
```

```
            # matrix with chi-squared distributed rv
            chi = np.random.chisquare(d - 1, I)
            x[t, :] = c * ((ran[t] + np.sqrt(l)) ** 2 + chi)
    else:
        for t in range(1, M + 1):
            l = x[t - 1, :] * math.exp(-kappa * dt) / c
            N = np.random.poisson(l / 2, I)
            chi = np.random.chisquare(d + 2 * N, I)
            x[t, :] = c * chi
    return x
```

An application of this function might look as follows:

```
In [34]: paths = generate_paths(v0, kappa, theta, sigma, T, M, I)
```

Figure 6.3 shows the first 10 simulated volatility paths.

```
In [35]: pd.DataFrame(paths[:, :10]).plot(legend=False, figsize=(10, 6));
```

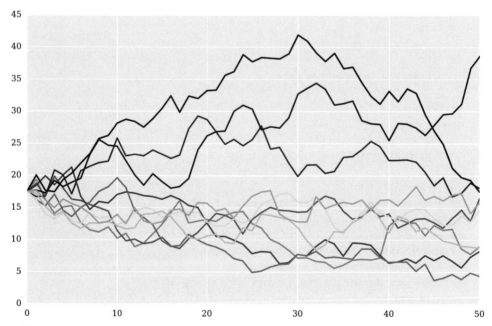

FIGURE 6.3   10 simulated volatility paths for GL96 model.

The Monte Carlo estimator for a European call option is defined by

$$C(v_0, K, T) = e^{-rT} \frac{1}{I} \sum_{i=1}^{I} \max(v_T^i - K, 0)$$

with $\max(v_T - K, 0)$ being the payoff function of the European call option. Here, v_T^i is the i-th simulated value for the volatility index at maturity. The function to calculate the Monte Carlo estimator for the value of the European call option is presented below.

```
def call_estimator(v0, kappa, theta, sigma, T, r, K, M, I):
    ''' Estimation of European call option price in GL96 Model
    via Monte Carlo simulation

    Parameters
    ==========
    v0: float (positive)
        current volatility level
    kappa: float (positive)
        mean-reversion factor
    theta: float (positive)
        long-run mean of volatility
    sigma: float (positive)
        volatility of volatility
    T: float (positive)
        time-to-maturity
    r: float (positive)
        risk-free short rate
    K: float (positive)
        strike price of the option
    M: int
        number of time intervals
    I: int
        number of simulation paths

    Returns
    =======
    callvalue: float
        MCS estimator for European call option
    '''
    V = generate_paths(v0, kappa, theta, sigma, T, M, I)
    callvalue = math.exp(-r * T) * np.sum(np.maximum(V[-1] - K, 0)) / I
    return callvalue
```

```
In [36]: call_estimator(v0, kappa, theta, sigma, T, r, K, M, I)
Out[36]: 3.3751776084056191
```

Again, let us calculate option prices over a wider range of strikes.

```
In [37]: %%time
    ....: estimates = []
    ....: for k in strikes:
    ....:     estimates.append(call_estimator(v0, kappa, theta, sigma,
    ....:                                     T, r, k, M, I))
    ....: data['estimates'] = estimates
    ....:
CPU times: user 11.4 s, sys: 38 us, total: 11.4 s
Wall time: 11.4 s
```

Figure 6.4 compares the Monte Carlo estimator values given the above parametrization with the European call option values obtained from the formula by Grünbichler and Longstaff (1996).

```
In [38]: data.plot(style=['b', 'r.'], figsize=(10, 6));
```

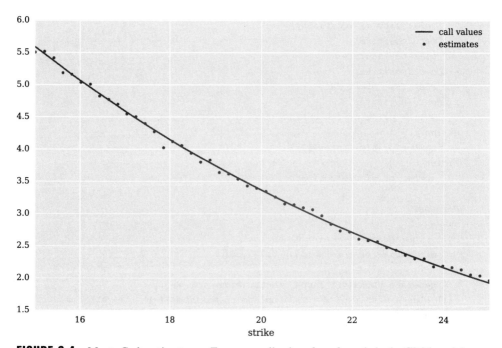

FIGURE 6.4   Monte Carlo estimates vs. European call values from formula in the GL96 model.

6.6 AUTOMATED MONTE CARLO TESTS

This section illustrates how to automate Monte Carlo-based valuation tests. Even if semi-analytical option pricing formulas are available – as in the Grünbichler and Longstaff (1996) model – in general one needs numerical methods as well. One of the most flexible and powerful methods when it comes to the valuation of more complex, exotic instruments is Monte Carlo simulation (MCS).

When implementing MCS algorithms it is generally advised to benchmark the results from these algorithms against results from other valuation methods which are known to deliver exact values. Therefore, this section implements MCS for the Grünbichler and Longstaff (1996) model and benchmarks the results against the semi-analytical formula for European volatility call options as presented earlier in this chapter.

In the previous section, MCS was introduced and some benchmark results presented. However, this section enhances the analysis and adds functionalities for the structured storage and systematic analysis of valuation results. In this regard, the Python library pandas is used in combination with the storage capabilities of PyTables, the Python wrapper for the HDF5 database file format.

6.6.1 The Automated Testing

The following test procedures are based on the Python script `srd_ simula-tion_analysis.py` (see sub-section 6.9.2, *srd simulation analysis.py* for the complete code). To automate the valuation for a significant number of options, a set of parameter values and lists has to be specified. First, some imports and the parametrization of the financial model.

```
import time
import math
import numpy as np
from datetime import datetime
from srd_functions import generate_paths, call_price
from srd_simulation_results import *

# Model Parameters
v0 = 20.0  # initial volatility
kappa = 3.0  # speed of mean reversion
theta = 20.0  # long-term volatility
sigma = 3.2  # standard deviation coefficient
zeta = 0.0  # factor of the expected volatility risk premium
r = 0.01  # risk-free short rate
```

The parameter values chosen are not too unrealistic, for example, for the VSTOXX volatility index. Second, the following simulation parameters are assumed:

```
# General Simulation Parameters
write = True
var_red = [(False, False), (False, True), (True, False), (True, True)]
```

```
    # 1st = mo_match -- random number correction (std + mean + drift)
    # 2nd = anti_paths -- antithetic paths for variance reduction
# number of time steps
steps_list = [25, 50, 75, 100]
# number of paths per valuation
paths_list = [2500, 50000, 75000, 100000, 125000, 150000]
SEED = 100000   # seed value
runs = 3   # number of simulation runs
PY1 = 0.010   # performance yardstick 1: abs. error in currency units
PY2 = 0.010   # performance yardstick 2: rel. error in decimals
maturity_list = [1.0 / 12, 1.0 / 4, 1.0 / 2, 1.0]   # maturity list
```

The single parameters and list objects have the following meanings:

- write is just a flag to indicate that the results should be stored on disk
- var_red contains the configuration for the variance reduction techniques, i.e. moment matching of pseudo-random numbers and antithetic variates
- steps_list is the list with the different numbers for the time steps to be used for the discretization
- paths_list contains the different numbers for the MCS paths for the volatility process
- runs is a parameter which says how often the same option is valued for a single parameter combination
- SEED is a seed value for NumPy's pseudo-random number generator; it is fixed to make it easier to compare results
- PY1 is the performance yardstick for absolute differences
- PY2 is the performance yardstick for relative differences
- maturity_list is the list with times-to-maturity
- strike_list finally is the list with the different strike prices.

For details on such Monte Carlo simulation analyses and the respective MCS background information refer to Hilpisch (2015, ch. 10). For a detailed exposition of Monte Carlo methods implemented in Python see also Hilpisch (2014, ch. 10).

The script srd_simulation_analysis.py used in this section relies on the MCS function from the previous section. In addition, it uses the following function which implements two variance reduction techniques, moment matching and antithetic variates:

```
def randoms(M, I):
    ''' Function to generate pseudo-random numbers with variance reduction.

    Parameters
    ==========
    M: int
        number of discrete time intervals
    I: int
        number of simulated paths
```

```
    Returns
    =======
    rand: Numpy ndarray object
        object with pseudo-random numbers
    '''
    if anti_paths is True:
        rand_ = np.random.standard_normal((M + 1, I / 2))
        rand = np.concatenate((rand_, -rand_), 1)
    else:
        rand = np.random.standard_normal((M + 1, I))
    if mo_match is True:
        rand = rand / np.std(rand)
        rand = rand - np.mean(rand)
    return rand
```

The main valuation and testing loop is implemented through the following code. Important passages are commented inline.

```
t0 = time.time()
sim_results = pd.DataFrame()

for vr in var_red:  # variance reduction techniques
    mo_match, anti_paths = vr
    for M in steps_list:  # number of time steps
        for I in paths_list:  # number of paths
            t1 = time.time()
            d1 = datetime.now()
            abs_errors = []
            rel_errors = []
            l = 0.0
            errors = 0
            # name of the simulation setup
            name = ('Call_' + str(runs) + '_'
                    + str(M) + '_' + str(I / 1000)
                    + '_' + str(mo_match)[0] + str(anti_paths)[0] +
                    '_' + str(PY1 * 100) + '_' + str(PY2 * 100))
            np.random.seed(SEED)  # RNG seed value
            for run in range(runs):  # simulation runs
                print "\nSimulation Run %d of %d" % (run + 1, runs)
                print "--------------------------------------------------------"
                print ("Elapsed Time in Minutes %8.2f"
                        % ((time.time() - t0) / 60))
                print " --------------------------------------------------------"
                z = 0
                for T in maturity_list:  # time-to-maturity
                    dt = T / M  # time interval in year fractions
                    V = generate_paths(v0, kappa, theta, sigma, T, M, I)
                        # volatility process paths
                    print "\n Results for Time-to-Maturity %6.3f" % T
```

```
                    print "  --------------------------------------------------"
            for K in strike_list:  # Strikes
                h = np.maximum(V[-1] - K, 0)  # inner value matrix
                # MCS estimator
                call_estimate = math.exp(-r * T) * np.sum(h) / I * 100
                # BSM analytical value
                callalue = call_price(v0, kappa, theta, sigma,
                                zeta, T, r, K) * 100
                # errors
                diff = call_estimate - callalue
                rdiff = diff / callalue
                abs_errors.append(diff)
                rel_errors.append(rdiff * 100)
                # output
                br = "    --------------------------------------------------"
                print "\n  Results for Strike %4.2f\n" % K
                print ("    European Op. Value MCS    %8.4f" %
                        call_estimate)
                print ("    European Op. Value Closed %8.4f" %
                        callalue)
                print "    Valuation Error (abs)   %8.4f" % diff
                print "    Valuation Error (rel)   %8.4f" % rdiff
                if abs(diff) < PY1 or abs(diff) / callalue < PY2:
                        print "      Accuracy ok!\n" + br
                        CORR = True
                else:
                        print "      Accuracy NOT ok!\n" + br
                        CORR = False
                        errors = errors + 1
                print "    %d Errors, %d Values, %.1f Min." \
                        % (errors, len(abs_errors),
                    float((time.time() - t1) / 60))
                print ("    %d Time Intervals, %d Paths"
                        % (M, I))
                z += 1
                l += 1
        t2 = time.time()
        d2 = datetime.now()
        if write is True:  # append simulation results
            sim_results = write_results(sim_results, name, SEED,
                    runs, M, I, mo_match, anti_paths,
                    l, PY1, PY2, errors,
                    float(errors) / l, np.array(abs_errors),
                    np.array(rel_errors), t2 - t1, (t2 - t1) / 60, d1, d2)
if write is True:
    # write/append DataFrame to HDFStore object
    write_to_database(sim_results)
```

6.6.2 The Storage Functions

The script `srd_simulation_analysis.py` from the previous sub-section generates a number of results and a lot of printed output during execution. However, one generally wants to store such results in a structured manner and maybe analyze it later on. To this end, we use the pandas library which provides convenient data storage and analysis features. In combination with the PyTables library, simulation results are easily stored on disk and read from disk later on.

Consider now the Python module `srd_simulation_results.py` with several functions to store and analyze the data generated through the other script (see sub-section 6.9.3, *srd_simulation_results.py* for the complete script). We will go through this script part by part. Of course, there are some necessary imports and a filename for the database is also specified:

```python
import numpy as np
import pandas as pd
import datetime as dt
import matplotlib.pyplot as plt


# filname for HDFStore to save results
filename = "../data/simulation_results.h5"
```

Having a `DataFrame` object instantiated (with results already stored or not), the following function allows us to add a set of valuation results to the `DataFrame` as an additional row:

```python
def write_results(sim_results, name, SEED, runs, steps, paths, mo_match,
                  anti_paths, l, PY1, PY2, errors, error_ratio,
                  abs_errors, rel_errors, t1, t2, d1, d2):
    ''' Appends simulation results to pandas DataFrame df and returns it.

    Parameters
    ==========
    see srd_simulation_analysis.py

    Returns
    =======
    df: pandas DataFrame object
        updated results object
    '''
    results = {
    'sim_name': name,
    'seed': SEED,
    'runs': runs,
    'time_steps': steps,
    'paths': paths,
    'mo_match': mo_match,
```

```
    'anti_paths': anti_paths,
    'opt_prices': l,
    'abs_tol': PY1,
    'rel_tol': PY2,
    'errors': errors,
    'error_ratio': error_ratio,
    'aval_err': sum(abs_errors) / l,
    'abal_err': sum(abs(rel_errors)) / l,
    'time_sec': t1,
    'time_min': t2,
    'time_opt': t1 / l,
    'start_date': d1,
    'end_date': d2
    }
    df = pd.concat([sim_results,
                    pd.DataFrame([results])],
                    ignore_index=True)
    return df
```

Once all the single simulation results have been added to the DataFrame sim_results, this should be stored on disk in a HDFStore file object. This is what the following function accomplishes:

```
def write_to_database(sim_results, filename=filename):
    ''' Write pandas DataFrame sim_results to HDFStore object.

    Parameters
    ==========
    sim_results: pandas DataFrame object
        object with simulation results
    filename: string
        name of the file for storage
    '''
    h5 = pd. HDFStore(filename, 'a')
    h5.append('sim_results', sim_results, min_itemsize={'values': 30},
              ignore_index=True)
    h5.close()
```

6.6.3 The Results

Let us now turn to the analysis of valuation results. To this end, we work with the Python module srd_simulation_results.py (see sub-section 6.9.3, *srd_simulation_results.py* for the code). The function `print_results()` prints simulation results stored in the HDFStore file object with name `filename`. If not otherwise parametrized, the function prints the first 50 results stored in the database (if that many exist).

```python
def print_results(filename=filename, idl=0, idh=50):
    ''' Prints valuation results in detailed form.

    Parameters
    ==========
    filename: string
        HDFStore with pandas.DataFrame with results
    idl: int
        start index value
    idh: int
        stop index value
    '''
    h5 = pd.HDFStore(filename, 'r')
    sim_results = h5['sim_results']
    br = "---------------------------------------------------------"
    for i in range(idl, min(len(sim_results), idh + 1)):
        row = sim_results.iloc[i]
        print br
        print "Start Calculations  %32s" % row['start_date'] + "\n" + br
        print "ID Number           %32d" % i
        print "Name of Simulation  %32s" % row['sim_name']
        print "Seed Value for RNG  %32d" % row['seed']
        print "Number of Runs      %32d" % row['runs']
        print "Time Steps          %32d" % row['time_steps']
        print "Paths               %32d" % row['paths']
        print "Moment Matching     %32s" % row['mo_match']
        print "Antithetic Paths    %32s" % row['anti_paths'] + "\n"
        print "Option Prices       %32d" % row['opt_prices']
        print "Absolute Tolerance  %32.4f" % row['abs_tol']
        print "Relative Tolerance  %32.4f" % row['rel_tol']
        print "Errors              %32d" % row['errors']
        print "Error Ratio         %32.4f" % row['error_ratio'] + "\n"
        print "Aver Val Error      %32.4f" % row['aval_err']
        print "Aver Abs Val Error  %32.4f" % row['abal_err']
        print "Time in Seconds     %32.4f" % row['time_sec']
        print "Time in Minutes     %32.4f" % row['time_min']
        print "Time per Option     %32.4f" % row['time_opt'] + "\n" + br
        print "End Calculations    %32s" % row['end_date']\
                    + "\n" + br + "\n"
    print "Total number of rows in table %d" % len(sim_results)
    h5.close()
```

Let us inspect selected valuation results from running the respective Python script `srd_simulation_analysis.py`:

```
-----------------------------------------------------------------
Start Calculations          2016-01-11 11:02:11.159464
-----------------------------------------------------------------

ID Number                                               2
Name of Simulation          Call_3_25_75_FF_1.0_1.0
Seed Value for RNG                                 100000
Number of Runs                                          3
Time Steps                                             25
Paths                                              75000
Moment Matching                                    False
Antithetic Paths                                   False

Option Prices                                         60
Absolute Tolerance                                0.0100
Relative Tolerance                                0.0100
Errors                                                 9
Error Ratio                                       0.1500

Aver Val Error                                   -0.1963
Aver Abs Val Error                                0.4773
Time in Seconds                                   4.1964
Time in Minutes                                   0.0699
Time per Option                                   0.0699
-----------------------------------------------------------------
End Calculations            2016-01-11 11:02:15.355906
-----------------------------------------------------------------


-----------------------------------------------------------------
Start Calculations          2016-01-11 11:02:15.362043
-----------------------------------------------------------------

ID Number                                               3
Name of Simulation          Call_3_25_100_FF_1.0_1.0
Seed Value for RNG                                 100000
Number of Runs                                          3
Time Steps                                             25
Paths                                             100000
Moment Matching                                    False
Antithetic Paths                                   False

Option Prices                                         60
Absolute Tolerance                                0.0100
Relative Tolerance                                0.0100
Errors                                                 5
```

```
Error Ratio                                0.0833

Aver Val Error                            -0.1645
Aver Abs Val Error                         0.3589
Time in Seconds                            5.7146
Time in Minutes                            0.0952
Time per Option                            0.0952
-------------------------------------------------------------
End Calculations          2016-01-11 11:02:21.076603
-------------------------------------------------------------


-------------------------------------------------------------
Start Calculations        2016-01-11 11:02:21.082678
-------------------------------------------------------------
ID Number                                        4
Name of Simulation        Call_3_25_125_FF_1.0_1.0
Seed Value for RNG                          100000
Number of Runs                                   3
Time Steps                                      25
Paths                                       125000
Moment Matching                              False
Antithetic Paths                             False

Option Prices                                   60
Absolute Tolerance                          0.0100
Relative Tolerance                          0.0100
Errors                                           2
Error Ratio                                 0.0333

Aver Val Error                              0.0043
Aver Abs Val Error                          0.2666
Time in Seconds                             6.9533
Time in Minutes                             0.1159
Time per Option                             0.1159
-------------------------------------------------------------
End Calculations          2016-01-11 11:02:28.035962
-------------------------------------------------------------
```

"Time in Minutes" and "Time per Option" values coincide since 60 options are valued per run.

In principle, the results from these three different parametrizations already illustrate that valuation accuracy is, in general, higher the higher the computational effort (in this case the number of paths). The number of errors drops from 9 for 75,000 paths to 2 for 125,000 paths.

Finally, the second major function contained in the Python module is `plot_error_ratio()` and plots the error ratios against the computational effort, i.e. (number of simulation paths) x (number of time steps).

```python
def plot_error_ratio(filename=filename):
    ''' Show error ratio vs. paths * time_steps (i.e.granularity).

    Parameters
    ==========
    filename: string
        name of file with data to be plotted
    '''
    h5 = pd. HDFStore(filename, mode='r')
    sim_results = h5['sim_results']
    x = np.array(sim_results['paths'] * sim_results['time_steps'], dtype='d')
    x = x / max(x)
    y = sim_results['error_ratio']
    plt.plot(x, y, 'bo', label=' error ratio')
    rg = np.polyfit(x, y, deg=1)
    plt.plot(np.sort(x), np.polyval(rg, np.sort(x)), 'r', label='regression',
            linewidth=2)
    plt.xlabel('time steps * paths (normalized)')
    plt.ylabel('errors / option valuations')
    plt.legend()
    plt.grid(True)
    h5.close()
```

Let us generate an overview plot with the above function. The graphical output is shown as
Figure 6.5.

```python
In [39]: from srd_simulation_results import plot_error_ratio

In [40]: plot_error_ratio(filename)
<matplotlib.figure.Figure at 0x2ab25e711950>
```

The linear regression illustrates graphically the statement that the higher the computational effort the higher in general the accuracy of the MCS valuations. The high variability of the error ratios stems from the fact that it is not only the computational effort which influences valuation accuracy. For example, the use of variance reduction techniques also has a significant influence.

This being said, one might be interested in analyzing the impact of the variance reduction techniques on valuation accuracy. To this end, pandas provides powerful grouping methods for the DataFrame object. First, we open the database in which the simulation results are stored and read them into an in memory object:

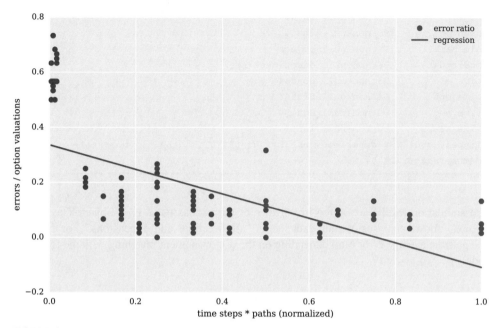

FIGURE 6.5   Error ratios of Monte Carlo valuation vs. computational effort.

```
In [41]: import pandas as pd

In [42]: h5 = pd.HDFStore(filename, 'r')

In [43]: data = h5['sim_results']

In [44]: h5.close()

In [45]: data.info()
<class 'pandas.core.frame.DataFrame'>
Int64Index: 96 entries, 0 to 95
Data columns (total 19 columns):
ab_val_err     96 non-null float64
abs_tol        96 non-null float64
anti_paths     96 non-null bool
av_val_err     96 non-null float64
end_date       96 non-null datetime64[ns]
error_ratio    96 non-null float64
errors         96 non-null int64
mo_match       96 non-null bool
opt_prices     96 non-null float64
paths          96 non-null int64
rel_tol        96 non-null float64
```

```
runs              96 non-null int64
seed              96 non-null int64
sim_name          96 non-null object
start_date        96 non-null datetime64[ns]
time_min          96 non-null float64
time_opt          96 non-null float64
time_sec          96 non-null float64
time_steps        96 non-null int64
dtypes: bool(2), datetime64[ns](2), float64(9), int64(5), object(1)
memory usage: 13.7+ KB
```

The simulation results are stored in 96 rows of the pandas `DataFrame` object. The method `groupby` allows analyses of such data sets in "all directions and dimensions." For example, one gets the average error ratio depending on the use of moment matching with the following code:

```
In [46]: data.groupby(['mo_match']).mean()[['error_ratio']]
Out[46]:
          error_ratio
mo_match
False        0.193750
True         0.169097
```

In the simulations, moment matching obviously reduces the error ratio by slightly more than 2 percentage points from above 19% to less than 17%.

The same analysis can be done with more data columns, both for the grouping and the output.

```
In [47]: data.groupby(['mo_match', 'anti_paths']).mean()[['error_ratio', 'errors']]
Out[47]:
                        error_ratio      errors
mo_match anti_paths
False    False             0.206944   12.416667
         True              0.180556   10.833333
True     False             0.159028    9.541667
         True              0.179167   10.750000
```

Here, the results indicate that moment matching alone should be used. Adding antithetic paths increases the error ratio *ceteris paribus*.

In similar fashion, the data can be grouped by time steps and paths – by analogy with the analysis above. Figure 6.6 presents the results.

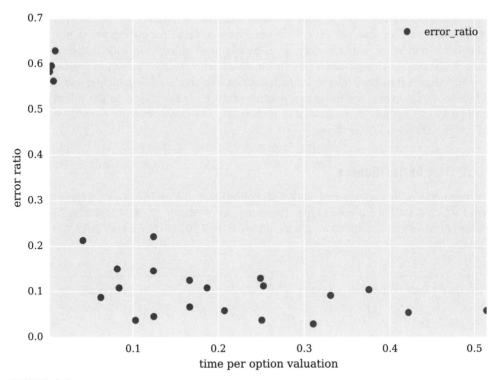

FIGURE 6.6 Error ratios of Monte Carlo valuation vs. time per option.

```
In [48]: df = data.groupby(['time_steps', 'paths']).mean()[['error_ratio',
         'time_opt']]

In [49]: df.plot(x='time_opt', y='error_ratio', style='bo');

In [50]: plt.xlabel('time per option valuation');

In [51]: plt.ylabel('error ratio');
```

As expected, the general rule that accuracy increases with increasing computational effort is again supported by this specific analysis. Of course, other analyses can be done with the data generated and stored on disk.

6.7 MODEL CALIBRATION

Previous sections implement a *theoretical* valuation approach in that a parametric model is given and parameter values are simply *assumed*. However, any realistic valuation of volatility options has to incorporate at least some information from the market itself. This is generally done by taking the quotes of liquidly traded vanilla options as input for a so-called *model calibration.* During the calibration of a financial model, parameters are determined for that model which best replicate the observed option quotes. These parameters are in turn used to value other, maybe more exotic, derivatives by means of numerical methods such as Monte Carlo simulation. Such a procedure is often termed a *market-based valuation approach.*

This section illustrates how to calibrate the financial model of Grünbichler and Longstaff (1996) to option quotes for European volatility calls traded at Eurex. In the following, the semi-analytical formula as introduced in section 6.4, *The Option Pricing Formula* is used to accomplish the model calibration.

6.7.1 The Option Quotes

The remainder of this section will work with option quotes of VSTOXX call options traded at Eurex which are all of European type. The data is as of March 31, 2014 and contains quotes for the options with maturities for each month from April 2014 to November 2014. Let us have a look at the data.

```
In [52]: import pandas as pd

In [53]: path = './source/data/'

In [54]: h5 = pd.HDFStore(path + 'vstoxx_option_quotes.h5', 'r')

In [55]: option_quotes = h5['option_quotes']

In [56]: option_quotes.info()
<class 'pandas.core.frame.DataFrame'>
Int64Index: 98 entries, 46219 to 46365
Data columns (total 8 columns):
DATE         98 non-null datetime64[ns]
EXP_YEAR     98 non-null int64
EXP_MONTH    98 non-null int64
TYPE         98 non-null object
STRIKE       98 non-null float64
PRICE        98 non-null float64
MATURITY     98 non-null datetime64[ns]
TTM          98 non-null float64
dtypes: datetime64[ns](2), float64(3), int64(2), object(1)
memory usage: 6.9+ KB

In [57]: option_quotes.iloc[25: 35]
Out[57]:
            DATE EXP_YEAR EXP_MONTH TYPE  STRIKE PRICE    MATURITY   TTM
46244 2014-03-31     2014         5    C    26.0  0.60  2014-05-16 0.126
46245 2014-03-31     2014         5    C    27.0  0.50  2014-05-16 0.126
46246 2014-03-31     2014         5    C    28.0  0.45  2014-05-16 0.126
46247 2014-03-31     2014         5    C    29.0  0.40  2014-05-16 0.126
```

46248	2014-03-31	2014	5	C	30.0	0.35	2014-05-16	0.126
46249	2014-03-31	2014	5	C	32.5	0.25	2014-05-16	0.126
46250	2014-03-31	2014	5	C	35.0	0.20	2014-05-16	0.126
46251	2014-03-31	2014	5	C	37.5	0.15	2014-05-16	0.126
46252	2014-03-31	2014	5	C	40.0	0.10	2014-05-16	0.126
46253	2014-03-31	2014	5	C	42.5	0.10	2014-05-16	0.126

As you can see, the data set comprises a total of 98 option quotes. Note that option quotes for Eurex volatility options have tick sizes of 5 cents, i.e. 0.05 EUR. A detailed overview of the terms of these options can be found in chapter 8, *Terms of the VSTOXX and its Derivatives*. In what follows, we assume that each option is written on a single unit of the underlying, i.e. 1 point of the VSTOXX index translates into 1 EUR.

6.7.2 The Calibration Procedure

In simple terms, the problem of calibration is to find parameters for an option model such that observed market quotes of liquidly traded plain vanilla options are replicated as closely as possible. To this end, one defines an error function that is to be minimized. Such a function could be the *Mean Squared Absolute Error (MSAE)*. The task is then to solve the problem

$$\min_{\kappa,\theta,\sigma} \frac{1}{N} \sum_{n=1}^{N} \left(C_n^* - C_n^{GL96}(\kappa,\theta,\sigma) \right)^2$$

with the C_n^* being the market or input prices and the C_n^{GL96} being the model or output prices for the options $n = 1, \dots, N$.

For some constellations, it might be more appropriate to minimize the *Mean Squared Relative Error (MSRE)*:

$$\min_{\kappa,\theta,\sigma} \frac{1}{N} \sum_{n=1}^{N} \left(\frac{C_n^* - C_n^{GL96}(\kappa,\theta,\sigma)}{C_n^*} \right)^2$$

The Python script (see sub-section 6.9.4, *srd_model_calibration.py*) that implements a procedure to calibrate the Grünbichler-Longstaff option pricing model is explained in the following step-by-step procedure.

First, some imports and parameter specifications.

```
import numpy as np
import pandas as pd
from srd_functions import call_price
import scipy.optimize as sco
import matplotlib.pyplot as plt


path = './source/data/'


# Fixed Parameters
```

```
v0 = 17.6639  # VSTOXX index on 31. March 2014
r = 0.01  # risk-less short rate
zeta = 0.  # volatility risk premium factor
```

The function `read_select_quotes()` reads and selects option quotes for the calibration.

```
def read_select_quotes(path=path, tol=0.2):
    ''' Selects and read options quotes.

    Parameters
    ==========
    path: string
        path to file with option quotes

    Returns
    =======
    option_data: pandas DataFrame object
        option data
    '''
    h5 = pd.HDFStore(path + 'vstoxx_march_2014.h5', 'r')

    # read option data from file and close it
    option_data = h5['vstoxx_options']
    h5.close()
    # select relevant date for call option quotes
    option_data = option_data[(option_data.DATE == '2014-3-31')
                              & (option_data.TYPE == 'C')]
    # calculate time-to-maturity in year fractions
    option_data['TTM'] = (option_data.MATURITY - option_data.DATE).apply (
                        lambda x: x / np.timedelta64(1, 'D') / 365.)

# only those options close enough to the ATM level
option_data = option_data[(option_data.STRIKE > (1 - tol) * v0)
                          & (option_data.STRIKE < (1 + tol) * v0)]
return option_data
```

However, the core functions of the calibration script are the following. On the one hand, `valuation_function()`.

```
def valuation_function(p0):
    ''' Valuation function for set of strike prices

    Parameters
    ==========
    p0: list
        set of model parameters
```

```
    Returns
    =======
    call_prices: NumPy ndarray object
        array of call prices
    '''
    kappa, theta, sigma = p0
    call_prices = []
    for strike in strikes:
        call_prices.append(call_price(v0, kappa, theta,
                                sigma, zeta, ttm, r, strike))
    call_prices = np.array(call_prices)
    return call_prices
```

On the other hand, `error_function()`.

```
def error_function(p0):
    ''' Error function for model calibration.

    Parameters
    ==========
    p0: tuple
        set of model parameters

    Returns
    =======
    MSE: float
        mean squared (relative/absolute) error
    '''
    global i
    call_prices = valuation_function(p0)
    kappa, theta, sigma = p0
    pen = 0.
    if 2 * kappa * theta < sigma ** 2:
        pen = 1000.0
    if kappa < 0 or theta < 0 or sigma < 0:
        pen = 1000.0
    if relative is True:
        MSE = (np.sum(((call_prices - call_quotes) / call_quotes) ** 2)
                / len(call_quotes) + pen)
    else:
        MSE = np.sum((call_prices - call_quotes) ** 2) / len(call_quotes) + pen
    if i == 0:
        print ("{:>6s}{:>6s}{:>6s}".format('kappa', 'theta', 'sigma')
            + "{:>12s}".format('MSE'))

    # print intermediate results: every 100th iteration
    if i % 100 == 0:
```

```
        print "{:6.3f}{:6.3f}{:6.3f}".format(*p0) + "{:>12.5f}". format(MSE)
    i += 1
    return MSE
```

Function `valuation_function()` implements a valuation for the array of strikes under consideration and the parameter values provided. Function `error_function()` calculates either the MSAE or the MSRE – given the array of strikes and the parameter vector p0. Some penalties are also added depending on the single parameter values or their constellation. For details and a number of similar examples, refer to the book Hilpisch (2015, ch. 11).

Then standard functions from the `scipy.optimize` library (see Hilpisch (2014), ch. 9) are used to implement both a *global* (i.e. via the `brute()` function) and a *local optimization* (i.e. via the `fmin()` function). This is all wrapped into the function `model_calibration()`.

```
def model_calibration(option_data, rel=False, mat='2014-07-18'):
    ''' Function for global and local model calibration.

    Parameters
    ==========
    option_data: pandas DataFrame object
        option quotes to be used
    relative: boolean
        relative or absolute MSE
    maturity: string
        maturity of option quotes to calibrate to

    Returns
    =======
    opt: tuple
        optimal parameter values
    '''
    global relative  # if True: MSRE is used, if False: MSAE
    global strikes
    global call_quotes
    global ttm
    global i

    relative = rel
    # only option quotes for a single maturity
    option_quotes = option_data[option_data.MATURITY == mat]

    # time-to-maturity from the data set
    ttm = option_quotes.iloc[0, -1]

    # transform strike column and price column in ndarray object
    strikes = option_quotes['STRIKE'].values
```

```
    call_quotes = option_quotes['PRICE'].values

    # global optimization
    i = 0   # counter for calibration iterations
    p0 = sco.brute(error_function, ((5.0, 20.1, 1.0), (10., 30.1, 1.25),
                                    (1.0, 9.1, 2.0)), finish=None)

    # local optimization
    i = 0
    opt = sco.fmin(error_function, p0, xtol=0.0000001, ftol=0.0000001,
                                   maxiter=1000, maxfun=1500)

    return opt
```

Finally, the results are visualized by plotting the model values against the market values and providing the absolute differences separately. This is accomplished by the function `plot_calibration_results()`.

```
def plot_calibration_results(opt):
    ''' Function to plot market quotes vs. model prices.

    Parameters
    ==========
    opt: list
        optimal parameters from calibration
    '''
    callalues = valuation_function(opt)
    diffs = callalues - call_quotes
    plt.figure()
    plt.subplot(211)
    plt.plot(strikes, call_quotes, label='market quotes')
    plt.plot(strikes, callalues, 'ro', label='model prices')
    plt.ylabel('option values')
    plt.grid(True)
    plt.legend()
    plt.axis([min(strikes) - 0.5, max(strikes) + 0.5,
            0.0, max(call_quotes) * 1.1])
    plt.subplot(212)
    wi = 0.3
    plt.bar(strikes - wi / 2, diffs, width=wi)
    plt.grid(True)
    plt.xlabel('strike price')
    plt.ylabel('difference')
    plt.axis([min(strikes) - 0.5, max(strikes) + 0.5,
            min(diffs) * 1.1, max(diffs) * 1.1])
    plt.tight_layout()
```

6.7.3 The Calibration Results

We start with a calibration run for the option quotes with shorter maturity and using the *MSAE* as a yardstick.

```
In [58]: from srd_model_calibration import *

In [59]: option_data = read_select_quotes()

In [60]: %time opt = model_calibration(option_data, rel=False, mat=
            '2014-05-16')
 kappa  theta  sigma        MSE
 5.000 10.000  1.000      7.78606
 6.000 12.500  9.000      0.23173
 7.000 16.250  9.000      0.40860
 8.000 20.000  9.000      2.54160
 9.000 23.750  9.000      9.70521
10.000 27.500  9.000     26.90758
12.000 10.000  9.000      3.75104
13.000 13.750  9.000      1.50070
14.000 17.500  9.000      0.06953
15.000 21.250  9.000      3.39340
16.000 25.000  9.000     18.12298
17.000 28.750  9.000     51.74883
19.000 11.250  9.000      5.14886
20.000 15.000  9.000      1.96050
 kappa  theta  sigma        MSE
15.000 18.750  7.000      0.01356
16.381 19.112  6.613      0.00834
27.671 18.969  8.513      0.00831
33.461 18.950  9.343      0.00831
33.457 18.950  9.342      0.00831
Optimization terminated successfully.
         Current function value: 0.008311
         Iterations: 247
         Function evaluations: 450
CPU times: user 5.53 s, sys: 0 ns, total: 5.53 s
Wall time: 5.54 s
```

Figure 6.7 shows the calibration results.

```
In [61]: plot_calibration_results(opt)
<matplotlib.figure.Figure at 0x2ab247cec750>
```

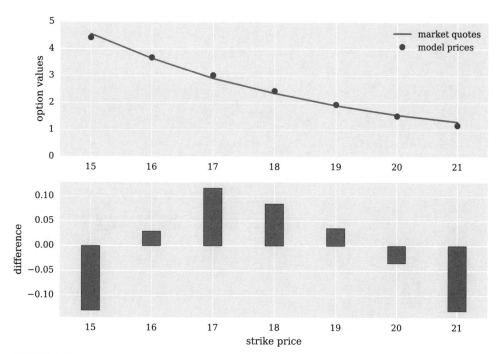

FIGURE 6.7   Calibration of option pricing model to option quotes for May 2014 maturity with MSAE.

Now the calibration to the option quotes with a longer time-to-maturity and using the *MSRE* as a yardstick.

```
In [62]: %time opt = model_calibration(option_data, rel=True, mat='2014-07-18')
 kappa  theta  sigma      MSE
 5.000 10.000  1.000    1.00000
 6.000 12.500  9.000    0.12866
 7.000 16.250  9.000    0.01167
 8.000 20.000  9.000    0.18546
 9.000 23.750  9.000    1.20473
10.000 27.500  9.000    3.86826
12.000 10.000  9.000    0.73475
13.000 13.750  9.000    0.41208
14.000 17.500  9.000    0.05791
15.000 21.250  9.000    0.15684
16.000 25.000  9.000    1.57671
17.000 28.750  9.000    5.26237
19.000 11.250  9.000    0.81013
20.000 15.000  9.000    0.45062
 kappa  theta  sigma      MSE
 5.000 20.000  5.000    0.00051
 5.848 19.927  5.295    0.00050
```

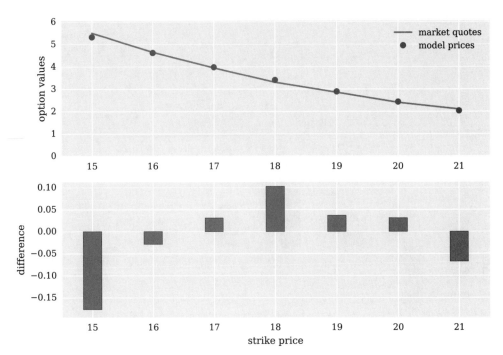

FIGURE 6.8   Calibration of option pricing model to option quotes for July 2014 maturity with MSRE.

```
11.500 19.608   7.260        0.00049
12.731 19.585   7.638        0.00049
12.732 19.585   7.638        0.00049
Optimization terminated successfully.
        Current function value: 0.000495
        Iterations: 252
        Function evaluations: 450
CPU times: user 5.6 s, sys: 0 ns, total: 5.6 s
Wall time: 5.61 s
```

The results of this calibration run are shown in Figure 6.8.

```
In [63]: plot_calibration_results(opt)
<matplotlib.figure.Figure at 0x2ab271446550>
```

Neither of the two fits is satisfactory for such small sets of option prices. The differences are often higher than the tick size of 5 cents. Therefore, this model obviously does not paint too realistic a picture of the real world. This may be due to the underlying, i.e. the VSTOXX volatility index, exhibiting more and/or other properties than the ones captured in the model of Grünbichler and Longstaff (1996). For example, a well documented stylized fact is that time series of volatility indexes, like the VSTOXX, exhibit (positive) *jumps* of significant size and with significant probability. Something that is, for example, not captured in the pricing model used in this chapter.

6.8 CONCLUSIONS

Volatility derivatives, like futures and options on a volatility index, and their arbitrage-free valuation are the focus of this chapter. The model of Grünbichler and Longstaff (1996) is introduced since it serves pretty well as a benchmark case – due to its simplicity – for volatility modeling and volatility derivatives valuation. The model uses a square-root diffusion or CIR process to describe the evolution of volatility (indexes) over time. Futures and European call option pricing formulas are presented. Based on an exact discretization scheme, Monte Carlo simulation is described as an alternative numerical pricing method. In addition, Python code to implement automated Monte Carlo simulation studies is provided and used for such a study. Finally, the GL96 model is calibrated to market quotes for European call options on the VSTOXX volatility index. The results illustrate that the model might not be rich enough to account for market realities.

6.9 PYTHON SCRIPTS

6.9.1 srd_functions.py

```
#
# Module with functions for
# Grünbichler and Longstaff (1996) model
#
# (c) Dr. Yves J. Hilpisch
# Listed Volatility and Variance Derivatives
#
import math
import numpy as np
import scipy.stats as scs


def futures_price(v0, kappa, theta, zeta, T):
    ''' Futures pricing formula in GL96 model.

    Parameters
    ==========
    v0: float (positive)
        current volatility level
    kappa: float (positive)
        mean-reversion factor
    theta: float (positive)
        long-run mean of volatility
```

```
        zeta: float (positive)
            volatility risk premium
        T: float (positive)
            time-to-maturity

        Returns
        =======
        future: float
            price of a future
        '''
        alpha = kappa * theta
        beta = kappa + zeta
        future = (alpha / beta * (1 - math.exp(-beta * T))
                                + math.exp(-beta * T) * v0)
        return future


def cx(K, gamma, nu, lamb):
    ''' Complementary distribution function of non-central chi-squared density.

    Parameters
    ==========
    K: float (positive)
        strike price
    gamma: float (positive)
        as defined in the GL96 model
    nu: float (positive)
        degrees of freedom
    lamb: float (positive)
        non-centrality parameter

    Returns
    =======
    complementary distribution of nc cs density
    '''
    return 1 - scs.ncx2.cdf(gamma * K, nu, lamb)


def call_price(v0, kappa, theta, sigma, zeta, T, r, K):
    ''' Call option pricing formula in GL96 Model

    Parameters
    ==========
    v0: float (positive)
        current volatility level
    kappa: float (positive)
        mean-reversion factor
    theta: float (positive)
        long-run mean of volatility
    sigma: float (positive)
        volatility of volatility
```

```
    zeta: float  (positive)
        volatility risk premium
    T: float  (positive)
        time-to-maturity
    r: float  (positive)
        risk-free short rate
    K: float (positive)
        strike price of the option

    Returns
    =======
    call: float
        present value of European call option
    '''
    D = math.exp(-r * T)   # discount factor

    alpha = kappa * theta
    beta = kappa + zeta
    gamma = 4 * beta / (sigma ** 2 * (1 - math.exp(-beta * T)))
    nu = 4 * alpha / sigma ** 2
    lamb = gamma * math.exp(-beta * T) * v0

    # the pricing formula
    call = (D * math.exp(-beta * T) * v0 * cx(K, gamma, nu + 4, lamb)
      + D * (alpha / beta) * (1 - math.exp(-beta * T))
      * cx(K, gamma, nu + 2, lamb)
      - D * K * cx(K, gamma, nu, lamb))
    return call

def generate_paths(x0, kappa, theta, sigma, T, M, I):
    ''' Simulation of square-root diffusion with exact discretization

    Parameters
    ==========
    x0: float  (positive)
        starting value
    kappa: float  (positive)
        mean-reversion factor
    theta: float  (positive)
        long-run mean
    sigma: float  (positive)
        volatility (of volatility)
    T: float  (positive)
        time-to-maturity
    M: int
        number of time intervals
    I: int
        number of simulation paths
```

```
    Returns
    =======
    x: NumPy ndarray object
        simulated paths
    '''
    dt = float(T) / M
    x = np.zeros((M + 1, I), dtype=np.float)
    x[0, :] = x0
    # matrix filled with standard normal distributed rv
    ran = np.random.standard_normal((M + 1, I))
    d = 4 * kappa * theta / sigma ** 2
     # constant factor in the integrated process of x
    c = (sigma ** 2 * (1 - math.exp(-kappa * dt))) / (4 * kappa)
    if d > 1:
        for t in range(1, M + 1):
            # non-centrality parameter
            l = x[t - 1, :] * math.exp(-kappa * dt) / c
            # matrix with chi-squared distributed rv
            chi = np.random.chisquare(d - 1, I)
            x[t, :] = c * ((ran[t] + np.sqrt(l)) ** 2 + chi)
    else:
        for t in range(1, M + 1):
            l = x[t - 1, :] * math.exp(-kappa * dt) / c
            N = np.random.poisson(l / 2, I)
            chi = np.random.chisquare(d + 2 * N, I)
            x[t, :] = c * chi
    return x


def call_estimator(v0, kappa, theta, sigma, T, r, K, M, I):
    ''' Estimation of European call option price in GL96 Model
    via Monte Carlo simulation

    Parameters
    ==========
    v0: float (positive)
        current volatility level
    kappa: float (positive)
        mean-reversion factor
    theta: float (positive)
        long-run mean of volatility
    sigma: float (positive)
        volatility of volatility
    T: float (positive)
        time-to-maturity
    r: float (positive)
        risk-free short rate
    K: float (positive)
        strike price of the option
```

```
    M: int
        number of time intervals
    I: int
        number of simulation paths

    Returns
    =======
    callvalue: float
        MCS estimator for European call option
    '''
    V = generate_paths(v0, kappa, theta, sigma, T, M, I)
    callvalue = math.exp(-r * T) * np.sum(np.maximum(V[-1] - K, 0)) / I
    return callvalue
```

6.9.2 srd_simulation_analysis.py

```
#
# Valuation of European volatility options
# by Monte Carlo simulation in
# Grünbichler and Longstaff (1996) model
# -- analysis of valuation results
#
# (c) Dr. Yves J. Hilpisch
# Listed Volatility and Variance Derivatives
#
import time
import math
import numpy as np
from datetime import datetime
from srd_functions import generate_paths, call_price
from srd_simulation_results import *


# Model Parameters
v0 = 20.0  # initial volatility
kappa = 3.0  # speed of mean reversion
theta = 20.0  # long-term volatility
sigma = 3.2  # standard deviation coefficient
zeta = 0.0  # factor of the expected volatility risk premium
r = 0.01  # risk-free short rate


# General Simulation Parameters
write = True
var_red = [(False, False), (False, True), (True, False), (True, True)]
    # 1st = mo_match -- random number correction (std + mean + drift)
    # 2nd = anti_paths -- antithetic paths for variance reduction
# number of time steps
steps_list = [25, 50, 75, 100]
```

```python
# number of paths per valuation
paths_list = [2500, 50000, 75000, 100000, 125000, 150000]
SEED = 100000   # seed value
runs = 3   # number of simulation runs
PY1 = 0.010   # performance yardstick 1: abs. error in currency units
PY2 = 0.010   # performance yardstick 2: rel. error in decimals
maturity_list = [1.0 / 12 , 1.0 / 4, 1.0 / 2, 1.0]   # maturity list
strike_list = [15.0, 17.5, 20.0, 22.5, 25.0]   # strike list

def generate_paths(x0, kappa, theta, sigma, T, M, I):
    ''' Simulation of square-root diffusion with exact discretization

    Parameters
    ==========
    x0: float (positive)
        starting value
    kappa: float (positive)
        mean-reversion factor
    theta: float (positive)
        long-run mean
    sigma: float (positive)
        volatility (of volatility)
    T: float (positive)
        time-to-maturity
    M: int
        number of time intervals
    I: int
        number of simulation paths

    Returns
    =======
    x: NumPy ndarray object
        simulated paths
    '''
    dt = float(T) / M
    x = np.zeros((M + 1, I), dtype=np.float)
    x[0, :] = x0
    # matrix filled with standard normally distributed rv
    ran = randoms(M, I)
    d = 4 * kappa * theta / sigma ** 2
    # constant factor in the integrated process of x
    c = (sigma ** 2 * (1 - math.exp(-kappa * dt))) / (4 * kappa)
    if d > 1:
        for t in range(1, M + 1):
            # non-centrality parameter
            l = x[t - 1, :] * math.exp(-kappa * dt) / c
            # matrix with chi-squared distributed rv
            chi = np.random.chisquare(d - 1, I)
            x[t, :] = c * ((ran[t] + np.sqrt(l)) ** 2 + chi)
```

```
        else:
            for t in range(1, M + 1):
                l = x[t - 1, :] * math.exp(-kappa * dt) / c
                N = np.random.poisson(l / 2, I)
                chi = np.random.chisquare(d + 2 * N, I)
                x[t, :] = c * chi
        return x

def randoms(M, I):
    ''' Function to generate pseudo-random numbers with variance reduction.

    Parameters
    ==========
    M: int
        number of discrete time intervals
    I: int
        number of simulated paths

    Returns
    =======
    rand: Numpy ndarray object
        object with pseudo-random numbers
    '''
    if anti_paths is True:
        rand_ = np.random.standard_normal((M + 1, I / 2))
        rand = np.concatenate((rand_, -rand_), 1)
    else:
        rand = np.random.standard_normal((M + 1, I))
    if mo_match is True:
        rand = rand / np.std(rand)
        rand = rand - np.mean(rand)
    return rand

t0 = time.time()
sim_results = pd.DataFrame()

for vr in var_red:  # variance reduction techniques
    mo_match, anti_paths = vr
    for M in steps_list:  # number of time steps
        for I in paths_list:  # number of paths
            t1 = time.time()
            d1 = datetime.now()
            abs_errors = []
            rel_errors = []
            l = 0.0
            errors = 0
            # name of the simulation setup
            name = ('Call_' + str(runs) + '_'
                    + str(M) + '_' + str(I / 1000))
```

```python
                        + '_' + str(mo_match)[0] + str(anti_paths)[0] +
                        '_' + str(PY1 * 100) + '-' + str(PY2 * 100))
np.random.seed(SEED)  # RNG seed value
for run in range(runs):  # simulation runs
    print "\nSimulation Run %d of %d" % (run + 1, runs)
    print "-----------------------------------------------------------"
    print ("Elapsed Time in Minutes %8.2f"
            % ((time.time() - t0) / 60))
    print "-----------------------------------------------------------"
    z = 0
    for T in maturity_list:  # time-to-maturity
        dt = T / M  # time interval in year fractions
        V = generate_paths(v0, kappa, theta, sigma, T, M, I)
            # volatility process paths
        print "\n Results for Time-to-Maturity %6.3f" % T
        print "----------------------------------------------------------"
        for K in strike_list:  # Strikes
            h = np.maximum(V[-1] - K, 0)  # inner value matrix
            # MCS estimator
            call_estimate = math.exp(-r * T) * np.sum(h) / I * 100
            # BSM analytical value
            callalue = call_price(v0, kappa, theta, sigma,
                            zeta, T, r, K) * 100
            # errors
            diff = call_estimate - callalue
            rdiff = diff / callalue
            abs_errors.append(diff)
            rel_errors.append(rdiff * 100)
            # output
            br = "    ----------------------------------------------"
            print "\n Results for Strike %4.2f\n" % K
            print ("    European Op. Value MCS    %8.4f" %
                        call_estimate)
            print ("    European Op. Value Closed %8.4f" %
                        callalue)
            print "    Valuation Error (abs)    %8.4f" % diff
            print "    Valuation Error (rel)    %8.4f" % rdiff
            if abs(diff) < PY1 or abs(diff) / callalue < PY2:
                    print "        Accuracy ok!\n" + br
                    CORR = True
            else:
                    print "        Accuracy NOT ok!\n" + br
                    CORR = False
                    errors = errors + 1
            print "    %d Errors, %d Values, %.1f Min. " \
                        % (errors, len(abs_errors),
                    float((time.time() - t1) / 60))
            print (" %d Time Intervals, %d Paths"
                        % (M, I))
```

```
                         z = z + 1
                         l = l + 1

             t2 = time.time()
             d2 = datetime.now()
             if write is True:  # append simulation results
                 sim_results = write_results(sim_results, name, SEED,
                         runs, M, I, mo_match, anti_paths,
                         l, PY1, PY2, errors,
                         float(errors) / l, np.array(abs_errors),
                         np.array(rel_errors), t2 - t1, (t2 - t1) / 60, d1, d2)

 if write is True:
     # write/append DataFrame to HDFStore object
     write_to_database(sim_results)
```

6.9.3 srd_simulation_results.py

```
#
# Valuation of European volatility options
# by Monte Carlo simulation in
# Grünbichler and Longstaff (1996) model
# -- Creating a database for simulation results
# with pandas and PyTables
#
# (c) Dr. Yves J. Hilpisch
# Listed Volatility and Variance Derivatives
#
import numpy as np
import pandas as pd
import datetime as dt
import matplotlib.pyplot as plt
# filname for HDFStore to save results
filename = "../data/simulation_results.h5"


def write_results(sim_results, name, SEED, runs, steps, paths, mo_match,
                  anti_paths, l, PY1, PY2, errors, error_ratio,
                  abs_errors, rel_errors, t1, t2, d1, d2):
    ''' Appends simulation results to pandas DataFrame df and returns it.

    Parameters
    ==========
    see srd_simulation_analysis.py


    Returns
    =======
```

```
    df: pandas DataFrame object
        updated results object
    '''
    results = {
    'sim_name': name,
    'seed': SEED,
    'runs': runs,
    'time_steps': steps,
    'paths': paths,
    'mo_match': mo_match,
    'anti_paths': anti_paths,
    'opt_prices': l,
    'abs_tol': PY1,
    'rel_tol': PY2,
    'errors': errors,
    'error_ratio': error_ratio,
    'aval_err': sum(abs_errors) / l,
    'abal_err': sum(abs(rel_errors)) / l,
    'time_sec': t1,
    'time_min': t2,
    'time_opt': t1 / l,
    'start_date': d1,
    'end_date': d2
    }
    df = pd.concat([sim_results,
                    pd.DataFrame([results])],
                    ignore_index=True)
    return df


def write_to_database(sim_results, filename=filename):
    ''' Write pandas DataFrame sim_results to HDFStore object.

    Parameters
    ==========
    sim_results: pandas DataFrame object
        object with simulation results
    filename: string
        name of the file for storage
    '''
    h5 = pd. HDFStore(filename, 'a')
    h5.append('sim_results', sim_results, min_itemsize={'values': 30},
        ignore_index=True)
    h5.close()


def print_results(filename=filename, idl=0, idh=50):
    ''' Prints valuation results in detailed form.

    Parameters
    ==========
```

```
        filename: string
            HDFStore with pandas.DataFrame with results
        idl: int
            start index value
        idh: int
            stop index value
        '''
        h5 = pd. HDFStore(filename, 'r')
        sim_results = h5['sim_results']
        br = "---------------------------------------------------------"
        for i in range(idl, min(len(sim_results), idh + 1)):
            row = sim_results.iloc[i]
            print br
            print "Start Calculations  %32s" % row['start_date'] + "\n" + br
            print "ID Number           %32d" % i
            print "Name of Simulation  %32s" % row['sim_name']
            print "Seed Value for RNG  %32d" % row['seed']
            print "Number of Runs      %32d" % row['runs']
            print "Time Steps          %32d" % row['time_steps']
            print "Paths               %32d" % row['paths']
            print "Moment Matching     %32s" % row['mo_match']
            print "Antithetic Paths    %32s" % row['anti_paths'] + "\n"
            print "Option Prices       %32d" % row['opt_prices']
            print "Absolute Tolerance  %32.4f" % row['abs_tol']
            print "Relative Tolerance  %32.4f" % row['rel_tol']
            print "Errors              %32d" % row['errors']
            print "Error Ratio         %32.4f" % row['error_ratio'] + "\n"
            print "Aver Val Error      %32.4f" % row['aval_err']
            print "Aver Abs Val Error  %32.4f" % row['abal_err']
            print "Time in Seconds     %32.4f" % row['time_sec']
            print "Time in Minutes     %32.4f" % row['time_min']
            print "Time per Option     %32.4f" % row['time_opt'] + "\n" + br
            print "End Calculations    %32s" % row['end_date'] \
                      + "\n" + br + "\n"
        print "Total number of rows in table %d" % len(sim_results)
        h5.close()


def plot_error_ratio(filename=filename):
    ''' Show error ratio vs. paths * time_steps (i.e. granularity).

    Parameters
    ==========
    filename: string
        name of file with data to be plotted
    '''
    h5 = pd. HDFStore(filename, mode='r')
    sim_results = h5['sim_results']
    x = np.array(sim_results['paths'] * sim_results['time_steps'], dtype='d')
    x = x / max(x)
```

```
    y = sim_results['error_ratio']
    plt.plot(x, y, 'bo', label='error ratio')
    rg = np.polyfit(x, y, deg=1)
    plt.plot(np.sort (x), np.polyval(rg, np.sort(x)), 'r', label='regression',
            linewidth=2)
    plt.xlabel('time steps * paths (normalized)')
    plt.ylabel('errors / option valuations')
    plt.legend()
    plt.grid(True)
    h5.close()
```

6.9.4 srd_model_calibration.py

```
#
# Calibration of Grünbichler and Longstaff (1996)
# square-root diffusion model to
# VSTOXX call options traded at Eurex
# Data as of 31. March 2014
# All data from www.eurexchange.com
#
# (c) Dr. Yves J. Hilpisch
# Listed Volatility and Variance Derivatives
#
import numpy as np
import pandas as pd
from srd_functions import call_price
import scipy.optimize as sco
import matplotlib.pyplot as plt


path = './source/data/'


# Fixed Parameters
v0 = 17.6639  # VSTOXX index on 31. March 2014
r = 0.01  # risk-less short rate
zeta = 0.  # volatility risk premium factor


def read_select_quotes(path=path, tol=0.2):
    ''' Selects and read options quotes.

    Parameters
    ==========
    path: string
        path to file with option quotes

    Returns
    =======
    option_data: pandas DataFrame object
```

```
              option data
        '''
    h5 = pd.HDFStore(path + 'vstoxx_march_2014.h5', 'r')

    # read option data from file and close it
    option_data = h5['vstoxx_options']
    h5.close()
    # select relevant date for call option quotes
    option_data = option_data[(option_data.DATE == '2014-3-31')
                             & (option_data.TYPE == 'C')]
    # calculate time-to-maturity in year fractions
    option_data['TTM'] = (option_data.MATURITY - option_data.DATE).apply(
                         lambda x: x / np.timedelta64(1, 'D') / 365.)
    # only those options close enough to the ATM level
    option_data = option_data[(option_data.STRIKE > (1 - tol) * v0)
                             & (option_data.STRIKE < (1 + tol) * v0)]
    return option_data

def valuation_function(p0):
    ''' Valuation function for set of strike prices

    Parameters
    ==========
    p0: list
        set of model parameters

    Returns
    =======
    call_prices: NumPy ndarray object
        array of call prices
    '''
    kappa, theta, sigma = p0
    call_prices = []
    for strike in strikes:
        call_prices.append(call_price(v0, kappa, theta,
                                  sigma, zeta, ttm, r, strike))
    call_prices = np.array(call_prices)
    return call_prices

def error_function(p0):
    ''' Error function for model calibration.

    Parameters
    ==========
    p0: tuple
        set of model parameters

    Returns
    =======
```

```
    MSE: float
        mean squared (relative/absolute) error
    '''
    global i
    call_prices = valuation_function(p0)
    kappa, theta, sigma = p0
     pen = 0.
    if 2 * kappa * theta < sigma ** 2:
        pen = 1000.0
    if kappa < 0 or theta < 0 or sigma < 0:
        pen = 1000.0
    if relative is True:
        MSE = (np.sum(((call_prices - call_quotes) / call_quotes) ** 2)
                / len(call_quotes) + pen)
    else:
        MSE = np.sum((call_prices - call_quotes) ** 2) / len(call_quotes) + pen

    if i == 0:
            print ("{:>6s}{:>6s}{:>6s}".format('kappa', 'theta', 'sigma')
                + "{:>12s}".format('MSE'))

    # print intermediate results: every 100th iteration
    if i % 100 == 0:
        print "{:6.3f} {:6.3f} {:6.3f}".format(*p0) + "{:>12.5f}".format(MSE)
    i += 1
    return MSE

def model_calibration(option_data, rel=False, mat=' 2014-07-18'):
    ''' Function for global and local model calibration.

    Parameters
    ==========
    option_data: pandas DataFrame object
        option quotes to be used
    relative: boolean
        relative or absolute MSE
    maturity: string
        maturity of option quotes to calibrate to

    Returns
    =======
    opt: tuple
        optimal parameter values
    '''
    global relative  # if True: MSRE is used, if False: MSAE
    global strikes
    global call_quotes
    global ttm
```

```
    global i

    relative = rel
    # only option quotes for a single maturity
    option_quotes = option_data[option_data.MATURITY == mat]

    # time-to-maturity from the data set
    ttm = option_quotes.iloc[0, -1]

    # transform strike column and price column in ndarray object
    strikes = option_quotes['STRIKE'].values
    call_quotes = option_quotes['PRICE'].values

    # global optimization
    i = 0  # counter for calibration iterations
    p0 = sco.brute(error_function, ((5.0, 20.1, 1.0), (10., 30.1, 1.25),
                            (1.0, 9.1, 2.0)), finish=None)

    # local optimization
    i = 0
    opt = sco.fmin(error_function, p0, xtol=0.0000001, ftol=0.0000001,
                            maxiter=1000, maxfun=1500)

    return opt

def plot_calibration_results(opt):
    ''' Function to plot market quotes vs. model prices.

    Parameters
    ==========
    opt: list
        optimal parameters from calibration
    '''
    callalues = valuation_function(opt)
    diffs = callalues - call_quotes
    plt.figure()
    plt.subplot(211)
    plt.plot(strikes, call_quotes, label='market quotes')
    plt.plot(strikes, callalues, 'ro', labe='model prices')
    plt.ylabel('option values')
    plt.grid(True)
    plt.legend()
    plt.axis([min(strikes) - 0.5, max(strikes) + 0.5,
            0.0, max(call_quotes) * 1.1])
    plt.subplot(212)
    wi = 0.3
    plt.bar(strikes - wi / 2, diffs, width=wi)
    plt.grid(True)
    plt.xlabel('strike price')
```

```python
    plt.ylabel('difference')
    plt.axis([min(strikes) - 0.5, max(strikes) + 0.5,
        min(diffs) * 1.1, max(diffs) * 1.1])
    plt.tight_layout()

if __name__ == '__main__':
    option_data = read_select_quotes()
    opt = model_calibration(option_data=option_data)
```

CHAPTER 7

Advanced Modeling of the VSTOXX Index

7.1 INTRODUCTION

This chapter is somewhat different in style compared to the other chapters about the VSTOXX volatility index and related derivatives. It introduces another parsimonious model, which is called square-root jump diffusion (SRJD) to model the VSTOXX volatility index. This model, which is essentially an extension of the Grünbichler and Longstaff (1996) model as analyzed in the previous chapter, is capable of reproducing prices of European options written on the VSTOXX reasonably well.

Two major enhancements characterize the SRJD model:

- **term structure**: it allows us to capture the term structure as observed in the prices of futures on the VSTOXX index
- **jump component**: including a jump component allows better replication of option prices in the short term

Adding these two components makes a market-consistent calibration of the model to a comprehensive set of European options on the VSTOXX index possible. For similar analyses and modeling approaches including jumps for the volatility index refer, for example, to Psychoyios (2005), Sepp (2008) or Psychoyios et al. (2010). For empirical evidence with regard to jumps in volatility see Todorov and Tauchen (2011).

7.2 MARKET QUOTES FOR CALL OPTIONS

Before we introduce the model, let us set the stage by revisiting market quotes for European call options written on the VSTOXX volatility index. First, we import the data:

```
In [1]: import pandas as pd

In [2]: path = './source/data/'

In [3]: h5 = pd. HDFStore(path + 'vstoxx_data_31032014.h5', 'r')
```

We have both options data and futures data stored in this file with quotes from March 31, 2014.

```
In [4]: h5
Out[4]:
<class 'pandas.io.pytables.HDFStore'>
File path: ./source/data/vstoxx_data_31032014.h5
/futures_data              frame       (shape->[8,6])
/options_data              frame       (shape->[395,8])
```

Option market quotes are what we are concerned with for the moment.

```
In [5]: option_quotes = h5['options_data']

In [6]: option_quotes.info()
<class 'pandas.core.frame.DataFrame'>
Int64Index: 395 entries, 46170 to 46564
Data columns (total 8 columns):
DATE         395 non-null datetime64[ns]
EXP_YEAR     395 non-null int64
EXP_MONTH    395 non-null int64
TYPE         395 non-null object
STRIKE       395 non-null float64
PRICE        395 non-null float64
MATURITY     395 non-null datetime64[ns]
TTM          395 non-null float64
dtypes: datetime64[ns](2), float64(3), int64(2), object(1)
memory usage: 27.8+ KB

In [7]: option_quotes.head()
Out[7]:
            DATE EXP_YEAR EXP_MONTH TYPE STRIKE PRICE   MATURITY  TTM
46170 2014-03-31     2014         4    C    1.0 16.85 2014-04-18 0.049
46171 2014-03-31     2014         4    C    2.0 15.85 2014-04-18 0.049
46172 2014-03-31     2014         4    C    3.0 14.85 2014-04-18 0.049
46173 2014-03-31     2014         4    C    4.0 13.85 2014-04-18 0.049
46174 2014-03-31     2014         4    C    5.0 12.85 2014-04-18 0.049
```

At any given point in time, there are options on the VSTOXX available for eight maturities.

```
In [8]: mats = sorted(set(option_quotes['MATURITY']))

In [9]: mats
Out[9]:
```

```
[Timestamp('2014-04-18 00:00:00'),
 Timestamp('2014-05-16 00:00:00'),
 Timestamp('2014-06-20 00:00:00'),
 Timestamp('2014-07-18 00:00:00'),
 Timestamp('2014-08-15 00:00:00'),
 Timestamp('2014-09-19 00:00:00'),
 Timestamp('2014-10-17 00:00:00'),
 Timestamp('2014-11-21 00:00:00')]
```

The spot level of the VSTOXX index on March 31, 2014 was 17.6639.

```
In [10]: v0 = 17.6639
```

In what follows, we only want to plot call option market quotes which are not too far in-the-money nor out-of-the-money.

```
In [11]: tol = 0.4

In [12]: to_plot = option_quotes[(option_quotes['STRIKE'] > (1 - tol) * v0)
    ....:                         & (option_quotes['STRIKE'] < (1 + tol) * v0)]
    ....:
```

Figure 7.1 shows the VSTOXX European call option quotes which fulfill the requirements. The goal of this chapter is to replicate "all these option quotes" as closely as possible.

```
In [13]: import matplotlib.pyplot as plt

In [14]: import seaborn as sns; sns.set()

In [15]: import matplotlib

In [16]: matplotlib.rcParams['font.family'] = 'serif'

In [17]: markers = ['.', 'o', '^', 'v', 'x', 'D', 'd', '>', '<']

In [18]: plt.figure(figsize=(10, 6));

In [19]: for i, mat in enumerate(mats):
    ....:     strikes = to_plot[(to_plot['MATURITY'] == mat)]['STRIKE']
    ....:     prices = to_plot[(to_plot['MATURITY'] == mat)]['PRICE']
    ....:     plt.plot(strikes, prices, 'b%s' % markers[i],
    ....:         label=str(mat)[:10])
    ....:
```

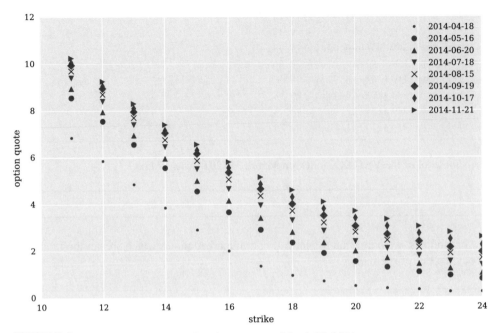

FIGURE 7.1   VSTOXX European call option quotes on March 31, 2014.

```
<matplotlib.figure.Figure at 0x2ab247d90d50>

In [20]: plt.legend();

In [21]: plt.xlabel('strike');

In [22]: plt.ylabel('option quote');
```

7.3 THE SRJD MODEL

A filtered probability space $\{\Omega, \mathcal{F}, \mathbb{F}, P\}$ representing uncertainty in the model economy is given with final date T where $0 < T < \infty$. Ω denotes the continuous state space, $\mathcal{F}$ a σ–algebra, $\mathbb{F}$ a filtration – i.e. a family of non-decreasing σ–algebras $\mathbb{F} \equiv \{\mathcal{F}_{t \in [0,T]}\}$ with $\mathcal{F}_0 \equiv \{\emptyset, \Omega\}$ and $\mathcal{F}_T \equiv \mathcal{F}$ – and P the real or objective probability measure.

In the SRJD model, which is an affine jump diffusion (see Duffie et al. (2000)), the risk-neutral dynamics of the VSTOXX volatility index are given by the following stochastic differential equation (SDE):

$$dv_t = \kappa(\theta - v_t)dt + \sigma\sqrt{v_t}dZ_t + J_t v_t dN_t - r_J dt$$

The meaning of the variables and parameters is:

- v_t volatility index level at date t
- κ speed of adjustment of v_t to...
- ... θ, the long-term mean of the index
- σ volatility coefficient of the index level
- Z_t standard Brownian motion
- J_t jump at date t with distribution...
- ... $\log(1 + J_t) \approx \mathbf{N}(\log(1 + \mu) - \frac{\delta^2}{2}, \delta^2)$
- $\mathbf{N}$ cumulative distribution function of a standard normal random variable
- N_t Poisson process with intensity λ
- $r_J \equiv \lambda \cdot (e^{\mu + \delta^2/2} - 1)$ drift correction for jump.

The stochastic process for v is adapted to the filtration $\mathbb{F}$. Moreover, Z and N are not correlated. The time t value of a zero-coupon bond paying one unit of currency at $T, 0 \leq t < T$, is $B_t(T) = e^{-r(T-t)}$ with $r \geq 0$ the constant risk-less short rate.

By the Fundamental Theorem of Asset Pricing, the time t value of an attainable, $\mathcal{F}_T$-measurable contingent claim $V_T \equiv h_T(X_T) \geq 0$ (satisfying suitable integrability conditions) is given by arbitrage as

$$V_t = \mathbf{E}_t^Q \left(B_t(T) V_T \right)$$

with $V_0 = \mathbf{E}_0^Q(B_0(T)V_T)$ as the important special case for valuation purposes. Q is a P-equivalent martingale measure. The contingent claim could be a European call option maturing at T with payoff $V_T = h_T(v_T) \equiv \max[v_T - K, 0]$. It could also be a European put with payoff $V_T = h_T(v_T) \equiv \max[K - v_T, 0]$. In both cases, K is the fixed strike price of the option.

To simulate the financial model, i.e. to generate numerical values for v_t, it has to be discretized. To this end, divide the given time interval $[0, T]$ in equidistant sub-intervals Δt such that now $t \in \{0, \Delta t, 2\Delta t, \ldots, T\}$, i.e. there are $M + 1$ points in time with $M \equiv T/\Delta t$. With $s = t - \Delta t$, a discretization of the continuous time market model is given by

$$\tilde{v}_t = \tilde{v}_s + \kappa(\theta - \tilde{v}_s^+)\Delta t + \sigma \sqrt{\tilde{v}_s^+} \sqrt{\Delta t} z_t^1$$
$$+ \left(e^{\mu_J + \delta^2 z_t^2} - 1 \right) \tilde{v}_s^+ y_t - r_J \Delta t$$
$$v_t = \tilde{v}_t^+$$

for $t \in \{\Delta t, \ldots, T\}$ with $x^+ \equiv \max[x, 0]$ and the z_t^n being standard normally distributed and y_t Poisson distributed. z_t^1, z_t^2 and y_t are uncorrelated. This discretization scheme is an Euler discretization and is generally called *full trunction* scheme. See Lord et al. (2008) for an analysis of this and other biased discretization schemes for the square-root diffusion process.

7.4 TERM STRUCTURE CALIBRATION

The first step in the calibration of the SRJD model is with regard to the futures term structure.

7.4.1 Futures Term Structure

It is difficult for parsimonious short rate models like that of Cox et al. (1985) to account for different term structures of the interest rate. A possible solution is the introduction of time-dependent parameters which, however, enlarges the number of parameters significantly, sacrificing at the same time the convenience of a limited number of economic parameters. Another solution is a *deterministic shift approach* according to Brigo and Mercurio (2001) which preserves the basic structure of the model with all its advantages and which nevertheless allows us to better account for different term structures of the short rate.

In this section, we transfer the deterministic shift approach for the short rate models of Brigo and Mercurio (2001) to the SRJD model. Since the square-root diffusion and the jumps are not correlated, we can first apply the approach to the diffusion part and use this enhanced component later on in conjunction with the jump component.

Before we present the theory, a look at the VSTOXX futures data first.

```
In [23]: futures_quotes = h5['futures_data']

In [24]: futures_quotes.info()
<class 'pandas.core.frame.DataFrame'>
Int64Index: 8 entries, 496 to 503
Data columns (total 6 columns):
DATE          8 non-null datetime64[ns]
EXP_YEAR      8 non-null int64
EXP_MONTH     8 non-null int64
PRICE         8 non-null float64
MATURITY      8 non-null datetime64[ns]
TTM           8 non-null float64
dtypes: datetime64[ns](2), float64(2), int64(2)
memory usage: 448.0 bytes
```

Figure 7.2 presents the futures quotes for all eight maturities.

```
In [25]: ax = futures_quotes.plot(x='MATURITY', y='PRICE',
    ....:                          figsize=(10, 6), legend=False)
    ....:
<matplotlib.figure.Figure at 0x2ab25d177c50>

In [26]: futures_quotes.plot(x='MATURITY', y='PRICE', style='ro', ax=ax);
```

Consider for now the square-root diffusion volatility model of Grünbichler and Longstaff (1996) as presented in the previous chapter, which is formally the same as the short rate model of Cox et al. (1985) and which is a special case of the SRJD model:

$$dv_t = \kappa(\theta - v_t)dt + \sigma\sqrt{v_t}dZ_t$$

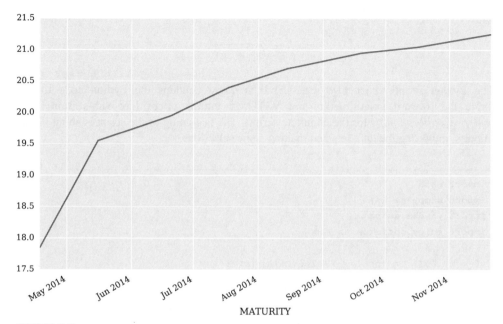

MATURITY

FIGURE 7.2 VSTOXX futures quotes on March 31, 2014.

We want to calibrate this model to the observed volatility term structure, given by the above presented set of prices for futures on the VSTOXX index with different maturities. We have to minimize for all considered times t and a parameter set $\alpha = (\kappa, \theta, \sigma, v_0)$ simultaneously the single differences

$$\Delta f(0, t) \equiv f(0, t) - f^{GL96}(0, t; \alpha)$$

where $f(0, t)$ is the time 0 market (instantaneous) forward volatility for time t and the quantity $f^{GL96}(0, t; \alpha)$ is the model (instantaneous) forward volatility for time t given parameter set α.

Assume that there is a continuously differentiable volatility term structure function $F(0, t)$ available (i.e. there are infinitely many volatility futures prices). The forward volatility then is

$$f(0, t) = \frac{\partial F(0, t)}{\partial t}$$

On the other hand, the model implied forward volatility is given as (see Brigo and Mercurio (2001))

$$f^{GL96}(0, t; \alpha) = \frac{\kappa\theta(e^{\gamma t} - 1)}{2\gamma + (\kappa + \gamma)(e^{\gamma t} - 1)}$$
$$+ v_0 \frac{4\gamma^2 e^{\gamma t}}{(2\gamma + (\kappa + \gamma)(e^{\gamma t} - 1))^2}$$

with

$$\gamma \equiv \sqrt{\kappa^2 + 2\sigma^2}$$

The Python script `srjd_fwd_calibration.py` contains the Python code to calibrate the forward volatilities to the VSTOXX futures prices (see sub-section 7.8.1, *srjd_fwd_calibration.py* for the complete script). The beginning of the script is about library imports, importing the data sets and making some selections.

```python
import math
import numpy as np
import pandas as pd
import scipy.optimize as sco


v0 = 17.6639  # initial VSTOXX index level
i = 0  # counter for calibration runs

# reading the VSTOXX futures quotes
path = 'source/data/'
h5 = pd.HDFStore(path + 'vstoxx_data_31032014.h5', 'r')
futures_quotes = h5['futures_data']
h5.close()

# selecting needed data columns and adding spot value
forwards = list(futures_quotes['PRICE'].values)
forwards.insert(0, v0)
forwards = np.array(forwards)
ttms = list(futures_quotes['TTM'].values)
ttms.insert(0, 0)
ttms = np.array(ttms)
```

The function `srd_forwards()` implements the forward formula from above for a given parameter set.

```python
def srd_forwards(p0):
    ''' Function for forward volatilities in GL96 Model.

    Parameters
    ==========
    p0: list
        set of model parameters, where

        kappa: float
            mean-reversion factor
```

```
        theta: float
            long-run mean
        sigma: float
            volatility factor

    Returns
    =======
    forwards: NumPy ndarray object
        forward volatilities
    '''
    t = ttms
    kappa, theta, sigma = p0
    g = math.sqrt(kappa ** 2 + 2 * sigma ** 2)
    sum1 = ((kappa * theta * (np.exp(g * t) - 1)) /
            (2 * g + (kappa + g) * (np.exp(g * t) - 1)))
    sum2 = v0 * ((4 * g ** 2 * np.exp(g * t)) /
                (2 * g + (kappa + g) * (np.exp(g * t) - 1)) ** 2)
    forwards = sum1 + sum2
    return forwards
```

To operationalize the calibration, we use the mean squared error (MSE) as our yardstick

$$\min_{\alpha} \frac{1}{N} \sum_{n=1}^{N} \left(f_n - f_n^{GL96}(\alpha) \right)^2$$

which is to be minimized. Here, we assume that we have N observations for the forward volatility. In Python this takes on the form of function `srd_fwd_error()`.

```
def srd_fwd_error(p0):
    ''' Error function for GL96 forward volatilities calibration.

    Parameters
    ==========
    p0: tuple
        parameter vector

    Returns
    =======
    MSE: float
        mean-squared error for p0
    '''
    global i
    kappa, theta, sigma = p0
    srd_fwds = srd_forwards(p0)
    MSE = np.sum((forwards - srd_fwds) ** 2) / len(forwards)
    if 2 * kappa * theta < sigma ** 2:
        MSE = MSE + 100      # penalty
```

```
    elif sigma < 0:
        MSE = MSE + 100
    # print intermediate results: every 50th iteration
    if i % 50 == 0:
        print "{:6.3f} {:6.3f} {:6.3f}".format(* p0) + "{:>12.5f}".format(MSE)
    i += 1
    return MSE
```

Executing the script yields optimal parameters for the Grünbichler and Longstaff (1996) model given the VSTOXX futures prices.

```
In [27]: %run source/scripts/srjd_fwd_calibration.py
 1.000 17.500  1.000     35.99817
 0.258 40.585  0.057      5.61895
 1.575 46.996  0.392      0.22958
 2.525 46.207  0.710      0.06348
 3.447 44.752  0.972      0.04264
 3.538 44.458  0.903      0.04261
 3.947 43.495  0.610      0.04243
 4.113 43.102  0.275      0.04219
 4.187 42.969  0.019      0.04213
 4.169 42.984  0.002      0.04213
 4.170 42.984  0.000      0.04213
Optimization terminated successfully.
         Current function value: 0.042129
         Iterations: 292
         Function evaluations: 526
```

```
In [28]: opt.round(3)
Out[28]: array([  4.17 ,  42.984,   0.  ])
```

These optimal values can be used to calculate the model forward volatilities using function srd_forwards().

```
In [29]: from srjd_fwd_calibration import *

In [30]: srd_fwds = srd_forwards(opt)

In [31]: srd_fwds
Out[31]:
array([ 17.6639    , 18.37130183, 19.22831373, 19.97504105,
        20.3916346, 20.69048824, 20.95488999, 21.10239774, 21.23092346])
```

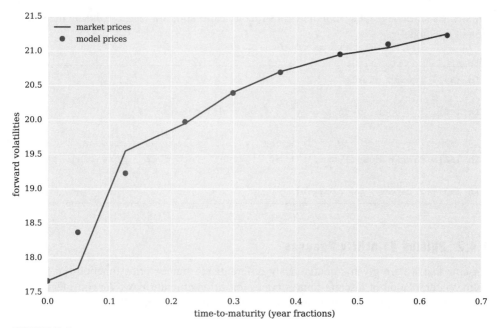

FIGURE 7.3 VSTOXX futures market quotes vs. model prices.

The numerical differences to the market futures prices are:

```
In [32]: srd_fwds - forwards
Out[32]:
array([ 0.        ,  0.52130183, -0.32168627,  0.02504105, -0.0083654,
       -0.00951176,  0.00488999,  0.05239774, -0.01907654])
```

Figure 7.3 compares the model futures prices (forward volatilities) with the VSTOXX futures market quotes. For longer maturities the fit is quite good.

```
In [33]: plt.figure(figsize=(10, 6));

In [34]: plt.plot(ttms, forwards, 'b', label='market prices');

In [35]: plt.plot(ttms, srd_fwds, 'ro', label='model prices');

In [36]: plt.legend(loc=0);

In [37]: plt.xlabel('time-to-maturity (year fractions)');

In [38]: plt.ylabel('forward volatilities');
```

Finally, we save the results from the term structure calibration for later use during the simulation of the model.

```
In [39]: import pickle

In [40]: f = open('varphi', 'w')   # open file on disk

# write ttms object and differences (varphi values) as dictionary
In [41]: pickle.dump({'ttms': ttms, 'varphi': srd_fwds - forwards}, f)

In [42]: f.close()   # close file
```

7.4.2 Shifted Volatility Process

Assume that we are given a continuously differentiable futures price function (i.e. through splines interpolation of discrete futures prices for different maturities). We consider now the deterministically shifted volatility process (see Brigo and Mercurio (2001))

$$\hat{v}_t \equiv v_t + \varphi(t, \alpha^*)$$

with $\varphi(t, \alpha^*) \equiv f(0, t) - f^{GL96}(0, t; \alpha^*)$, the difference at time t between the market implied forward volatility and the model implied forward volatility after calibration, i.e. for the optimal parameter set α^*. $\varphi(t, \alpha^*)$ corresponds to the differences (bars) in Figure 7.4.

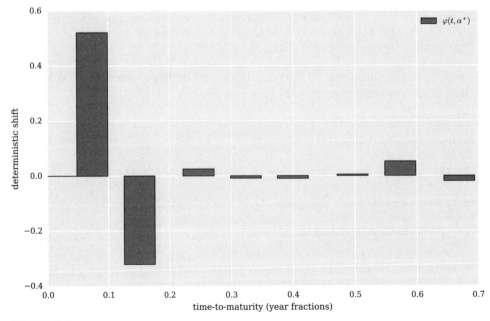

FIGURE 7.4 Deterministic shift values to account for VSTOXX futures term structure.

```
In [43]: plt.figure(figsize=(10, 6));

In [44]: plt.bar(ttms, srd_fwds - forwards,
   ....:         width=0.05, label='$\\varphi(t,\\alpha^*)$');
   ....:

In [45]: plt.legend(loc=0);

In [46]: plt.xlabel('time-to-maturity (year fractions)');

In [47]: plt.ylabel('deterministic shift');
```

The SRJD model discretization can now be adjusted as follows:

$$\tilde{v}_t = \tilde{v}_s + \kappa(\theta - \tilde{v}_s^+)\Delta t + \sigma\sqrt{\tilde{v}_s^+}\sqrt{\Delta t}z_t^1$$

$$+ \left(e^{\mu_J + \delta^2 z_t^2} - 1\right)\tilde{v}_s^+ y_t - r_J \Delta t \tag{7.1}$$

$$\hat{v}_t = \tilde{v}_t^+ + \varphi(t, \alpha^*) \tag{7.2}$$

This is consistent since the diffusion and jump parts are not correlated and since the jump part is added in such a way that the first moment of the stochastic volatility process does not change.

7.5 OPTION VALUATION BY MONTE CARLO SIMULATION

This section implements Monte Carlo simulation procedures for the SRJD model.

7.5.1 Monte Carlo Valuation

In what follows, the model option values are computed by Monte Carlo simulation (MCS). Given the discrete version of the financial model, the value of a European call option on the volatility index is estimated by MCS as follows:

Algorithm 1: Simulation algorithm

---
for $i = 1, 2, \ldots, I$ **do**
     for $t = \Delta t, \ldots, T$ **do**
1   draw pseudo-random numbers $z_t^1(i), z_t^2(i), y_t(i)$
2   apply these to equations (7.1) and (7.2) to calculate $v_t(i)$
3   calculate $V_T(i) = h_T(i) \equiv \max[v_T(i) - K, 0]$
4 sum up all payoffs at T, take the average and discount back to $t = 0$:

$$V_0(K, T) \approx e^{-rT} \cdot \frac{1}{I} \sum_I \max[v_T(i) - K, 0]$$

V_0 is the MCS estimator for the European call option value.

7.5.2 Technical Implementation

Because we are using a numerical method like MCS for all valuation and calibration tasks, the parametrization and implementation of the MCS algorithm play an important role. Some major features of our implementation are:

- **discretization**: the algorithm uses the Euler discretization scheme which is an approximation only but which might bring performance benefits
- **random numbers**: for every single option valuation the seed can be held constant such that every option is valued with the same set of (pseudo-)random numbers
- **variance reduction**: both antithetic variates and moment matching (for the first two moments of the pseudo-random numbers) are used as generic variance reduction techniques
- **deterministic shift**: the deterministic shift values φ are determined only once through a separate calibration and are held constant afterwards (even if model parameters change).

φ only has to be deterministic and integrable on closed intervals (see Brigo and Mercurio (2001)), which is of course the case. For the approach to be valid, it is not important how we originally came up with the φ.

The Python code for simulating the SRJD model is found in the script srjd_simulation.py (see sub-section 7.8.2, *srjd_simulation.py* for the complete script). The beginning of the script shows several imports, the definition of example parameters and also the cubic splines interpolation to be used for the estimation of the deterministic shift parameters.

```
import math
import pickle
import numpy as np
import scipy.interpolate as scint


v0 = 17.6639  # initial VSTOXX index level


# parameters of square-root diffusion
kappa = 2.0  # speed of mean reversion
theta = 15.0  # long-term volatility
sigma = 1.0  # standard deviation coefficient


# parameters of log-normal jump
lamb = 0.4  # intensity (jumps per year)
mu = 0.4  # average jump size
delta = 0.1  # volatility of jump size


# general parameters
r = 0.01  # risk-free interest rate
K = 17.5  # strike
T = 0.5  # time horizon
M = 150  # time steps
```

```
I = 10000   # number of MCS paths
anti_paths = True   # antithetic variates
mo_match = True   # moment matching


# deterministic shift parameters
varphi = pickle.load(open('varphi'))
tck = scint.splrep(varphi['ttms'], varphi['varphi'], k=1)
  # linear splines interpolation of
  # term structure calibration differences
```

The Python function `random_number_gen()` generates arrays of standard normally distributed pseudo-random numbers using both antithetic variates and moment matching as generic variance reduction techniques.

```
def random_number_gen(M, I, fixed_seed=False):
    ''' Generate standard normally distributed pseudo-random numbers

    Parameters
    ==========
    M: int
        number of time intervals
    I: int
        number of paths

    Returns
    =======
    ran: NumPy ndarrayo object
        random number array
    '''
    if fixed_seed  is True:
        np.random.seed(10000)
    if anti_paths  is True:
        ran = np.random.standard_normal((M + 1, I / 2))
        ran = np.concatenate((ran, -ran), axis=1)
    else:
        ran = np.standard_normal((M + 1, I))
    if mo_match is True:
        ran = ran / np.std(ran)
        ran -= np.mean(ran)
    return ran
```

The major function of this script is `srjd_simulation()` which implements the Monte Carlo simulation for the SRJD model based on an Euler discretization scheme. The scheme used here is usually called a *full truncation* scheme.

```
def srjd_simulation(x0, kappa, theta, sigma,
                    lamb, mu, delta, T, M, I, fixed_seed=False):
    ''' Function to simulate square-root jump Difusion.

    Parameters
    ==========
    x0: float
        initial value
    kappa: float
        mean-reversion factor
    theta: float
        long-run mean
    sigma: float
        volatility factor
    lamb: float
        jump intensity
    mu: float
        expected jump size
    delta: float
        standard deviation of jump
    T: float
        time horizon/maturity
    M: int
        time steps
    I: int
        number of simulation paths

    Returns
    =======
    x: NumPy ndarray object
        array with simulated SRJD paths
    '''
    dt = float(T) / M  # time interval
    shift = scint.splev(np.arange(M + 1) * dt, tck, der=0)
      # deterministic shift values
    xh = np.zeros((M + 1, I), dtype=np.float)
    x = np.zeros((M + 1, I), dtype=np.float)
    xh[0, :] = x0
    x[0, :] = x0
    # drift contribution of jump p.a.
    rj = lamb * (math.exp(mu + 0.5 * delta ** 2) - 1)
    # 1st matrix with standard normal rv
    ran1 = random_number_gen(M + 1, I, fixed_seed)
    # 2nd matrix with standard normal rv
    ran2 = random_number_gen(M + 1, I, fixed_seed)
    # matrix with Poisson distributed rv
```

```
    ran3 = np.random.poisson(lamb * dt, (M + 1, I))
    for t in range(1, M + 1):
        xh[t, :] = (xh[t - 1, :] +
                    kappa * (theta - np.maximum(0, xh[t - 1, :]))) * dt
                + np.sqrt(np.maximum(0, xh[t - 1, :])) * sigma
                * ran1[t] * np.sqrt(dt)
                + (np.exp(mu + delta * ran2[t]) - 1) * ran3[t]
                * np.maximum(0, xh[t - 1, :]) - rj * dt)
        x[t, :] = np.maximum(0, xh[t, :]) + shift[t]
    return x
```

Finally, the function `srjd_call_valuation()` estimates the value of a European call option given the simulated volatility paths from `srjd_simulation()`.

```
def srjd_call_valuation(v0, kappa, theta, sigma,
                        lamb, mu, delta, T, r, K, M=M, I=I,
                        fixed_seed=False):
    ''' Function to value European volatility call option in SRDJ model.
    Parameters see function srjd_simulation.

    Returns
    =======
    call_value: float
        estimator for European call present value for strike K
    '''
    v = srjd_simulation(v0, kappa, theta, sigma,
                        lamb, mu, delta, T, M, I, fixed_seed)
    call_value = np.exp(- r * T) * sum(np.maximum(v[-1] - K, 0)) / I
    return call_value
```

Executing the script yields a MCS estimator for the European call option with the parameters as assumed in the script of about 1 currency unit.

```
In [48]: %run source/scripts/srjd_simulation.py
Value of European call by MCS:    0.9959
```

7.6 MODEL CALIBRATION

This section now calibrates the SRJD model to market quotes for European call options on VSTOXX futures. It considers calibrations to a single maturity as well as to multiple maturities.

7.6.1 The Python Code

The calibration of the SRJD model is similar to the procedure for the Grünbichler and Lonstaff (1996) square-root diffusion model as presented in the previous chapter. The major difference now is that we have to take into account more parameter values for the optimization. The Python code is contained in script `srjd_model_calibration.py` (see sub-section 7.8.3, *srjd_model_calibration.py* for the complete script). As usual a few imports and parameter definitions first.

```python
import numpy as np
import pandas as pd
import scipy.optimize as sco
import matplotlib.pyplot as plt
from srd_model_calibration import path, read_select_quotes
from srjd_simulation import srjd_call_valuation


# fixed parameters
r = 0.01  # risk-less short rate
v0 = 17.6639  # VSTOXX index at 31.03.2014
M = 15  # number of time intervals
I = 100  # number of simulated paths
```

In what follows, we want to calibrate the model simultaneously to multiple maturities for the VSTOXX European call options. The valuation function `srjd_valuation_function()` therefore now calculates the differences between model and market values directly and returns an array with all differences (relative or absolute).

```python
def srjd_valuation_function(p0):
    ''' Valuation ('difference') function for all options
        of a given DataFrame object.

    Parameters
    ==========
    p0: list
        set of model parameters

    Returns
    =======
    diffs: NumPy ndarray object
        array with valuation differences
    '''
    global relative, option_data
    kappa, theta, sigma, lamb, mu, delta = p0
    diffs = []
    for i, option in option_data.iterrows():
```

```
            value = srjd_call_valuation(v0, kappa, theta, sigma,
                                         lamb, mu, delta,
                                         option['TTM'], r, option['STRIKE'],
                                         M=M, I=I, fixed_seed=True)
        if relative is True:
            diffs.append((value - option['PRICE']) / option['PRICE'])
        else:
            diffs.append(value - option['PRICE'])
    diffs = np.array(diffs)
    return diffs
```

The error function `srjd_error_function()` for the SRJD model has to be enhanced compared to the SRD case to account for the additional parameters of the model.

```
def srjd_error_function(p0):
    ''' Error function for model calibration.

    Parameters
    ==========
    p0: tuple
        set of model parameters

    Returns
    =======
    MSE: float
        mean squared (relative/absolute) error
    '''
    global i, min_MSE, option_data
    OD = len(option_data)
    diffs = srjd_valuation_function(p0)
    kappa, theta, sigma, lamb, mu, delta = p0

    # penalties
    pen = 0.
    if 2 * kappa * theta < sigma ** 2:
        pen = 1000.0
    if kappa < 0 or theta < 0 or sigma < 0 or lamb < 0 or delta < 0:
        pen = 1000.0

    MSE = np.sum(diffs ** 2) / OD + pen   # mean squared error

    min_MSE = min(min_MSE, MSE)   # running minimum value

    if i == 0:
        print \'n' + ('{:>5s}'.format('its')
                      + '{:>7s} {:>6s} {:>6s} {:>6s} {:>6s} {:>6s}'.format(
```

```
            'kappa', 'theta', 'sigma', 'lamb', 'mu', 'delta')
        + '{:>12s}'.format('MSE') + '{:>12s}'.format('min_MSE'))
# print intermediate results: every 100th iteration
if i % 100 == 0:
    print ('{:>5d}'.format(i)
            + '{:7.3f} {:6.3f} {:6.3f} {:6.3f} {:6.3f} {:6.3f}'.format(*p0)
            + '{:>12.5f}'.format(MSE) + '{:>12.5f}'.format(min_MSE))
i += 1
return MSE
```

The same holds true for the calibration function `srjd_model_calibration()` itself. This function allows us to select certain maturities for the calibration.

```
def srjd_model_calibration(data, p0=None, rel=False, mats=None):
    ''' Function for global and local model calibration.

    Parameters
    ==========
    option_data: pandas DataFrame object
        option quotes to be used
    relative: bool
        relative or absolute MSE
    mats: list
        list of maturities of option quotes to calibrate to

    Returns
    =======
    opt: tuple
        optimal parameter values
    '''
    global i, min_MSE, option_data
    global relative  # if True: MSRE is used, if False: MSAE

    min_MSE = 5000.  # dummy value
    relative = rel  # relative or absolute
    option_data = data

    if mats is not None:
        # select the option data for the given maturities
        option_data = option_data[option_data['MATURITY'].isin(mats)]

    # global optimization
    if p0 is None:
        i = 0  # counter for calibration iterations
        p0 = sco.brute(srjd_error_function, (
            (1.0, 9.1, 4.0),  # kappa
```

```
                (10., 20.1, 10.0),   # theta
                (1.0, 3.1, 2.0),   # sigma
                (0.0, 0.81, 0.4),   # lambda
                (-0.2, 0.41, 0.3),   # mu
                (0.0, 0.31, 0.15)),   # delta
            finish=None)


    # local optimization
    i = 0
    opt = sco.fmin(srjd_error_function, p0,
                   xtol=0.0000001, ftol=0.0000001,
                   maxiter=550, maxfun=700)

    return opt
```

7.6.2 Short Maturity

The addition of a jump component shall allow a better fit to short-term call option market quotes. Therefore, consider the following calibration to the shortest option maturity available:

```
In [49]: from srjd_model_calibration import *

# read option data, allow for 30% moneyness tolerance
In [50]: option_data = read_select_quotes(tol=0.3)
```

```
In [51]: %%time
    ....: opt_1 = srjd_model_calibration(option_data, p0=None,
    ....:                                rel=False, mats=['2014-4-18'])
    ....:
```

its	kappa	theta	sigma	lamb	mu	delta	MSE	min_MSE
0	1.000	10.000	1.000	0.000	-0.200	0.000	0.15785	0.15785
100	1.000	20.000	3.000	0.800	-0.200	0.000	0.10867	0.01976
200	5.000	20.000	3.000	0.400	-0.200	0.150	0.27793	0.01976
300	9.000	20.000	3.000	0.000	-0.200	0.300	0.70669	0.01976

its	kappa	theta	sigma	lamb	mu	delta	MSE	min_MSE
0	1.000	10.000	3.000	0.400	-0.200	0.000	0.01976	0.01976
100	1.016	9.216	2.996	0.476	-0.124	0.001	0.01956	0.01955
200	1.020	9.213	3.006	0.494	-0.128	0.001	0.01955	0.01955
300	0.976	8.895	3.000	0.392	-0.128	0.001	0.02214	0.01955
400	0.977	8.869	3.002	0.394	-0.128	0.001	0.01955	0.01955
500	0.976	8.866	3.002	0.394	-0.128	0.001	0.01955	0.01955

```
   600  0.976  8.867  3.002  0.394 -0.128  0.001     0.01955      0.01955
Warning: Maximum number of function evaluations has been exceeded.
CPU times: user 14.7 s, sys: 7.97 ms, total: 14.7 s
Wall time: 14.7 s
```

The optimal parameter values are:

```
In [52]: opt_1
Out[52]:
array([ 9.75770825e-01,   8.86539094e+00,   3.00188833e+00,
        3.93539089e-01,  -1.28094441e-01,   1.26180667e-03])
```

Using these optimal parameter values, add the model prices to the `DataFrame` object containing the option data.

```
In [53]: values = []

In [54]: kappa, theta, sigma, lamb, mu, delta = opt_1

In [55]: for i, option  in option_data.iterrows():
    ....:     value = srjd_call_valuation(v0, kappa, theta, sigma,
    ....:                                 lamb, mu, delta,
    ....:                                 option['TTM'], r, option['STRIKE'],
    ....:                                 M=M, I=I, fixed_seed=True)
    ....:     values.append(value)
    ....:

In [56]: option_data['MODEL'] = values
```

Figure 7.5 shows the calibration results graphically. Indeed, the fit seems to be quite good, reflecting a MSAE of about 0.0015 only.

```
# selecting the data for the shortest maturity
In [57]: os = option_data[option_data.MATURITY == '2014-4-18']

# selecting corresponding strike prices
In [58]: strikes = os.STRIKE.values

# comparing the model prices with the market quotes
In [59]: fig, ax = plt.subplots(2, 1, sharex=True, figsize=(10, 6));

In [60]: ax[0].plot(strikes, os.PRICE.values, label='market quotes');

In [61]: ax[0].plot(strikes, os.MODEL.values, 'ro', label='model prices');
```

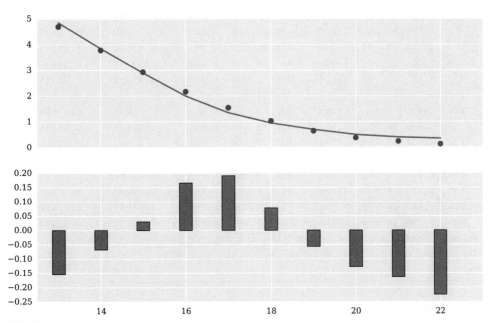

FIGURE 7.5 Calibration of SRJD model to European call options on the VSTOXX for shortest option maturity (April 2014).

```
In [62]: ax[1].bar(strikes - 0.15, os.MODEL.values - os.PRICE.values,
   ....:                              width=0.3);
   ....:

In [63]: ax[1].set_xlim(12.5, 23);
```

7.6.3 Two Maturities

Let us proceed with the simultaneous calibration of the model to the May and July maturities. The MSE is also pretty low in this case (i.e. below 0.01).

```
# read option data, allow for 17.5% moneyness tolerance
In [64]: option_data = read_select_quotes(tol=0.175)
```

```
In [65]: %%time
   ....: opt_2 = srjd_model_calibration(option_data, rel=False,
   ....:                           mats=['2014-5-16', '2014-7-18'])
   ....:
```

```
its  kappa  theta  sigma   lamb    mu   delta       MSE     min_MSE
  0  1.000 10.000  1.000  0.000 -0.200  0.000   8.71137     8.71137
100  1.000 20.000  3.000  0.800 -0.200  0.000   0.85126     0.10351
200  5.000 20.000  3.000  0.400 -0.200  0.150   0.59218     0.09015
300  9.000 20.000  3.000  0.000 -0.200  0.300   0.45081     0.01539

its  kappa  theta  sigma   lamb    mu   delta       MSE     min_MSE
  0  5.000 20.000  3.000  0.800  0.400  0.000   0.01539     0.01539
100  4.471 19.655  3.256  0.762  0.424  0.000   0.00892     0.00892
200  4.010 19.231  2.730  0.761  0.575  0.002   0.00792     0.00792
300  4.023 18.987  2.321  0.721  0.668  0.003   0.01182     0.00688
400  3.803 18.830  2.115  0.722  0.701  0.003   0.00660     0.00660
500  3.823 18.799  2.106  0.723  0.706  0.003   0.00644     0.00644
600  3.998 18.681  1.916  0.728  0.749  0.003   0.00598     0.00598
Warning: Maximum number of function evaluations has been exceeded.
CPU times: user 17.1 s, sys: 10 us, total: 17.1 s
Wall time: 17.1 s
```

The optimal parameter values are:

```
In [66]: opt_2
Out[66]:
array([  3.99997568e+00,   1.86836808e+01,   1.91679210e+00,
         7.28298815e-01,   7.48260996e-01,   3.26197421e-03])
```

In what follows, we use the Python function `plot_calibration_results()` to generate the plots for the different valuation runs. This function allows for different numbers of sub-plots, i.e. when the number of option maturities is changed. It is mainly a generalization of the plotting code used above.

```
def plot_calibration_results(option_data, opt, mats):
    ''' Function to plot market quotes vs. model prices.

    Parameters
    ==========
    option_data: pandas DataFrame object
        option data to plot
    opt: list
        optimal results from calibration
    mats: list
        maturities to be plotted
    '''
    kappa, theta, sigma, lamb, mu, delta = opt
    # adding model values for optimal parameter set
```

```
# to the DataFrame object
values = []
for i, option in option_data.iterrows():
    value = srjd_call_valuation(v0, kappa, theta, sigma,
                                lamb, mu, delta,
                                option['TTM'], r, option['STRIKE'],
                                M=M, I=I, fixed_seed=True)
    values.append(value)
option_data['MODEL'] = values

# plotting the market and model values
height = min(len(mats) * 3, 12)
fig, axarr = plt.subplots(len(mats), 2, sharex=True, figsize=(10, height))
for z, mat in enumerate(mats):
    if z == 0:
        axarr[z, 0].set_title('values')
        axarr[z, 1].set_title('differences')
    os = option_data[option_data.MATURITY == mat]
    strikes = os.STRIKE.values
    axarr[z, 0].set_ylabel('%s' % str(mat)[: 10])
    axarr[z, 0].plot(strikes, os.PRICE.values, label='market quotes')
    axarr[z, 0].plot(strikes, os.MODEL.values, 'ro', label='model prices')
    axarr[z, 0].legend(loc=0)
    wi = 0.3
    axarr[z, 1].bar(strikes - wi / 2, os.MODEL.values - os.PRICE.values,
                    width=wi)
    if mat == mats[- 1]:
        axarr[z, 0].set_xlabel('strike')
        axarr[z, 1].set_xlabel('strike')
```

Figure 7.6 shows the results of the calibration graphically. It is obvious that the SRJD model is able to account for multiple maturities at the same time which is mainly due to the term structure component introduced by the deterministic shift approach.

```
In [67]: plot_calibration_results(option_data, opt_2, ['2014-5-16',
                                   '2014-7-18'])
<matplotlib.figure.Figure at 0x2ab25d1b0190>
```

7.6.4 Four Maturities

In a next step, we consider four maturities – before we try to calibrate the model to all eight maturities.

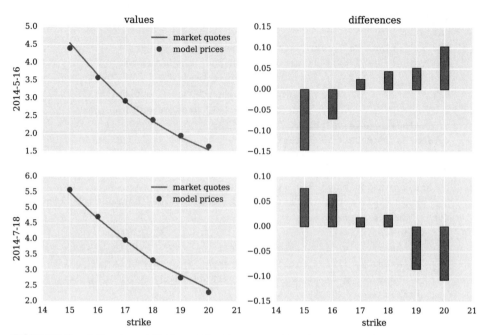

FIGURE 7.6 Calibration of SRJD model to European call options on the VSTOXX for May and July 2014 maturities.

```
In [68]: mats = sorted(set(option_data['MATURITY']))

In [69]: mats
Out[69]:
[Timestamp('2014-04-18 00:00:00'),
 Timestamp('2014-05-16 00:00:00'),
 Timestamp('2014-06-20 00:00:00'),
 Timestamp('2014-07-18 00:00:00'),
 Timestamp('2014-08-15 00:00:00'),
 Timestamp('2014-09-19 00:00:00'),
 Timestamp('2014-10-17 00:00:00'),
 Timestamp('2014-11-21 00:00:00')]
```

The four maturities for this particular calibration run are:

```
In [70]: mats[::2]
Out[70]:
[Timestamp('2014-04-18 00:00:00'),
 Timestamp('2014-06-20 00:00:00'),
 Timestamp('2014-08-15 00:00:00'),
 Timestamp('2014-10-17 00:00:00')]
```

For this calibration run, we use the optimal parameters from the previous calibration to two maturities. Obviously, the more options to calibrate the model to, the longer the procedure takes.

```
In [71]: %%time
   ....: opt_4 = srjd_model_calibration(option_data, p0=opt_2,
   ....:                                rel=False, mats=mats[::2])
   ....:

 its  kappa  theta  sigma   lamb     mu   delta        MSE      min_MSE
   0  4.000 18.684  1.917  0.728  0.748   0.003    0.52345      0.52345
 100  4.202 18.938  1.980  0.727  0.623   0.003    0.27887      0.27681
 200  3.650 21.465  3.293  0.744 -0.075   0.002    0.18617      0.18617
 300  3.195 22.481  2.867  0.743 -0.223   0.000    0.14915      0.14915
 400  3.107 22.191  2.990  0.745 -0.141   0.000    0.14609      0.14608
 500  3.081 22.162  3.028  0.743 -0.138   0.000    0.14572      0.14570
 600  3.057 22.100  3.041  0.738 -0.124   0.000    0.14521      0.14521
 700  3.061 22.110  3.034  0.738 -0.126   0.000    0.14517      0.14517
Warning: Maximum number of function evaluations has been exceeded.
CPU times: user 22.9 s, sys: 16 ms, total: 22.9 s
Wall time: 22.9 s
```

```
In [72]: opt_4
Out[72]:
array([  3.06082557e+00,   2.21100415e+01,   3.03422643e+00,
         7.38054016e-01,  -1.25823900e-01,   1.19890649e-06])
```

Even calibrating the model to four maturities yields quite a good fit over these maturities as Figure 7.7 illustrates.

```
In [73]: plot_calibration_results(option_data, opt_4, mats[::2])
<matplotlib.figure.Figure at 0x2ab247bec510>
```

7.6.5 All Maturities

Finally, let us attack the hardest calibration problem – the one involving all eight option maturities.

```
In [74]: %%time
   ....: opt_8_MSAE = srjd_model_calibration(option_data,
   ....:                                rel=False, mats=mats)
   ....:
```

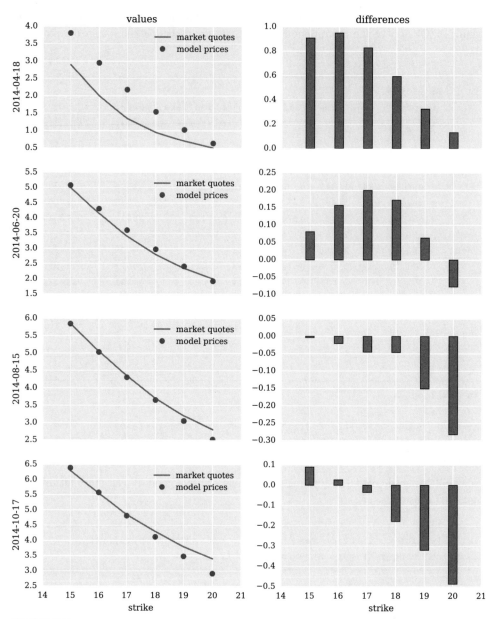

FIGURE 7.7 Calibration of SRJD model to European call options on the VSTOXX for four maturities.

its	kappa	theta	sigma	lamb	mu	delta	MSE	min_MSE
0	1.000	10.000	1.000	0.000	-0.200	0.000	12.79035	12.79035
100	1.000	20.000	3.000	0.800	-0.200	0.000	1.13623	0.13849
200	5.000	20.000	3.000	0.400	-0.200	0.150	1.08765	0.13849
300	9.000	20.000	3.000	0.000	-0.200	0.300	1.27175	0.13849

```
  its  kappa  theta  sigma   lamb     mu  delta        MSE     min_MSE
    0  1.000 20.000  3.000  0.400  0.400  0.150    0.13849     0.13849
  100  1.007 20.567  2.921  0.396  0.326  0.155    0.12039     0.11935
  200  1.018 21.609  3.266  0.404  0.032  0.163    0.10182     0.10096
  300  1.033 22.713  3.222  0.407 -0.123  0.155    0.09869     0.09863
  400  1.542 23.755  3.235  0.409 -0.985  0.067    0.08329     0.08120
  500  1.860 23.848  2.967  0.410 -1.297  0.002    0.07686     0.07686
  600  1.868 23.863  2.956  0.410 -1.303 -0.000 1000.07683     0.07683
Warning: Maximum number of function evaluations has been exceeded.
CPU times: user 1min 7s, sys: 16 ms, total: 1min 7s
Wall time: 1min 7s
```

```
In [75]: opt_8_MSAE
Out[75]:
array([  1.86781293e+00,    2.38625952e+01,    2.95539873e+00,
         4.10158642e-01,   -1.30281337e+00,    8.30841775e-08])
```

Figure 7.8 shows that the fit is still reasonable for eight maturities and that many options.

```
In [76]: plot_calibration_results(option_data, opt_8_MSAE, mats)
<matplotlib.figure.Figure at 0x2ab247b94250>
```

To check whether there is a (larger) difference when we calibrate the model using relative differences (i.e. the MSRE) as a yardstick, consider the following calibration run:

```
In [77]: %%time
   ....: opt_8_MSRE = srjd_model_calibration(option_data, p0=opt_8_MSAE,
   ....:                                      rel=True, mats=mats)
   ....:

  its  kappa  theta  sigma   lamb     mu  delta      MSE    min_MSE
    0  1.868 23.863  2.955  0.410 -1.303  0.000  0.02551    0.02551
  100  1.599 24.888  2.619  0.392 -1.381  0.000  0.02099    0.02099
  200  1.015 26.443  2.737  0.388 -1.676  0.000  0.02017    0.02017
  300  0.915 27.147  2.723  0.388 -1.947  0.000  0.02046    0.02011
  400  0.920 27.175  2.719  0.388 -2.142  0.000  0.02010    0.02010
  500  0.927 27.082  2.724  0.389 -2.373  0.000  0.02009    0.02009
  600  0.925 27.083  2.722  0.389 -2.409  0.000  0.02009    0.02009
  700  0.925 27.086  2.722  0.389 -2.409  0.000  0.02009    0.02009
Warning: Maximum number of function evaluations has been exceeded.
CPU times: user 46.9 s, sys: 16 ms, total: 46.9 s
Wall time: 46.9 s
```

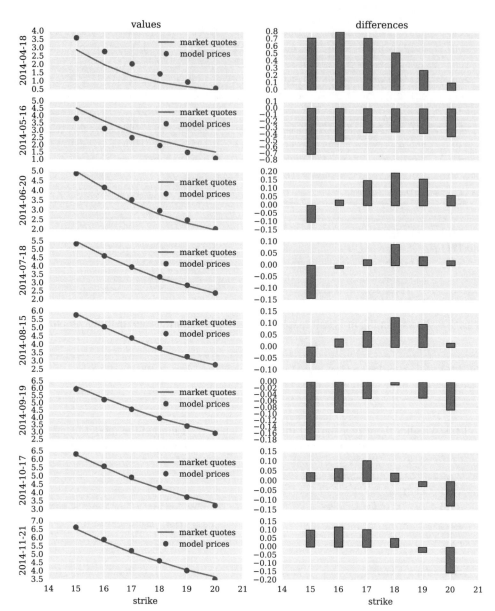

FIGURE 7.8   Calibration of SRJD model to European call options on the VSTOXX for all eight maturities (MSAE used).

Figure 7.9 presents the results. They are not too dissimilar to the ones obtained using the MSAE as a yardstick. The major difference is the weighting of the options in that now those options with lower market quotes (higher strikes) get more weight.

```
In [78]: plot_calibration_results(option_data, opt_8_MSRE, mats)
<matplotlib.figure.Figure at 0x2ab25d453250>
```

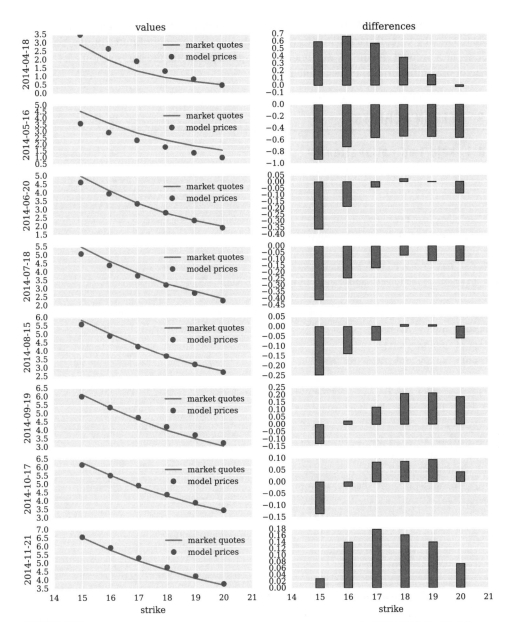

FIGURE 7.9 Calibration of SRJD model to European call options on the VSTOXX for all eight maturities (MSRE used).

7.7 CONCLUSIONS

This chapter introduces a more sophisticated model, the so-called square-root jump diffusion model (SRJD), for the evolution of the VSTOXX volatility index over time. It enhances the Grünbichler and Longstaff (1996) square-root diffusion model by two components: a log normally distributed *jump component* and a *deterministic shift component*. While the first allows us to better calibrate the model to short term option quotes, the latter makes it possible to take the volatility term structure – as embodied by the eight futures on the VSTOXX index – into account. All in all, the model yields good calibration results even in cases where all eight option maturities are accounted for.

7.8 PYTHON SCRIPTS

7.8.1 srjd_fwd_calibration.py

```
#
# Script for term structure calibration of
# Square-Root Jump Diffusion (SRJD) model
#
# (c) Dr. Yves J. Hilpisch
# Listed Volatility and Variance Derivatives
#
import math
import numpy as np
import pandas as pd
import scipy.optimize as sco


v0 = 17.6639  # initial VSTOXX index level
i = 0  # counter for calibration runs

# reading the VSTOXX futures quotes
path = 'source/data/'
h5 = pd.HDFStore(path + 'vstoxx_data_31032014.h5', 'r')
futures_quotes = h5['futures_data']
h5.close()

# selecting needed data columns and adding spot value
forwards = list(futures_quotes['PRICE'].values)
forwards.insert(0, v0)
forwards = np.array(forwards)
ttms = list(futures_quotes['TTM'].values)
ttms.insert(0, 0)
ttms = np.array(ttms)


def srd_forwards(p0):
    ''' Function for forward volatilities in GL96 Model.

    Parameters
    ==========
    p0: list
```

```
        set of model parameters, where

        kappa: float
            mean-reversion factor
        theta: float
            long-run mean
        sigma: float
            volatility factor

    Returns
    =======
    forwards: NumPy ndarray object
        forward volatilities
    '''
    t = ttms
    kappa, theta, sigma = p0
    g = math.sqrt(kappa ** 2 + 2 * sigma ** 2)
    sum1 = ((kappa * theta * (np.exp(g * t) - 1)) /
            (2 * g + (kappa + g) * (np.exp(g * t) - 1)))
    sum2 = v0 * ((4 * g ** 2 * np.exp(g * t)) /
                (2 * g + (kappa + g) * (np.exp(g * t) - 1)) ** 2)
    forwards = sum1 + sum2
    return forwards


def srd_fwd_error(p0):
    ''' Error function for GL96 forward volatilities calibration.

    Parameters
    ==========
    p0: tuple
        parameter vector

    Returns
    =======
    MSE: float
        mean-squared error for p0
    '''
    global i
    kappa, theta, sigma = p0
    srd_fwds = srd_forwards(p0)
    MSE = np.sum((forwards - srd_fwds) ** 2) / len(forwards)
    if 2 * kappa * theta < sigma ** 2:
        MSE = MSE + 100   # penalty
    elif sigma < 0:
        MSE = MSE + 100
    # print intermediate results: every 50th iteration
```

```
    if i % 50 == 0:
        print "{:6.3f} {:6.3f} {:6.3f}".format(*p0) + "{:>12.5f}".format(MSE)
    i += 1
    return MSE


if __name__ is '__main__':
    p0 = 1.0, 17.5, 1.0
    opt = sco.fmin(srd_fwd_error, p0,
                   xtol=0.00001, ftol=0.00001,
                   maxiter=1500, maxfun=2000)
```

7.8.2 srjd_simulation.py

```
#
# Module with simulation functions for
# Square-Root Jump Diffusion (SRJD) model
#
# (c) Dr. Yves J. Hilpisch
# Listed Volatility and Variance Derivatives
#
import math
import pickle
import numpy  as np
import scipy.interpolate as scint


v0 = 17.6639  # initial VSTOXX index level


# parameters of square-root diffusion
kappa = 2.0  # speed of mean reversion
theta = 15.0  # long-term volatility
sigma = 1.0  # standard deviation coefficient


# parameters of log-normal jump
lamb = 0.4  # intensity (jumps per year)
mu = 0.4  # average jump size
delta = 0.1  # volatility of jump size


# general parameters
r = 0.01  # risk-free interest rate
K = 17.5  # strike
T = 0.5  # time horizon
M = 150  # time steps
I = 10000  # number of MCS paths
anti_paths = True  # antithetic variates
mo_match = True  # moment matching
```

```
# deterministic shift parameters
varphi = pickle.load(open('varphi'))
tck = scint.splrep(varphi['ttms'], varphi['varphi'], k=1)
  # linear splines interpolation of
  # term structure calibration differences


def random_number_gen(M, I, fixed_seed=False):
    ''' Generate standard normally distributed pseudo-random numbers

    Parameters
    ==========
    M: int
        number of time intervals
    I: int
        number of paths

    Returns
    =======
    ran: NumPy ndarrayo object
        random number array
    '''
    if fixed_seed  is True:
        np.random.seed(10000)
    if anti_paths  is True:
        ran = np.random.standard_normal((M + 1, I / 2))
        ran = np.concatenate((ran, -ran), axis=1)
    else:
        ran = np.standard_normal((M + 1, I))
    if mo_match is True:
        ran = ran / np.std(ran)
        ran -= np.mean(ran)
    return ran


def srjd_simulation(x0, kappa, theta, sigma,
                    lamb, mu, delta, T, M, I, fixed_seed=False):
    ''' Function to simulate square-root jump Difusion.

    Parameters
    ==========
    x0: float
        initial value
    kappa: float
        mean-reversion factor
```

```
    theta: float
        long-run mean
    sigma: float
        volatility factor
    lamb: float
        jump intensity
    mu: float
        expected jump size
    delta: float
        standard deviation of jump
    T: float
        time horizon/maturity
    M: int
        time steps
    I: int
        number of simulation paths

    Returns
    =======
    x: NumPy ndarray object
        array with simulated SRJD paths
    '''
    dt = float(T) / M  # time interval
    shift = scint.splev(np.arange (M + 1) * dt, tck, der=0)
      # deterministic shift values
    xh = np.zeros((M + 1, I), dtype=np.float)
    x = np.zeros((M + 1, I), dtype=np.float)
    xh[0, :] = x0
    x[0, :] = x0
    # drift contribution of jump p.a.
    rj = lamb * (math.exp(mu + 0.5 * delta ** 2) - 1)
    # 1st matrix with standard normal rv
    ran1 = random_number_gen(M + 1, I, fixed_seed)
    # 2nd matrix with standard normal rv
    ran2 = random_number_gen(M + 1, I, fixed_seed)
    # matrix with Poisson distributed rv
    ran3 = np.random.poisson(lamb * dt, (M + 1, I))
    for t in range(1, M + 1):
        xh[t, :] = (xh[t - 1, :] +
                    kappa * (theta - np.maximum(0, xh[t - 1, :])) * dt
                + np.sqrt(np.maximum(0, xh[t - 1, :])) * sigma
                * ran1[t] * np.sqrt(dt)
                + (np.exp(mu + delta * ran2[t]) - 1) * ran3[t]
                * np.maximum(0, xh[t - 1, :]) - rj * dt)
        x[t, :] = np.maximum(0, xh[t, :]) + shift[t]
    return x
```

```
def srjd_call_valuation(v0, kappa, theta, sigma,
                        lamb, mu, delta, T, r, K, M=M, I=I,
                        fixed_seed=False):
    ''' Function to value European volatility call option in SRDJ model.
    Parameters see function srjd_simulation.

    Returns
    =======
    call_value: float
        estimator for European call present value for strike K
    '''
    v = srjd_simulation(v0, kappa, theta, sigma,
                        lamb, mu, delta, T, M, I, fixed_seed)
    call_value = np.exp(-r * T) * sum(np.maximum(v[-1] - K, 0)) / I
    return call_value

if __name__ is '__main__':
    call_value = srjd_call_valuation(v0, kappa, theta, sigma,
                                     lamb, mu, delta, T, r, K, M, I)
    print "Value of European call by MCS: %10.4f" % call_value
```

7.8.3 srjd_model_calibration.py

```
#
# Calibration of square-root jump diffusion (SRJD) model
# to VSTOXX European call options traded at Eurex
# Data as of 31. March 2014
# All data from www.eurexchange.com
#
# (c) Dr. Yves J. Hilpisch
# Listed Volatility and Variance Derivatives
#
import numpy as np
import pandas as pd
import scipy.optimize as sco
import matplotlib.pyplot as plt
from srd_model_calibration import path, read_select_quotes
from srjd_simulation import srjd_call_valuation

# fixed parameters
r = 0.01  # risk-less short rate
v0 = 17.6639  # VSTOXX index at 31.03.2014
M = 15  # number of time intervals
I = 100  # number of simulated paths
```

```
def srjd_valuation_function(p0):
    ''' Valuation ('difference') function for all options
        of a given DataFrame object.

    Parameters
    ==========
    p0: list
        set of model parameters

    Returns
    =======
    diffs: NumPy ndarray object
        array with valuation differences
    '''
    global relative, option_data
    kappa, theta, sigma, lamb, mu, delta = p0
    diffs = []
    for i, option in option_data.iterrows():
        value = srjd_call_valuation(v0, kappa, theta, sigma,
                                    lamb, mu, delta,
                                    option['TTM'], r, option['STRIKE'],
                                    M=M, I=I, fixed_seed=True)
        if relative is True:
            diffs.append((value - option['PRICE']) / option['PRICE'])
        else:
            diffs.append(value - option['PRICE'])
    diffs = np.array(diffs)
    return diffs


def srjd_error_function(p0):
    ''' Error function for model calibration.

    Parameters
    ==========
    p0: tuple
        set of model parameters

    Returns
    =======
    MSE: float
        mean squared (relative/absolute) error
    '''
    global i, min_MSE, option_data
    OD = len(option_data)
    diffs = srjd_valuation_function(p0)
    kappa, theta, sigma, lamb, mu, delta = p0
```

```
      # penalties
      pen = 0.
      if 2 * kappa * theta < sigma ** 2:
          pen = 1000.0
      if kappa < 0 or theta < 0 or sigma < 0 or lamb < 0 or delta < 0:
          pen = 1000.0

      MSE = np.sum(diffs ** 2) / OD + pen   # mean squared error

      min_MSE = min(min_MSE, MSE)   # running minimum value

      if i == 0:
          print '\n' + ('{:>5s}'.format('its')
                      + '{:>7s} {:>6s} {:>6s} {:>6s} {:>6s} {:>6s}'.format(
              'kappa', 'theta', 'sigma', 'lamb', 'mu', 'delta')
                      + '{:>12s}'.format('MSE') + '{:>12s}'.format('min_MSE'))
      # print intermediate results: every 100th iteration
      if i % 100 == 0:
          print ('{:>5d}'.format(i)
                  + '{:7.3f} {:6.3f} {:6.3f} {:6.3f} {:6.3f} {:6.3f}'.format(*p0)
                  + '{:>12.5f}'.format(MSE) + '{:>12.5f}'.format(min_MSE))
      i += 1
      return MSE

def srjd_model_calibration(data, p0= None, rel=False, mats=None):
    ''' Function for global and local model calibration.


    Parameters
    ==========
    option_data: pandas DataFrame object
        option quotes to be used
    relative: bool
        relative or absolute MSE
    mats: list
        list of maturities of option quotes to calibrate to

    Returns
    =======
    opt: tuple
        optimal parameter values
    '''
    global i, min_MSE, option_data
    global relative   # if True: MSRE is used, if False: MSAE

    min_MSE = 5000.   # dummy value
    relative = rel   # relative or absolute
    option_data = data
```

```python
    if mats is not None:
        # select the option data for the given maturities
        option_data = option_data[option_data['MATURITY'].isin(mats)]

    # global optimization
    if p0 is None:
        i = 0  # counter for calibration iterations
        p0 = sco.brute(srjd_error_function, (
            (1.0, 9.1, 4.0),   # kappa
            (10., 20.1, 10.0),  # theta
            (1.0, 3.1, 2.0),   # sigma
            (0.0, 0.81, 0.4),  # lambda
            (-0.2, 0.41, 0.3),  # mu
            (0.0, 0.31, 0.15)),  # delta
            finish=None)

    # local optimization
    i = 0
    opt = sco.fmin(srjd_error_function, p0,
                   xtol=0.0000001, ftol=0.0000001,
                   maxiter=550, maxfun=700)

    return opt


def plot_calibration_results(option_data, opt, mats):
    ''' Function to plot market quotes vs. model prices.

    Parameters
    ==========
    option_data: pandas DataFrame object
        option data to plot
    opt: list
        optimal results from calibration
    mats: list
        maturities to be plotted
    '''
    kappa, theta, sigma, lamb, mu, delta = opt
    # adding model values for optimal parameter set
    # to the DataFrame object
    values = []
    for i, option in option_data.iterrows():
        value = srjd_call_valuation(v0, kappa, theta, sigma,
                                    lamb, mu, delta,
                                    option['TTM'], r, option['STRIKE'],
                                    M=M, I=I, fixed_seed=True)
        values.append(value)
    option_data['MODEL'] = values
```

```python
# plotting the market and model values
height = min(len(mats) * 3, 12)
fig, axarr = plt.subplots(len(mats), 2, sharex=True,
                figsize=(10, height))
for z, mat in enumerate(mats):
    if z == 0:
        axarr[z, 0].set_title('values')
        axarr[z, 1].set_title('differences')
    os = option_data[option_data. MATURITY == mat]
    strikes = os. STRIKE.values
    axarr[z, 0].set_ylabel('%s' % str(mat)[:10])
    axarr[z, 0].plot(strikes, os.PRICE.values, label='market quotes')
    axarr[z, 0].plot(strikes, os.MODEL.values, 'ro', label='model prices')
    axarr[z, 0].legend(loc=0)
    wi = 0.3
    axarr[z, 1].bar(strikes - wi / 2, os. MODEL.values - os.PRICE.values,
                    width=wi)
if mat == mats[-1]:
    axarr[z, 0].set_xlabel('strike')
    axarr[z, 1].set_xlabel('strike')

if __name__ == '__main__':
    option_data = read_select_quotes('./source/data/', tol=0.1)
    option_data['VALUE'] = 0.0
    opt = srjd_model_calibration()
```

## CHAPTER 8

Terms of the VSTOXX and its Derivatives

This brief chapter is about the terms of the VSTOXX volatility index as well as futures and options traded on it. The chapter starts, however, with a brief review of some facts about the EURO STOXX 50 index whose options build the basis for the VSTOXX.

8.1 THE EURO STOXX 50 INDEX

The EURO STOXX 50 index is a European blue chip index introduced in February 1998 by STOXX Limited, a company of Deutsche Boerse Group. It comprises the stocks of the 50 largest companies by market capitalization in the euro zone given their free float. The weighting of the single components is also according to the market capitalization with a 10% cap for any given stock. The composition and single memberships are reviewed on an annual basis in September. The index level itself is calculated during trading days between 9 am and 6 pm CET. Although it was only introduced in 1998, it has been recalculated on a daily basis dating back to December 31, 1986.

Table 8.1 shows the composition of the index by sector.

Table 8.2 shows the composition of the index by country. Note that countries like the United Kingdom or Switzerland are not represented due to the euro zone criterion.

While the VSTOXX is based on an equity index with 50 stocks only, the VIX index is on a broader index, namely the S&P 500 which comprises 500 companies. This and the fact that the EURO STOXX 50 index is heavy on the financial sector gives a generally higher level for the VSTOXX index compared to the VIX index. In other words, 30 day implied volatility for the EURO STOXX 50 index is on average higher than for the S&P 500 index.

8.2 THE VSTOXX INDEX

The calculation of the *VSTOXX index* is explained in detail in Chapter 5, *VSTOXX Index*. Its calculation is based on out-of-the-money put and call options on the EURO STOXX 50 index.

TABLE 8.1   Industry sector weighting in the
EURO STOXX 50 index.

Sector	Weight
Banks	16.9%
Industrial Goods & Services	9.9%
Chemicals	9.5%
Insurance	8.0%
Health Care	6.8%
Oil & Gas	6.8%
Personal & Household Goods	6.5%
Automobiles & Parts	6.2%
Telecommunications	6.1%
Food & Beverage	5.9%

Data source: STOXX Limited, data as of 30
November 2015.

The methodology for its calculation makes use of the model-free replication approach for variance swaps (see Chapter 3, *Model-Free Replication of Variance*). It yields an estimate for the 30 day implied volatility by interpolating in general the implied volatilities from the two nearby maturity months.

In addition to the main VSTOXX 30-day index with ticker symbol V2TX, eight sub-indexes are calculated with maturities of 1, 2, 3, 6, 9, 12, 18 and 24 months reflecting the option series available for the EURO STOXX 50 index (see also Chapter 5, *VSTOXX Index* for more details). There are other main VSTOXX indexes available with time ranges from 60 to 360 days (in intervals of 30 days).

Figure 8.1 shows the starting screen for the VSTOXX index at the Thomson Reuters Eikon terminal. As you can see in the figure, the index mainly varied between 15% and 40% over the period shown.

TABLE 8.2   Country weighting in the EURO
STOXX 50 index.

Country	Weight
France	36.6%
Germany	32.1%
Spain	10.9%
Italy	7.7%
Netherlands	7.6%
Belgium	4.1%
Finland	1.1%

Data source: STOXX Limited, data as of 30
November 2015

FIGURE 8.1 Thomson Reuters Eikon starting screen for the VSTOXX volatility index (vendor code: .V2TX).

8.3 VSTOXX FUTURES CONTRACTS

VSTOXX (mini) futures contracts, in the form they are traded today, were introduced in 2009. Their product ID is FVS. Their main contract terms are described in the following list:

- **contract value**: 100 EUR per index point of the underlying
- **settlement**: cash settlement, on the first day after final settlement day
- **price quotation**: the price quotation is in (volatility) points to two decimal places
- **minimum price change**: the minimum price change is 0.05 (volatility) points, i.e. 5 EUR
- **contract months**: the eight nearest successive calendar months
- **last trading day**: last trading day is the final settlement day
- **final settlement day**: 30 calendar days before the expiration day of the underlying options, i.e. 30 calendar days before the third Friday of the expiration month of the underlying options
- **daily settlement price**: determinded for the current maturity month during the closing auction of the respective futures contract; for the other maturity months it is determined by the average bid/ask spread of the combination order book
- **final settlement price**: determined by Eurex Exchange on the last trading day based on the values of the underlying VSTOXX index between 11:30 am and 12:00 pm CET
- **trading hours**: 9 am to 10 pm CET (order book and Eurex Trade Entry Services)
- **block trade size**: 1,000 contracts
- **vendor codes**: FVSA Index (Bloomberg) and 0#FVS (Thomson Reuters).

Figure 8.2 shows a screen from the Thomson Reuters Eikon terminal with data about the VSTOXX futures contracts.

FIGURE 8.2 Thomson Reuters Eikon screen with VSTOXX futures contract information (vendor code: 0#FVS).

8.4 VSTOXX OPTIONS CONTRACTS

The VSTOXX options contracts, with product ID OVS, were introduced in 2010. Their main contract terms are described in the following list. They are mainly the same as for the futures contracts:

- **contract value**: 100 EUR per index point of the underlying
- **settlement**: cash settlement, on the first day after final settlement day
- **price quotation**: the price quotation is in (volatility) points with two decimal places
- **minimum price change**: the minimum price change is 0.05 (volatility) points, i.e. 5 EUR
- **contract months**: the eight nearest successive calendar months
- **last trading day**: last trading day is the final settlement day
- **final settlement day**: 30 calendar days before the expiration day of the underlying options, i.e. 30 calendar days before the third Friday of the expiration month of the underlying options
- **daily settlement price**: determined by Eurex Exchange on the basis of the Black (1976) model
- **final settlement price**: determined by Eurex Exchange on the last trading day based on the values of the underlying VSTOXX index between 11:30 am and 12:00 pm CET
- **exercise**: European style; exercise only on the final settlement day of the option series until 9 pm CET
- **exercise prices**: minimum exercise price difference of 1 volatility point
- **number of exercise prices**: at least 11 different exercise prices for both calls and puts such that 5 are in-the-money, 1 at-the-money, 5 out-of-the-money
- **trading hours**: 9 am to 10 pm CET (order book and Eurex Trade Entry Services)
- **block trade size**: 1,000 contracts
- **vendor codes**: V2X Index OMON (Bloomberg) and <0#FVS+> (Thomson Reuters).

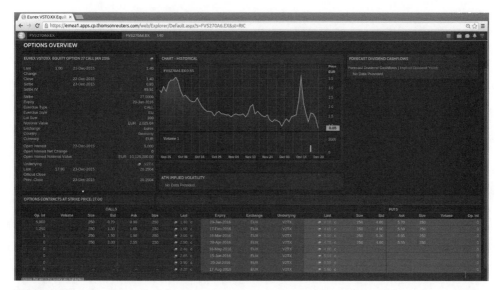

FIGURE 8.3   Thomson Reuters Eikon screen with VSTOXX options contract information (vendor code: `FVS270A6.EX`).

Figure 8.3 shows a screen from the Thomson Reuters Eikon terminal with VSTOXX call and put options data for an exercise price of 27.

8.5 CONCLUSIONS

The previous three chapters cover the VSTOXX volatility index and derivatives written on it from a conceptual and valuation point of view. This chapter adds information about the concrete terms of the contracts to the mix. While perhaps not as important from an academic point of view, they are of paramount importance for practitioners.

Listed Variance Derivatives

Realized Variance and Variance Swaps

9.1 INTRODUCTION

This chapter discusses basic notions and concepts needed in the context of variance swaps and futures. It covers among others the following topics:

- **realized variance**: the basic measure on which variance swaps and variance futures are defined
- **variance swap**: the definition of a variance swap and some numerical examples
- **mark-to-market**: the mark-to-market valuation approach for a variance swap
- **variance swap on EURO STOXX 50**: simple re-calculation of a variance swap given historical data
- **variance vs. volatility**: major differences between the two measures.

9.2 REALIZED VARIANCE

Historical or realized variance σ^2 generally is defined as

$$\sigma^2 \equiv \frac{252}{N} \cdot \sum_{n=1}^{N} R_n^2$$

where, for a time series $S_n, n = 0, 1, ..., N$, the log returns are given by

$$R_n \equiv \log \frac{S_n}{S_{n-1}}$$

Here, it is assumed that there are 252 trading days per year and that the average daily return is zero. The simple application of these definitions yields values as decimals. Scaling by a factor of $100^2 = 10,000$ gives values in percent.

$$\sigma^2 \equiv 10000 \cdot \frac{252}{N} \cdot \sum_{n=1}^{N} R_n^2$$

To simplify notation, we use the notation σ^2 instead of $\hat{\sigma}^2$ for the realized variance from here on.

The concept of realized variance is easily illustrated by the use of historical data for the EURO STOXX 50 stock index. To this end, we read data from the index provider's website http://www.stoxx.com with Python and the pandas library. For details on using the pandas library for interactive financial analytics see chapter 2, *Introduction to Python* or refer to Hilpisch (2014). As usual, we start with some Python library imports.

```
In [1]: import math

In [2]: import numpy as np

In [3]: import pandas as pd
```

First, we need the complete URL of the data set.

```
# text/csv file containing daily closing levels of EURO STOXX 50 index
In [4]: path = 'https://www.stoxx.com/document/Indices/Current/HistoricalData/'

In [5]: es_url = path + 'hbrbcpe.txt'
```

Second, we read the data with the pandas library from that source. The row structure of that file changes at the end of 2001 such that we need to define a helper column which is to be deleted after importing the data (see also chapter 4, *Data Analysis and Strategies*).

```
# column names for the data set
In [6]: cols = ['Date', 'SX5P', 'SX5E', 'SXXP', 'SXXE',
    ...:         'SXXF', 'SXXA', 'DK5F', 'DKXF', 'DEL']
    ...:


In [7]: try:  # reading the data with pandas
    ...:     es = pd.read_csv(es_url,  # filename
    ...:                      header=None,  # ignore column names
    ...:                      index_col=0,  # index column (dates)
    ...:                      parse_dates=True,  # parse these dates
    ...:                      dayfirst=True,  # format of dates
    ...:                      skiprows=4,  # ignore these rows
    ...:                      sep=';',  # data separator
    ...:                      names=cols)  # use these column names
    ...:     del es['DEL']
    ...: except:  # read stored data if there is no Internet connection
    ...:     es = pd.HDFStore('./source/data/SX5E.h5', 'r')['SX5E']
    ...:


In [8]: es = es[es.index < '2015-12-31']
```

Let us inspect the final five data rows.

```
In [9]: es.tail()
Out[9]:
               SX5P      SX5E     SXXP     SXXE     SXXF     SXXA      DK5F     DKXF
Date
2015-12-23  3109.23   3286.68   366.39   346.14   433.58   375.53   9927.33   614.12
2015-12-24  3108.11   3284.47   366.28   346.05   433.43   375.39   9931.72   614.38
2015-12-28  3093.61   3256.49   364.49   343.54   431.26   374.32   9873.94   611.58
2015-12-29  3139.28   3314.28   369.68   349.29   438.43   378.86  10023.66   620.66
2015-12-30  3118.07   3287.98   367.70   347.02   435.82   377.20   9956.22   617.48
```

Third, we select the EURO STOXX 50 index data from the data set just downloaded and imported, i.e. the data sub-set for the symbol SX5E. Using this sub-set, we generate a new pandas `DataFrame` object to store the data. The historical time series of daily closing levels of the EURO STOXX 50 can then easily be inspected by a call of the `plot` method. Figure 9.1 shows the graphical output.

```
In [10]: import seaborn as sns; sns.set()

In [11]: import matplotlib

In [12]: matplotlib.rcParams['font.family'] = 'serif'

In [13]: data = pd.DataFrame({'SX5E': es['SX5E']})

In [14]: data.plot(figsize=(10, 6));
```

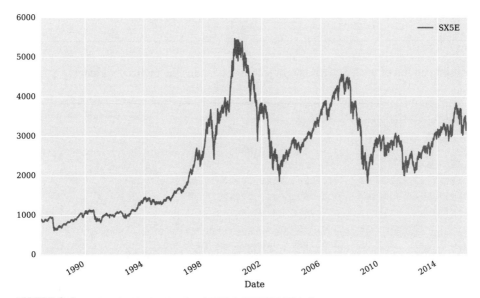

FIGURE 9.1 Historical index levels of EURO STOXX 50 index.

Fourth, the log returns are calculated (in vectorized fashion, i.e. simultaneously over the whole time series) and stored as a new column in the pandas `DataFrame` object.

```
In [15]: data['R_n'] = np.log(data['SX5E'] / data['SX5E'].shift(1))
```

Let us inspect the last five data rows of this new DataFrame object.

```
In [16]: data.tail()
Out[16]:
                 SX5E          R_n
Date
2015-12-23    3286.68     0.022262
2015-12-24    3284.47    -0.000673
2015-12-28    3256.49    -0.008555
2015-12-29    3314.28     0.017590
2015-12-30    3287.98    -0.007967
```

In the fifth step, we calculate the realized variance, again in vectorized fashion. With the following code we calculate the realized variance for every single date of the time series.

```
# np.cumsum calculates the element-wise cumulative sum of an array/time series
# np.arange(N) gives an array of the form [0, 1, ..., N-1]
In [17]: data['sigma**2'] = 10000 * 252 * (np.cumsum(data['R_n'] ** 2)
    ....:                                  / np.arange(len(data)))
    ....:
```

The third column of the `DataFrame` object now contains the realized variance.

```
In [18]: data.tail()
Out[18]:
                 SX5E          R_n     sigma**2
Date
2015-12-23    3286.68     0.022262   446.280005
2015-12-24    3284.47    -0.000673   446.220423
2015-12-28    3256.49    -0.008555   446.185389
2015-12-29    3314.28     0.017590   446.230025
2015-12-30    3287.98    -0.007967   446.191722
```

In the sixth and final step, one can now compare the index level time series with the realized variance over time graphically – see Figure 9.2.

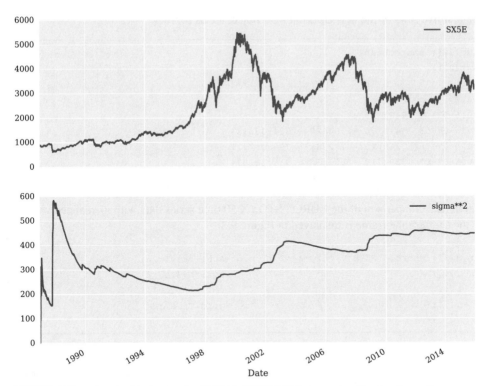

FIGURE 9.2 Historical index levels of EURO STOXX 50 index and realized variance (long term).

```
In [19]: data[['SX5E', 'sigma**2']].plot(subplots=True,
   ....:                                  figsize=(10, 8),
   ....:                                  color='blue',
   ....:                                  grid=True);
   ....:
```

Now let us implement the same approach for a shorter, recent period of time, i.e. the second half of the year 2015. The realized variance has to be re-calculated since there is now a new starting date.

```
# select time series data with date later/earlier than given dates
In [20]: short = data[['SX5E', 'R_n']][(data.index > '2015-7-1')
   ....:                                & (data.index <= '2015-12-31')]
   ....:

# calculate the realized variance in percent values
In [21]: short['sigma**2'] = 10000 * 252 * (np.cumsum(short['R_n'] ** 2)
   ....:                                     / np.arange(len(short)))
   ....:
```

The first five rows of the new `DataFrame` object are as follows:

```
In [22]: short.head()
Out[22]:
                 SX5E       R_n      sigma**2
Date
2015-07-02    3463.25  -0.009492          inf
2015-07-03    3441.76  -0.006224   324.686954
2015-07-06    3365.20  -0.022496   799.967421
2015-07-07    3294.19  -0.021327   915.381074
2015-07-08    3327.50   0.010061   750.306250
```

A graphical comparison of the EUROS STOXX 50 time series data with its realized variance for the shorter time frame is displayed in Figure 9.3.

```
In [23]: short[['SX5E', 'sigma**2']].plot(subplots=True,
    ....:                                 figsize=(10, 8),
    ....:                                 color='blue',
    ....:                                 grid=True);
    ....:
```

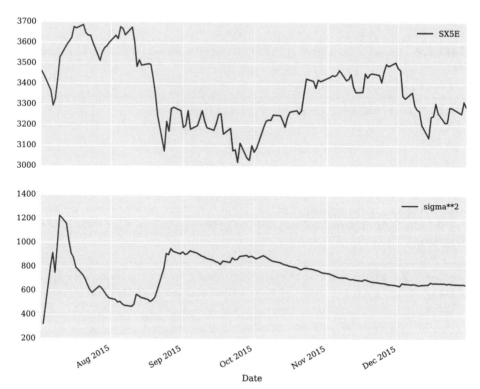

FIGURE 9.3 Historical index levels of EURO STOXX 50 index and realized variance (short term).

9.3 VARIANCE SWAPS

Nowadays, variance swaps are popular financial instruments for volatility/variance trading and hedging purposes. See, for instance, the paper of Bossu et al. (2005) for an overview of the features and characteristics of variance swaps.

9.3.1 Definition of a Variance Swap

A variance swap is a financial instrument that allows investors to trade future realized variance against current implied volatility (the "strike"). The characteristics and payoff of a variance swap are more like those of a forward contract than those of a typical swap on interest rates, currencies, equities, etc.

The payoff h_T of a variance swap maturing at some future date T is

$$h_T = \sigma_{0,T}^2 - \sigma_K^2$$

with σ_K^2 being the variance strike and σ_K the volatility strike.

At inception, i.e. at $t = 0$, the volatility strike is set such that the value of the variance swap is zero. This implies that the volatility strike is set equal to the implied volatility $\sigma_i(0, T)$ for the maturity T.

9.3.2 Numerical Example

Consider a Black-Scholes-Merton (1973) world with a geometric Brownian motion driving uncertainty for the index level of relevance (see Black and Scholes (1973) and Merton (1973)). The risk-neutral stochastic differential equation (SDE) in this model (without dividends) is given by:

$$dS_t = rS_t dt + \sigma S_t dZ_t$$

S_t is the index level at time t, r the constant risk-less short rate, σ the instantaneous volatility and Z_t a standard Brownian motion. For a comprehensive treatment of this and other continuous time financial models refer, for example, to Björk (2009).

Instantaneous volatility (and variance) in this model world is constant which makes implied volatility also constant, say $\sigma_t = \sigma_i = \sigma = 0.2$. Given, for example, a Monte Carlo simulation of this model, realized variance might deviate from $\sigma^2 = 0.2^2 = 0.04$. Let us implement such a Monte Carlo simulation for the model. An Euler discretization scheme for the above SDE is given for $t \geq \Delta t$ by

$$S_t = S_{t-\Delta t} \exp\left(\left(r - \frac{\sigma^2}{2}\right)\Delta t + \sigma\sqrt{\Delta t}z_t\right)$$

with Δt being the fixed time interval used for the discretization and z_t a standard normally distributed random variable.

A Python implementation might look as follows (refer to Hilpisch (2014) for details on Monte Carlo simulation with Python):

```python
def generate_path(S0, r, sigma, T, M):
    ''' Function to simulate a geometric Brownian motion.

    Parameters
    ==========
    S0: float
        initial index level
    r: float
        constant risk-less short rate
    sigma: float
        instantaneous volatility
    T: float
        date of maturity (in year fractions)
    M: int
        number of time intervals

    Returns
    =======
    path: pandas DataFrame object
        simulated path
    '''
    # length of time interval
    dt = float(T) / M
    # random numbers
    np.random.seed(100000)
    rn = np.random.standard_normal(M + 1)
    rn[0] = 0  # to keep the initial value
    # simulation of path
    path = S0 * np.exp(np.cumsum((r - 0.5 * sigma ** 2) * dt
                                 + sigma * math.sqrt(dt) * rn))
    # setting initial value
    path = pd.DataFrame(path, columns=['index'])
    return path
```

Using this function and providing numerical parameters returns a pandas `DataFrame` with a single simulated path for the model. A sample path is shown in Figure 9.4.

```python
In [24]: S0 = 100  # initial index level

In [25]: r = 0.005  # risk-less short rate

In [26]: sigma = 0.2  # instantaneous volatility

In [27]: T = 1.0  # maturity date
```

```
In [28]: M = 50   # number of time intervals

In [29]: data = generate_path(S0, r, sigma, T, M)

In [30]: data.plot(figsize=(10, 5));
```

Given such a simulated path, one can calculate realized variance over time in the same fashion as above for the EURO STOXX 50 index.

```
In [31]: data['R_t'] = np.log(data['index'] / data['index'].shift(1))

# scaling now by M / T since returns are not necessarily daily returns

In [32]: data['sigma**2'] = 10000 * M / T * (np.cumsum(data['R_t'] ** 2)
    ....:                                    / np.arange(len(data)))
    ....:

In [33]: data.tail()
Out[33]:
         index        R_t     sigma**2
46    86.914274  -0.020492   462.916655
47    86.263467  -0.007516   453.668339
48    87.101314   0.009666   445.190118
49    87.020414  -0.000929   436.113416
50    83.157399  -0.045408   448.009603
```

Figure 9.5 shows the results graphically.

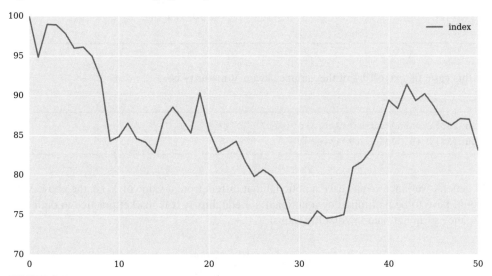

FIGURE 9.4 Sample path based on geometric Brownian motion.

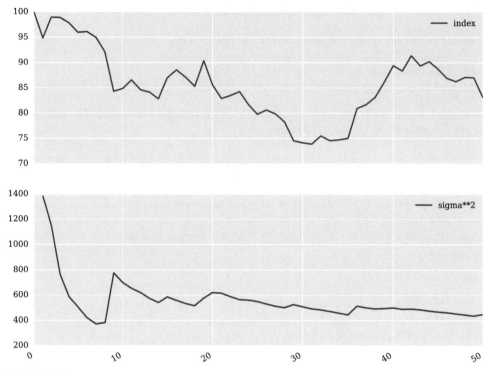

FIGURE 9.5   Geometric Brownian motion sample path with realized variance.

```
In [34]: data[['index', 'sigma**2']].plot(subplots=True,
    ....:                                  figsize=(10, 8),
    ....:                                  color='blue',
    ....:                                  grid=True);
    ....:
```

In this case, the payoff h_T of the variance swap at maturity is:

```
In [35]: data['sigma**2'].iloc[-1] - 20 ** 2
Out[35]: 48.009603247833468
```

In general, variance swaps have a notional that differs from a value of 1, i.e. the above value would have to be multiplied by a notional not equal to 1. It is market practice to define the variance swap notional in volatility terms:

$$Notional = \frac{VegaNotional}{2 \cdot Strike}$$

This can be done consistently due to the following relationship for a derivative instrument f depending on some underlying S with volatility σ (and satisfying further technical assumptions):

$$\frac{\partial f}{\partial \sigma} = \frac{\partial f}{\partial(\sigma^2)} \cdot 2\sigma$$

$$\Leftrightarrow \frac{\partial f}{\partial(\sigma^2)} = \frac{\frac{\partial f}{\partial \sigma}}{2\sigma}$$

Say we want a vega notional of 100,000 currency units, i.e.we want a payoff of 100,000 currency units per volatility point difference (e.g.when realized volatility is 1 percentage point above the volatility strike). The variance notional then is

$$Notional = \frac{100000}{2 \cdot 20} = 2500$$

```
In [36]: Notional = 100000. / (2 * 20)

In [37]: Notional
Out[37]: 2500.0
```

Given this value for the variance notional, the payoff of the variance swap in the above numerical example would be:

```
In [38]: Notional * (data['sigma**2'].iloc[-1] - 20 ** 2)
Out[38]: 120024.00811958367
```

9.3.3 Mark-to-Market

What about the value of a variance swap over time? A major advantage of working with variance (instead of volatility) is that variance is additive over time (when a mean of about zero is assumed). This gives rise to the following present value of a variance swap at time t, for a constant short rate r:

$$V_t = Notional \cdot e^{-r(T-t)} \cdot \left(\frac{t \cdot \sigma_{0,t}^2 + (T-t) \cdot \sigma_i^2(t,T)}{T} - \sigma_K^2 \right)$$

The major component of the mark-to-market value of the variance swap is the time weighted average of realized variance $\sigma_{0,t}^2$ up until time t and implied variance $\sigma_i^2(t,T)$ for the remaining life time from t onwards.

In the model economy, $\sigma_i^2(t, T) = \sigma_K^2 = \sigma^2 = 400$. Therefore:

$$V_t = Notional \cdot e^{-r(T-t)} \cdot \left(\frac{t \cdot \sigma_{0,t}^2 + (T - t) \cdot 400}{T} - 400 \right)$$

For $t = 0$, this obviously gives $V_t = 0$ as desired.

This is readily implemented in Python given that we already have realized variance in a pandas DataFrame object. We calculate it again in vectorized fashion for $t = 0, \Delta t, 2\Delta t..., T$.

```
In [39]: dt = T / M

In [40]: t = np.arange(M + 1) * dt

In [41]: t
Out[41]:
array([0.  ,  0.02,  0.04,  0.06,  0.08,  0.1 ,  0.12,  0.14,  0.16,
       0.18,  0.2 ,  0.22,  0.24,  0.26,  0.28,  0.3 ,  0.32,  0.34,
       0.36,  0.38,  0.4 ,  0.42,  0.44,  0.46,  0.48,  0.5 ,  0.52,
       0.54,  0.56,  0.58,  0.6 ,  0.62,  0.64,  0.66,  0.68,  0.7 ,
       0.72,  0.74,  0.76,  0.78,  0.8 ,  0.82,  0.84,  0.86,  0.88,
       0.9 ,  0.92,  0.94,  0.96,  0.98,  1.  ])

In [42]: sigma_K = 20

In [43]: data['V_t'] = Notional * np.exp(-r * (T - t)) * ((t * data['sigma**2']
   ....:             + (T - t) * sigma_K ** 2) / T - sigma_K ** 2)
   ....:

In [44]: data.tail()
Out[44]:
        index        R_t    sigma**2           V_t
46  86.914274  -0.020492  462.916655  144650.434548
47  86.263467  -0.007516  453.668339  126082.766551
48  87.101314   0.009666  445.190118  108434.594165
49  87.020414  -0.000929  436.113416   88469.022898
50  83.157399  -0.045408  448.009603  120024.008120
```

Graphically, we get the result as presented in Figure 9.6.

```
In [45]: data[['index', 'sigma**2', 'V_t']].plot(subplots=True,
   ....:                                          figsize=(10, 8),
   ....:                                          color='blue',
   ....:                                          grid=True);
   ....:
```

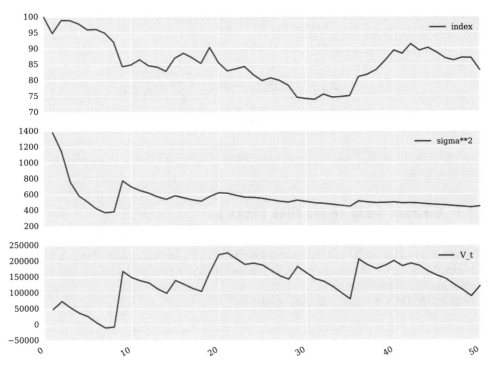

FIGURE 9.6 Geometric Brownian motion sample path with realized variance and variance swap mark-to-market values.

9.3.4 Vega Sensitivity

What is the sensitivity of the mark-to-market value of a variance swap with regard to implied volatility? Recall that the value itself is given by

$$V_t = Notional \cdot e^{-r(T-t)} \cdot \left(\frac{t \cdot \sigma_{0,t}^2 + (T-t) \cdot \sigma_i^2(t,T)}{T} - \sigma_K^2 \right)$$

Differentiation with respect to σ_i gives a vega of

$$Vega_t = \frac{\partial V_t}{\partial \sigma_i} = Notional \cdot e^{-r(T-t)} \cdot \frac{T-t}{T} \cdot 2\sigma_i(t,T)$$

At inception of the variance swap, we have a vega of

$$\begin{aligned}
Vega_0 &= \frac{\partial V_0}{\partial \sigma_i} \\
&= \frac{VegaNotional}{2 \cdot \sigma_i(0,T)} \cdot e^{-r(T-t)} \cdot \frac{T-t}{T} \cdot 2\sigma_i(0,T) \\
&= e^{-rT} \cdot VegaNotional
\end{aligned}$$

In this case, vega equals the discounted vega notional. For general t, we get

$$Vega_t = \frac{\partial V_t}{\partial \sigma_i}$$

$$= \frac{VegaNotional}{2 \cdot \sigma_i(t, T)} \cdot e^{-r(T-t)} \cdot \frac{T-t}{T} \cdot 2\sigma_i(t, T)$$

$$= e^{-r(T-t)} \cdot VegaNotional \cdot \frac{T-t}{T}$$

This illustrates that vega sensitivity diminishes over time and that it is proportional to the time-to-maturity.

9.3.5 Variance Swap on the EURO STOXX 50

We are now ready to do a historical re-calculation of a variance swap on the EURO STOXX 50. We will re-calculate a variance swap during June 2015. To this end we also use VSTOXX sub-index data for the shortest maturity available which provides us with a time series for the correct implied volatilities.

EURO STOXX 50 data is already available.

```
In [46]: es.info()
<class 'pandas.core.frame.DataFrame'>
DatetimeIndex: 7475 entries, 1986-12-31 to 2015-12-30
Data columns (total 8 columns):
SX5P    7475 non-null float64
SX5E    7475 non-null float64
SXXP    7475 non-null float64
SXXE    7475 non-null float64
SXXF    7475 non-null float64
SXXA    7475 non-null float64
DK5F    7475 non-null float64
DKXF    7475 non-null float64
dtypes: float64(8)
memory usage: 525.6 KB
```

The VSTOXX data can be read from the same source (see chapter 4, *Data Analysis and Strategies*).

```
In [47]: vs_url = path + 'h_vstoxx.txt'

In [48]: try:  # reading the data with pandas
    ....:     vs = pd.read_csv(vs_url,  # filename
    ....:                      index_col=0,  # index column (dates)
    ....:                      parse_dates=True,  # parse date information
```

```
     ....:                            dayfirst=True,  # day before month
     ....:                            header=2,  # header/column names
     ....:                            sep=',')  # separator character
     ....: except:  # read stored data if there is no Internet connection
     ....:       vs = pd. HDFStore ('./source/data/V2TX.h5', 'r')
     ....:

In [49]: vs.info()
<class 'pandas.core.frame.DataFrame'>
DatetimeIndex: 4357 entries, 1999-01-04 to 2016-02-12
Data columns (total 9 columns):
V2TX    4357 non-null float64
V6I1    3906 non-null float64
V6I2    4357 non-null float64
V6I3    4296 non-null float64
V6I4    4357 non-null float64
V6I5    4357 non-null float64
V6I6    4340 non-null float64
V6I7    4357 non-null float64
V6I8    4343 non-null float64
dtypes: float64(9)
memory usage: 340.4 KB
```

The data column V6I2 contains the index values (= implied volatility) for the nearest option series maturity available (i.e within a maximum of one month). For example, on June 1, 2015, the index values represent implied volatilities for the maturity on the third Friday in June 2015, i.e. June 19. Maturity T then is:

```
# 15 trading days
In [50]: T = 15.
```

The variance swap we want to re-calculate should start on June 1, 2015 and will have a maturity until June 19. It will have a vega notional of 100,000 EUR.

First, let us select and collect the data needed from the available data sets.

```
In [51]: data = pd.DataFrame(es['SX5E'][(es.index > '2015-5-31')
     ....:                      & (es.index < '2015-6-20')])
     ....:
```

```
In [52]: data['V6I1'] = vs['V6I1'][(vs.index > '2015-5-31')
     ....:                      & (vs.index < '2015-6-20')]
     ....:
```

The new data set looks as follows. Note that the VSTOXX sub-index is only available up until two days before the maturity date.

```
In [53]: data
Out[53]:
                SX5E      V6I1
Date
2015-06-01   3575.04   25.8710
2015-06-02   3561.89   25.9232
2015-06-03   3583.82   25.7958
2015-06-04   3556.38   26.2418
2015-06-05   3510.01   27.4496
2015-06-08   3468.31   27.2996
2015-06-09   3456.79   26.8020
2015-06-10   3526.48   25.8610
2015-06-11   3551.91   26.3897
2015-06-12   3502.77   29.7725
2015-06-15   3438.07   34.5593
2015-06-16   3454.09   36.2222
2015-06-17   3428.76   34.7235
2015-06-18   3450.45       NaN
2015-06-19   3455.80       NaN
```

We forward fill the NA values since for the vectorized calculations to follow we want to use these data points but they will have a negligible or zero influence anyway.

```
In [54]: data = data.fillna(method='ffill')
```

We save the data set for later re-use.

```
In [55]: h5 = pd.HDFStore('./source/data/SX5E_V6I1.h5')

In [56]: h5['SX5E_V6I1'] = data

In [57]: h5.close()
```

The implied volatility on June 1 was 25.871%. This gives rise to a variance swap strike of $\sigma_K^2 = 25.871^2 = 669.31$. For a vega notional of 100,000, the variance notional therefore is

$$Notional = \frac{100000}{2 \cdot 25.871} = 1932.67$$

```
In [58]: data['V6I1'][0]
Out[58]: 25.870999999999999


In [59]: sigma_K = data['V6I1'][0]


In [60]: Notional = 100000 / (2. * sigma_K)


In [61]: Notional
Out[61]: 1932.665919369178
```

Three time series now have to be calculated:

- log returns of the EURO STOXX 50 index
- realized variance of the EURO STOXX 50 index
- mark-to-market values of the variance swap.

First, the log returns.

```
In [62]: data['R_t'] = np.log(data['SX5E'] / data['SX5E'].shift(1))
```

Second, the realized variance which we scale by a factor of 10,000 to end up with percentage values and not decimal values.

```
In [63]: data['sigma**2'] = 10000 * 252 * (np.cumsum(data['R_t'] ** 2)
   ....:                                   / np.arange(len(data)))
   ....:
```

Third, the mark-to-market values. We start with the array of elapsed days.

```
In [64]: t = np.arange(1, 16)


In [65]: t
Out[65]: array([ 1, 2, 3, 4, 5, 6, 7, 8, 9, 10, 11, 12, 13, 14, 15])
```

We assume a fixed short rate of 0.1%.

```
In [66]: r = 0.001


In [67]: data['V_t'] = np.exp(-r * (T - t) / 365.) * ((t * data['sigma**2']
   ....:                  + (T - t) * data['V6I1'] ** 2) / T - sigma_K ** 2)
   ....:
```

The initial value of the variance swap is zero.

```
In [68]: data['V_t'].loc['2015-06-01'] = 0.0
```

The complete results data set is given below.

```
In [69]: data
Out[69]:
                SX5E      V6I1        R_t    sigma**2           V_t
Date
2015-06-01  3575.04   25.8710        NaN         NaN      0.000000
2015-06-02  3561.89   25.9232  -0.003685   34.220799    -82.332277
2015-06-03  3583.82   25.7958   0.006138   64.580457   -124.049833
2015-06-04  3556.38   26.2418  -0.007686   92.677552   -139.593571
2015-06-05  3510.01   27.4496  -0.013124  178.023718   -107.644092
2015-06-08  3468.31   27.2996  -0.011951  214.408816   -136.380856
2015-06-09  3456.79   26.8020  -0.003327  183.323049   -200.634978
2015-06-10  3526.48   25.8610   0.019960  300.555651   -196.905901
2015-06-11  3551.91   26.3897   0.007185  279.249096   -223.189008
2015-06-12  3502.77   29.7725  -0.013931  302.564935   -172.129074
2015-06-15  3438.07   34.5593  -0.018644  359.901600    -86.887791
2015-06-16  3454.09   36.2222   0.004649  332.134168   -141.190592
2015-06-17  3428.76   34.7235  -0.007360  315.833038   -234.822528
2015-06-18  3450.45   34.7235   0.006306  299.246550   -309.629583
2015-06-19  3455.80   34.7235   0.001549  278.303868   -391.004773
```

The payoff of the variance swap at maturity given the variance notional then is:

```
In [70]: Notional * data['V_t'][-1]
Out[70]: -755681.59959400445
```

Finally, a plot of the major results is presented as Figure 9.7.

```
In [71]: data[['SX5E', 'sigma**2', 'V_t']].plot(subplots=True,
    ....:                                       color='blue',
    ....:                                       figsize=(10, 8));
    ....:
```

We save the data for use in the next chapter.

```
In [72]: h5 = pd.HDFStore('./source/data/var_data.h5', 'a')

In [73]: h5['var_swap'] = data

In [74]: h5.close()
```

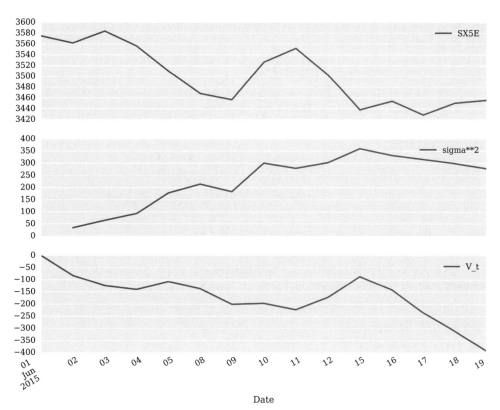

FIGURE 9.7 EURO STOXX 50 historical index levels with realized variance and futures prices.

9.4 VARIANCE VS. VOLATILITY

Both variance and volatility are tradable asset classes. The following sub-sections discuss some differences between the two measures of variability and the two asset classes, respectively. See also Bennett and Gil (2012) on this topic.

9.4.1 Squared Variations

Squared variations are in many application scenarios the better measure for variability compared to simple variations. By squaring variations, one makes sure that variations do not cancel each other out. Since volatility is generally defined as the square root of variance, both measures avoid the cancelling of positive and negative variations.

9.4.2 Additivity in Time

Although both volatility and variance avoid the cancelling out of variations, there is a major difference between both when it comes to additivity. While variance is additive (linear) in time, volatility is convex (nonlinear) in time.

Assume we have N return observations and assume $0 < M < N$. We then have:

$$\sigma^2 \equiv \frac{252}{N} \cdot \sum_{n=1}^{N} R_n^2$$

$$= \frac{252}{N} \cdot \left(\sum_{n=1}^{M} R_n^2 + \sum_{n=M+1}^{N} R_n^2 \right)$$

$$= \frac{252}{N} \cdot \sum_{n=1}^{M} R_n^2 + \frac{252}{N} \cdot \sum_{n=M+1}^{N} R_n^2$$

$$\equiv \sigma_1^2 + \sigma_2^2$$

Here, σ_1^2 is the variance for the first part and σ_2^2 for the second part of the return observations. Note that one needs to keep the weighting factor constant at $\frac{252}{N}$ in order to retain additivity.

This aspect can be illustrated by a simple numerical example. Consider first a function to calculate realized variance that we can re-use.

```
# function to calculate the realized variance
In [75]: rv = lambda ret_dat: 10000 * 252. / N * np.sum(ret_dat ** 2)
```

Second, a simple example data set...

```
In [76]: data = np.array([0.01, 0.02, 0.03, 0.04, 0.05])
```

... of length $N = 5$.

```
In [77]: N = len(data)

In [78]: N
Out[78]: 5
```

Then, we can easily see additivity.

```
In [79]: rv(data[:2]) + rv(data[2:])
Out[79]: 2772.0000000000005
```

```
In [80]: rv(data)
Out[80]: 2772.0000000000005
```

Next, we use the EURO STOXX 50 index data from before. Let us have a look at the year 2013 and the two halves of the year.

```
In [81]: data = pd.DataFrame(es['SX5E'][(es.index > '31-12-2012')
    ....:                                & (es.index < '01-01-2014')])
    ....:

# we need log returns
In [82]: data['R_t'] = np.log(data['SX5E'] / data['SX5E'].shift(1))
```

We have 256 index level observations and 255 return observations.

```
In [83]: N = len(data) - 1

In [84]: N
Out[84]: 255

In [85]: var_1st = rv(data['R_t'][data.index < '2013-07-01'])

In [86]: var_1st
Out[86]: 159.1490165508348

In [87]: var_2nd = rv(data['R_t'][data.index > '2013-06-30'])

In [88]: var_2nd
Out[88]: 98.3424775210876
```

Again, additivity is given for the realized variance.

```
In [89]: var_1st + var_2nd
Out[89]: 257.4914940719224

In [90]: var_full = rv(data['R_t'])

In [91]: var_full
Out[91]: 257.4914940719223
```

Obviously, this is different when considering realized volatility instead of variance.

```
In [92]: vol_1st = math.sqrt(rv(data['R_t'][data.index < '2013-07-01']))

In [93]: vol_1st
Out[93]: 12.615427719694438
```

```
In [94]: vol_2nd = math.sqrt(rv(data['R_t'][data.index > '2013-06-30']))

In [95]: vol_2nd
Out[95]: 9.916777577473823

In [96]: vol_1st + vol_2nd
Out[96]: 22.53220529716826

In [97]: vol_full = math.sqrt(rv(data['R_t']))

In [98]: vol_full
Out[98]: 16.04654149877544
```

This is something to be expected due to the sub-additivity $\sqrt{a+b} \leq \sqrt{a} + \sqrt{b}$ of the square-root function.

9.4.3 Static Hedges

Realized variance can be statically replicated (hedged) by positions in out-of-the money put and call options. This is a well-known result which is presented in detail in chapter 3, *Model-Free Replication of Variance*. It is the basic idea and approach underlying volatility indexes like the VSTOXX and the VIX. This also makes it possible to statically replicate and hedge variance swaps by the use of options – something not true for volatility swaps, for example.

9.4.4 Broad Measure of Risk

Implied volatility generally is only defined for a certain maturity and a certain strike. When the spot moves, at-the-money implied volatility changes as well. By contrast, (implied) variance is a measure taking into account all strikes for a given maturity. This can be seen from the fact that the traded variance level of a variance swap is applicable independently of the spot of the underlying (index).

9.5 CONCLUSIONS

This chapter introduces variance swaps both theoretically as well as based on concrete numerical examples. Central notions are realized variance, variance/volatility strike and variance notional. Mark-to-market valuations of such instruments are easily accomplished due to their very nature. As a consequence, sensitivities of variance swaps, for example, with regard to vega are also easily derived. The major numerical example is based on EURO STOXX 50 index and log return data. A hypothetical variance swap with inception on June 1, 2015 and maturity on June 19, 2015 is valued by the mark-to-market approach using VSTOXX sub-index data with the very same maturity as a proxy for the implied volatility during the life time of the variance swap.

## CHAPTER 10

Variance Futures at Eurex

10.1 INTRODUCTION

Based on the previous chapter, this chapter introduces the Eurex variance futures contracts and their major characteristics. It covers mainly the following topics:

- introduction to and motivation for Eurex variance futures
- variance futures concepts needed to understand and trade in Eurex variance futures
- example calculation for a variance future illustrating the concepts by numerical results
- comparison between variance swaps and futures based on the numerical example.

By introducing variance futures on the EURO STOXX 50 stock index, Eurex standardizes one of the most popular types of volatility/variance derivatives, namely variance swaps. Such a standardization brings a number of benefits to the markets:

- **unified terms**: standardization leads to unified, well-documented terms
- **transparency**: centralized trading at Eurex increases transparency for all market participants
- **liquidity**: standardization and centralization increase liquidity (market depth) in the variance futures
- **fungibility**: variance futures are fully fungible and can be traded in and out at any point over their life time
- **increased market integrity**: clearing by Eurex ensures, among other things, low counterparty risk and high risk management standards.

Variance futures replicate the payoff of Over-the-Counter (OTC) variance swaps and are traded based on OTC conventions in vega notional and at volatility strikes. Daily margin payments based on settlement prices add up to the final settlement payoff of the OTC variance swap. The start of trading for the variance futures of Eurex was September 22, 2014.

Net present value (NPV) effects are accounted for by two different pricing components:

- discount factor as for the mark-to-market for variance swaps
- accumulated return on modified variation margin (ARMVM) for the daily margin payments.

In order to perfectly mimic the cash flow of a variance swap with the same terms, variance futures trading makes certain conversions necessary. This is mainly due to the variance swaps being based on end-of-day returns of the respective index (which cannot be exactly known during the day). Therefore, there are two conversions:

- **intraday**: intraday trades are booked with the desired quantity and at preliminary futures prices
- **end-of-day**: at the end of the day, intraday trades are cancelled and re-booked with the same quantity at the futures settlement prices (taking into account the realized variance for the rest of the day, i.e. since the time the trade was initially booked).

All trades are booked and conversions are made by the Eurex T7 trading system. While variance futures are quoted in vega notional and volatility strikes, bookings and clearings are made only in futures and futures prices.

10.2 VARIANCE FUTURES CONCEPTS

Standardized trading and settlement in variance futures is based on a number of financial concepts. This section introduces all necessary concepts and provides formal definitions.

10.2.1 Realized Variance

Realized variance σ^2 for the Eurex variance futures is defined as

$$\sigma^2 \equiv 10000 \cdot \frac{252}{N} \cdot \sum_{n=1}^{N} R_n^2$$

where, for a time series $S_n, n = 0, 1, \ldots, N$, of daily EURO STOXX 50 closing values, the log returns are given by

$$R_n \equiv \log \frac{S_n}{S_{n-1}}$$

Here, it is assumed that there are 252 trading days per year and that the average daily return is zero. Note the scaling factor of 10,000 to get to the market convention of quoting variance in percent and not in decimal values.

10.2.2 Net Present Value Concepts

There are two concepts that take into account that the daily margin cash flows of trading futures leads, time-wise, to a different cash flow profile than the single payoff of a variance future at maturity.

Discount Factor The first is the discount factor DF_t which is defined for a maturity date T and a current date t by

$$DF_t = e^{-\frac{r(T-t)}{365}}$$

Here, r is the relevant interest rate to be applied to the remaining time-to-maturity $(T - t)$, calculated in days. Eurex uses Euribor rates to calculate the discount factor.

Let us have a look at the development of the Euribor rates in 2014 from January to the beginning of September. Euribor rates are available on the website www.euribor-rates.eu or in a slightly more convenient form as Excel spreadsheet files for download on the website www.emmi-benchmarks.eu/euribor-org/euribor-rates.html. From this last website, we have downloaded Euribor rates data for 2014 which we use in the following. For details on the Python usage that follows, see chapter 2, *Introduction to Python* or refer to Hilpisch (2014). pandas is once again the library we are working with.

```
In [1]: import pandas as pd
```

With pandas, you can read data from a spreadsheet file as follows:

```
# read data from CSV file
In [2]: eb = pd.read_csv('./source/data/hist_EURIBOR_2015.csv',   # filename
    ...:                 index_col=0,     # index column
    ...:                 parse_dates=True,    # parsing date information
    ...:                 dayfirst=True)   # European date convention
    ...:

In [3]: eb. info()
<class 'pandas.core.frame.DataFrame'>
DatetimeIndex: 135 entries, 2015-01-02 to 2015-07-14
Data columns (total 8 columns):
1w      135 non-null float64
2w      135 non-null float64
1m      135 non-null float64
2m      135 non-null float64
3m      135 non-null float64
6m      135 non-null float64
9m      135 non-null float64
12m     135 non-null float64
dtypes: float64(8)
memory usage: 9.5 KB
```

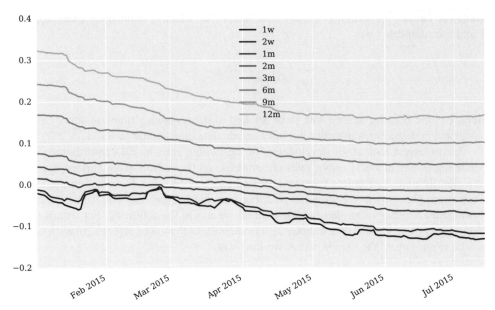

FIGURE 10.1   Historical Euribor rates.

Figure 10.1 shows the evolution of the eight different rates over time (values in percent).

```
In [4]: import seaborn as sns; sns. set()

In [5]: import matplotlib

In [6]: matplotlib.rcParams['font.family'] = 'serif'

In [7]: eb.plot(figsize=(10, 6));
```

Short term interest rates are pretty low, leading to a rather low impact of the discount factor in such an environment. Let us calculate the discount factor for the longest maturity with the last available rate for the 12 month horizon.

```
In [8]: eb.tail()
Out[8]:
                    1w      2w      1m      2m      3m      6m      9m     12m
2015-07-08  -0.131  -0.118  -0.071  -0.038  -0.018   0.049   0.101   0.164
2015-07-09  -0.131  -0.118  -0.071  -0.039  -0.018   0.049   0.100   0.163
2015-07-10  -0.133  -0.118  -0.071  -0.039  -0.018   0.049   0.101   0.164
2015-07-13  -0.131  -0.118  -0.071  -0.038  -0.019   0.049   0.102   0.166
2015-07-14  -0.131  -0.118  -0.071  -0.039  -0.019   0.049   0.101   0.168
```

For a 12 month period the discount effect is less than half a percent.

```
In [9]: import math

In [10]: math.exp(-0.00168 * 365. / 365)
Out[10]: 0.9983214104100598
```

ARMVM   The accumulated return on modified variation margin (ARMVM) takes into account that variance futures trading leads to daily margin payments that have an impact on the present value of the variance future. For given dates t and $t - 1$, ARMVM is given by

$$ARMV\ M_t = ARMV\ M_{t-1} \cdot e^{\frac{r\Delta t}{365}} + \left(F_{t-1}^S - C\right) \left(e^{\frac{r\Delta t}{365}} - 1\right)$$

Here, r is the relevant interest rate to be used, Δt is the difference between dates t and $t - 1$ in days, F_{t-1}^S is the variance futures settlement price at $t - 1$ and C is a constant fixed at a level of 3,000. If $t = 1$, i.e. on the first settlement day (say Monday), $ARMVM_1 \equiv 0$ and $F_1^S \equiv C$.

The relevant rate for the ARMVM calculation is the Eonia rate. On the website www.emmi-benchmarks.eu/euribor-eonia-org/about-eonia.html you find the following explanation:

> *"Eonia® (Euro OverNight Index Average) is the effective overnight reference rate for the euro. It is computed as a weighted average of all overnight unsecured lending transactions in the interbank market, undertaken in the European Union and European Free Trade Association (EFTA) countries."*

This website also provides historical Eonia data for download. Let us have a look at the historical development of the Eonia rates for a couple of weeks in 2015.

```
# read data from Excel spreadsheet file
In [11]: eo = pd.read_csv('./source/data/hist_EONIA_2015.csv',  # filename
    ....:                 index_col=0,  # index column
    ....:                 parse_dates=True,  # parsing date information
    ....:                 dayfirst=True)  # European date convention
    ....:

In [12]: eo. info()
<class 'pandas.core.frame.DataFrame'>
DatetimeIndex: 60 entries, 2015-04-21 to 2015-07-14
Data columns (total 1 columns):
EONIA    60 non-null float64
dtypes: float64(1)
memory usage: 960.0 bytes
```

Again, we can easily visualize the data set (see Figure 10.2).

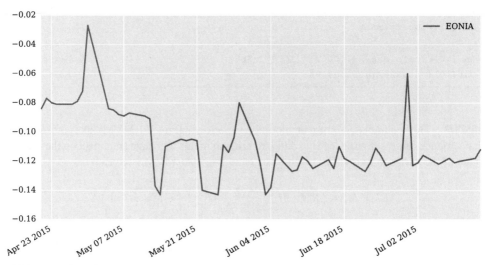

FIGURE 10.2 Historical Eonia rates.

```
In [13]: eo.plot(figsize=(10, 5))
Out[13]: <matplotlib.axes._subplots.AxesSubplot at 0x2ab2484c2d50>
<matplotlib.figure.Figure at 0x2ab247dd0050>
```

The last available values in the data set for Eonia are:

```
In [14]: eo.tail()
Out[14]:
                EONIA
2015-07-08 -0.118
2015-07-09 -0.121
2015-07-10 -0.120
2015-07-13 -0.118
2015-07-14 -0.112
```

Let us work with a value (in decimals) of $r_{eo} = -0.001$.

```
In [15]: r_eo = -0.001
```

Now consider the second settlement day $t = 2$ (say Tuesday), assume that a rate of r_{eo} applies and remember that $F_1^S = 3000$. We then have

$$ARMV\ M_2 = 0 \cdot e^{\frac{r_{eo} \cdot 1}{365}} + (3000 - 3000)\left(e^{\frac{r_{eo} \cdot 1}{365}} - 1\right) = 0$$

Consider now the third settlement day $t = 3$ (say Wednesday). Assume that the futures settlement price has risen the day before to $F_2^S = 3100$. Now

$$ARMV\ M_3 = 0 \cdot e^{\frac{r_{eo} \cdot 1}{365}} + (3100 - 3000)\left(e^{\frac{r_{eo} \cdot 1}{365}} - 1\right)$$

The effect is rather small.

```
In [16]: ARMVM3 = 0 * math.exp(r_eo / 365) + (3100 - 3000)
                  * (math.exp(r_eo / 365) - 1)

In [17]: ARMVM3
Out[17]: -0.0002739722274380796
```

One day later, on the fourth settlement day $t = 4$, and assuming that the variance futures settlement price has fallen the day before to $F_3 = 3050$, we get

$$ARMV\ M_4 = ARMV\ M_3 \cdot e^{\frac{r_{eo} \cdot 1}{365}} + (3050 - 3000)\left(e^{\frac{r_{eo} \cdot 1}{365}} - 1\right)$$

```
In [18]: ARMVM4 = (ARMVM3 * math.exp(r_eo / 365)
    ....:          + (3050 - 3000) * (math.exp(r_eo / 365) - 1))
    ....:

In [19]: ARMVM4
Out[19]: -0.0004109575905493053
```

10.2.3 Traded Variance Strike

The traded variance strike σ_t^2 at date t is the time weighted average of the realized variance $\sigma_{0,t}^2$ weighted by the number of elapsed days t and the traded implied variance $\sigma_i^2(t, T)$ weighted by the remaining life time of the variance future in days:

$$\sigma_t^2 = \frac{t \cdot \sigma_{0,t}^2 + (T - t) \cdot \sigma_i^2(t, T)}{T}$$

10.2.4 Traded Futures Price

The traded futures price F_t given the other quantities from before is then defined as

$$F_t = DF_t \cdot \left(\sigma_t^2 - \sigma_i^2(t, T)\right) - ARMV\ M_t + 3000$$

The scaling constant $C = 3000$ is chosen to ensure that the futures price cannot become negative.

10.2.5 Number of Futures

Variance futures are traded in vega notional and volatility strikes. However, settlement takes place in futures (or variance notional) and variance strikes. The number of futures is calculated according to the formula

$$futures = \frac{VegaNotional}{2 \cdot \sigma_i(t,T)} \cdot \frac{T}{T-t}$$

with $\sigma_i(t,T)$ as the traded implied volatility strike.

10.2.6 Par Variance Strike

At daily settlement, i.e. when the log return for the EURO STOXX 50 for that day is known, the par variance strike σ_p^2 is calculated using the then current settled implied volatility σ_i.

$$\sigma_p^2 = \frac{t \cdot \sigma_{0,t}^2 + (T-t) \cdot \sigma_i^2}{T}$$

10.2.7 Futures Settlement Price

Finally, the daily futures settlement price F_t^S is calculated according to the following formula where all components are as defined as before:

$$F_t^S = DF_t \cdot \left(\sigma_p^2 - \sigma_K^2\right) - ARMV\,M_t + 3000$$

The futures settlement price is the mark-to-market value of the corresponding variance swap minus the ARMVM plus the scaling factor of 3,000.

10.3 EXAMPLE CALCULATION FOR A VARIANCE FUTURE

In this section, we conduct an example calculation for the Eurex variance futures contract given historical data as used in sub-section 9.3.5, *Variance Swap on the EURO STOXX 50*.

```
In [20]: import pandas as pd

In [21]: h5 = pd.HDFStore('./source/data/SX5E_V6I1.h5', 'r')

In [22]: data = h5['SX5E_V6I1']

In [23]: h5.close()

In [24]: data
```

```
Out[24]:
              SX5E      V6I1
Date
2015-06-01  3575.04  25.8710
2015-06-02  3561.89  25.9232
2015-06-03  3583.82  25.7958
2015-06-04  3556.38  26.2418
2015-06-05  3510.01  27.4496
2015-06-08  3468.31  27.2996
2015-06-09  3456.79  26.8020
2015-06-10  3526.48  25.8610
2015-06-11  3551.91  26.3897
2015-06-12  3502.77  29.7725
2015-06-15  3438.07  34.5593
2015-06-16  3454.09  36.2222
2015-06-17  3428.76  34.7235
2015-06-18  3450.45  34.7235
2015-06-19  3455.80  34.7235
```

We add Euribor and Eonia data to the pandas `DataFrame` object. For simplicity, we use the 2 week Euribor values throughout.

```
In [25]: data = data.join(eb['2w'], how='left')

In [26]: data = data.join(eo, how='left')

In [27]: data
Out[27]:
              SX5E      V6I1      2w     EONIA
Date
2015-06-01  3575.04  25.8710  -0.108   -0.106
2015-06-02  3561.89  25.9232  -0.109   -0.122
2015-06-03  3583.82  25.7958  -0.109   -0.143
2015-06-04  3556.38  26.2418  -0.109   -0.138
2015-06-05  3510.01  27.4496  -0.109   -0.115
2015-06-08  3468.31  27.2996  -0.110   -0.127
2015-06-09  3456.79  26.8020  -0.110   -0.126
2015-06-10  3526.48  25.8610  -0.111   -0.117
2015-06-11  3551.91  26.3897  -0.111   -0.120
2015-06-12  3502.77  29.7725  -0.113   -0.125
2015-06-15  3438.07  34.5593  -0.108   -0.119
2015-06-16  3454.09  36.2222  -0.109   -0.125
2015-06-17  3428.76  34.7235  -0.109   -0.110
2015-06-18  3450.45  34.7235  -0.109   -0.118
2015-06-19  3455.80  34.7235  -0.108   -0.120
```

Let us add the log returns to the data set as well as the realized variance.

```
In [28]: import numpy as np

In [29]: data['R_t'] = np.log(data['SX5E'] / data['SX5E'].shift(1))

In [30]: data['sigma**2'] = 10000 * 252 * (np.cumsum(data['R_t'] ** 2)
   ....:                                  / np.arange(len(data)))
   ....:

In [31]: data
Out[31]:
                SX5E      V6I1      2w    EONIA        R_t     sigma**2
Date
2015-06-01  3575.04   25.8710  -0.108  -0.106        NaN          NaN
2015-06-02  3561.89   25.9232  -0.109  -0.122  -0.003685    34.220799
2015-06-03  3583.82   25.7958  -0.109  -0.143   0.006138    64.580457
2015-06-04  3556.38   26.2418  -0.109  -0.138  -0.007686    92.677552
2015-06-05  3510.01   27.4496  -0.109  -0.115  -0.013124   178.023718
2015-06-08  3468.31   27.2996  -0.110  -0.127  -0.011951   214.408816
2015-06-09  3456.79   26.8020  -0.110  -0.126  -0.003327   183.323049
2015-06-10  3526.48   25.8610  -0.111  -0.117   0.019960   300.555651
2015-06-11  3551.91   26.3897  -0.111  -0.120   0.007185   279.249096
2015-06-12  3502.77   29.7725  -0.113  -0.125  -0.013931   302.564935
2015-06-15  3438.07   34.5593  -0.108  -0.119  -0.018644   359.901600
2015-06-16  3454.09   36.2222  -0.109  -0.125   0.004649   332.134168
2015-06-17  3428.76   34.7235  -0.109  -0.110  -0.007360   315.833038
2015-06-18  3450.45   34.7235  -0.109  -0.118   0.006306   299.246550
2015-06-19  3455.80   34.7235  -0.108  -0.120   0.001549   278.303868
```

Assume that the variance future comes to life on June 1, 2015 and that it matures on June 19, 2015. This is a maturity of $T = 15$ trading days. Let us generate in addition an array with all (elapsed) trading days over time.

```
In [32]: T = 15.

In [33]: data['t'] = np. arange(1, 16)

In [34]: data['t']
Out[34]:
Date
2015-06-01    1
2015-06-02    2
2015-06-03    3
```

```
2015-06-04     4
2015-06-05     5
2015-06-08     6
2015-06-09     7
2015-06-10     8
2015-06-11     9
2015-06-12    10
2015-06-15    11
2015-06-16    12
2015-06-17    13
2015-06-18    14
2015-06-19    15
Name: t, dtype: int64
```

Assuming a constant Euribor rate of -0.1%, we can add a new column to the `DataFrame` object with the discount factors in vectorized fashion (see chapter 11, *Trading and Settlement* for further details on the discount factor calculation).

```
In [35]: r_eb = -0.001

In [36]: data['DF_t'] = np.exp(-r_eb * (T - data['t']) / 365.)

In [37]: data
Out[37]:
                 SX5E     V6I1     2w   EONIA      R_t   sigma**2    t       DF_t
Date
2015-06-01  3575.04  25.8710  -0.108  -0.106      NaN        NaN    1   1.000038
2015-06-02  3561.89  25.9232  -0.109  -0.122  -0.003685  34.220799   2   1.000036
2015-06-03  3583.82  25.7958  -0.109  -0.143   0.006138  64.580457   3   1.000033
2015-06-04  3556.38  26.2418  -0.109  -0.138  -0.007686  92.677552   4   1.000030
2015-06-05  3510.01  27.4496  -0.109  -0.115  -0.013124 178.023718   5   1.000027
2015-06-08  3468.31  27.2996  -0.110  -0.127  -0.011951 214.408816   6   1.000025
2015-06-09  3456.79  26.8020  -0.110  -0.126  -0.003327 183.323049   7   1.000022
2015-06-10  3526.48  25.8610  -0.111  -0.117   0.019960 300.555651   8   1.000019
2015-06-11  3551.91  26.3897  -0.111  -0.120   0.007185 279.249096   9   1.000016
2015-06-12  3502.77  29.7725  -0.113  -0.125  -0.013931 302.564935  10   1.000014
2015-06-15  3438.07  34.5593  -0.108  -0.119  -0.018644 359.901600  11   1.000011
2015-06-16  3454.09  36.2222  -0.109  -0.125   0.004649 332.134168  12   1.000008
2015-06-17  3428.76  34.7235  -0.109  -0.110  -0.007360 315.833038  13   1.000005
2015-06-18  3450.45  34.7235  -0.109  -0.118   0.006306 299.246550  14   1.000003
2015-06-19  3455.80  34.7235  -0.108  -0.120   0.001549 278.303868  15   1.000000
```

The standard volatility strike is $\sigma_K = 25.871$ and the standard variance strike is $\sigma_K^2 = 25.871^2 = 669.31$.

```
In [38]: sigma_K = data['V6I1'][0]

In [39]: sigma_K
Out[39]: 25.870999999999999
```

Assume a vega notional of 100,000. This translates into a variance notional of:

```
In [40]: Notional = 100000 / (2 * sigma_K)

In [41]: Notional
Out[41]: 1932.665919369178
```

The settlement price on the first trading day is standardized to 3,000. We generate a new column in the pandas DataFrame object and initialize the first value (and all the others) accordingly.

```
In [42]: data['F_tS'] = 3000

In [43]: data
Out[43]:
                 SX5E     V6I1      2w    EONIA       R_t    sigma**2    t \
Date
2015-06-01    3575.04  25.8710  -0.108  -0.106       NaN         NaN    1
2015-06-02    3561.89  25.9232  -0.109  -0.122  -0.003685   34.220799   2
2015-06-03    3583.82  25.7958  -0.109  -0.143   0.006138   64.580457   3
2015-06-04    3556.38  26.2418  -0.109  -0.138  -0.007686   92.677552   4
2015-06-05    3510.01  27.4496  -0.109  -0.115  -0.013124  178.023718   5
2015-06-08    3468.31  27.2996  -0.110  -0.127  -0.011951  214.408816   6
2015-06-09    3456.79  26.8020  -0.110  -0.126  -0.003327  183.323049   7
2015-06-10    3526.48  25.8610  -0.111  -0.117   0.019960  300.555651   8
2015-06-11    3551.91  26.3897  -0.111  -0.120   0.007185  279.249096   9
2015-06-12    3502.77  29.7725  -0.113  -0.125  -0.013931  302.564935  10
2015-06-15    3438.07  34.5593  -0.108  -0.119  -0.018644  359.901600  11
2015-06-16    3454.09  36.2222  -0.109  -0.125   0.004649  332.134168  12
2015-06-17    3428.76  34.7235  -0.109  -0.110  -0.007360  315.833038  13
2015-06-18    3450.45  34.7235  -0.109  -0.118   0.006306  299.246550  14
2015-06-19    3455.80  34.7235  -0.108  -0.120   0.001549  278.303868  15

                 DF_t   F_tS
Date
2015-06-01    1.000038   3000
2015-06-02    1.000036   3000
2015-06-03    1.000033   3000
2015-06-04    1.000030   3000
2015-06-05    1.000027   3000
```

```
2015-06-08   1.000025   3000
2015-06-09   1.000022   3000
2015-06-10   1.000019   3000
2015-06-11   1.000016   3000
2015-06-12   1.000014   3000
2015-06-15   1.000011   3000
2015-06-16   1.000008   3000
2015-06-17   1.000005   3000
2015-06-18   1.000003   3000
2015-06-19   1.000000   3000
```

The ARMVM on the first settlement day is zero. We again generate a new column and initialize all values with zero.

```
In [44]: data['ARMVM_t'] = 0.0
```

The futures price on the second settlement day is given as:

```
In [45]: data['F_tS'][1] = data['DF_t'][1] * ((data['t'][1] * data['sigma**2'][1]
    ....:                   + (T - data['t'][1]) * data['V6I1'][1] ** 2) / T
    ....:                   - sigma_K ** 2) + 3000
    ....:

In [46]: data['F_tS'][1]
Out[46]: 2917
```

Analogously, we can calculate the settlement prices for all other settlement days. Note that we take the index level of the EURO STOXX 50 at close and not the average of its level between 11:50 and 12:00 CET at the final settlement day (see chapter 11, *Trading and Settlement*).

```
In [47]: for t in data.index[1:]:
    ....:         data['ARMVM_t'][t] = (data['ARMVM_t'].shift(1)[t]
    ....:                              * math.exp(data['EONIA'].shift(1)[t] / 252)
    ....:                              + (data['F_tS'].shift(1)[t] - 3000)
    ....:                              * (math.exp(data['EONIA'].shift(1)[t] / 252) - 1))
    ....:         data['F_tS'][t] = data['DF_t'][t] * ((data['t'][t] * data['sigma**2'][t]
    ....:                           + (T - data['t'][t]) * data['V6I1'][t] ** 2) / T
    ....:                           -sigma_K ** 2) - data['ARMVM_t'][t] + 3000
    ....:
```

We end up with a complete data set, and in particular the simulated variance futures settlement values.

```
In [48]: data
Out[48]:
                   SX5E      V6I1       2w    EONIA         R_t      sigma**2    t  \
Date
2015-06-01      3575.04   25.8710   -0.108   -0.106         NaN           NaN    1
2015-06-02      3561.89   25.9232   -0.109   -0.122   -0.003685     34.220799    2
2015-06-03      3583.82   25.7958   -0.109   -0.143    0.006138     64.580457    3
2015-06-04      3556.38   26.2418   -0.109   -0.138   -0.007686     92.677552    4
2015-06-05      3510.01   27.4496   -0.109   -0.115   -0.013124    178.023718    5
2015-06-08      3468.31   27.2996   -0.110   -0.127   -0.011951    214.408816    6
2015-06-09      3456.79   26.8020   -0.110   -0.126   -0.003327    183.323049    7
2015-06-10      3526.48   25.8610   -0.111   -0.117    0.019960    300.555651    8
2015-06-11      3551.91   26.3897   -0.111   -0.120    0.007185    279.249096    9
2015-06-12      3502.77   29.7725   -0.113   -0.125   -0.013931    302.564935   10
2015-06-15      3438.07   34.5593   -0.108   -0.119   -0.018644    359.901600   11
2015-06-16      3454.09   36.2222   -0.109   -0.125    0.004649    332.134168   12
2015-06-17      3428.76   34.7235   -0.109   -0.110   -0.007360    315.833038   13
2015-06-18      3450.45   34.7235   -0.109   -0.118    0.006306    299.246550   14
2015-06-19      3455.80   34.7235   -0.108   -0.120    0.001549    278.303868   15


                    DF_t   F_tS    ARMVM_t
Date
2015-06-01      1.000038   3000   0.000000
2015-06-02      1.000036   2917   0.000000
2015-06-03      1.000033   2875   0.040173
2015-06-04      1.000030   2860   0.111062
2015-06-05      1.000027   2892   0.187647
2015-06-08      1.000025   2863   0.236836
2015-06-09      1.000022   2799   0.305743
2015-06-10      1.000019   2802   0.406065
2015-06-11      1.000016   2776   0.497784
2015-06-12      1.000014   2827   0.604188
2015-06-15      1.000011   2912   0.689681
2015-06-16      1.000008   2858   0.730901
2015-06-17      1.000005   2764   0.800957
2015-06-18      1.000003   2689   0.903601
2015-06-19      1.000000   2607   1.048771
```

Figure 10.3 shows the results graphically.

```
In [49]: data[['SX5E', 'sigma**2', 'F_tS']].plot(subplots=True,
    ....:                                        color='blue',
    ....:                                        figsize=(10, 9));
    ....:
```

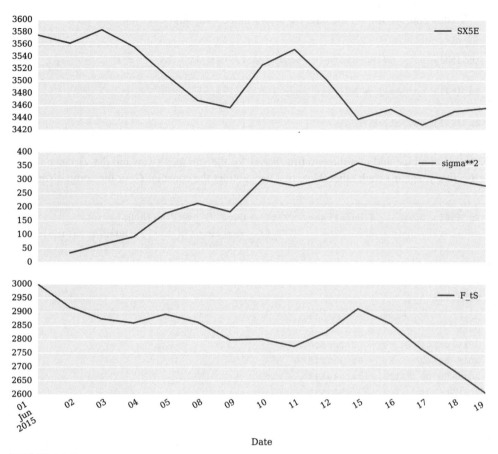

FIGURE 10.3 Calculated variance futures settlement values for the EURO STOXX 50.

We save the generated data set for re-use in the next section.

```
In [50]: h5 = pd.HDFStore('./source/data/var_data.h5', 'a')

In [51]: h5['var_future'] = data

In [52]: h5.close()
```

10.4 COMPARISON OF VARIANCE SWAP AND FUTURE

Eurex variance futures are a means to replicate the payoff of OTC-traded variance swaps with a listed, standardized product. Let us compare the mark-to-market values of the variance swap from sub-section 9.3.5, *Variance Swap on the EURO STOXX 50* with the settlement values calculated in the previous section.

To this end, we import the data for the variance swap first.

```
In [53]: h5 = pd.HDFStore('./source/data/var_data.h5', 'r')

In [54]: var_swap = h5['var_swap']

In [55]: h5.close()
```

Next, we combine and plot the two time series for the variance swap and the variance future, respectively, against each other. Note that we subtract the constant C for the comparison.

```
In [56]: comp = pd.DataFrame({'F_tS': data['F_tS'] - 3000,
    ....:                      'V_t': var_swap['V_t']}, index=data.index)
    ....:

In [57]: comp
Out[57]:
                F_tS          V_t
Date
2015-06-01        0     0.000000
2015-06-02      -83   -82.332277
2015-06-03     -125  -124.049833
2015-06-04     -140  -139.593571
2015-06-05     -108  -107.644092
2015-06-08     -137  -136.380856
2015-06-09     -201  -200.634978
2015-06-10     -198  -196.905901
2015-06-11     -224  -223.189008
2015-06-12     -173  -172.129074
2015-06-15      -88   -86.887791
2015-06-16     -142  -141.190592
2015-06-17     -236  -234.822528
2015-06-18     -311  -309.629583
2015-06-19     -393  -391.004773
```

Figure 10.4 compares the two time series.

```
In [58]: comp.plot(style=['b', 'ro'], figsize=(9, 5));
```

Finally, Figure 10.5 presents the absolute differences which are quite small.

```
In [59]: (comp['F_tS'] - comp['V_t']).plot(style='r^', figsize=(9, 5));
```

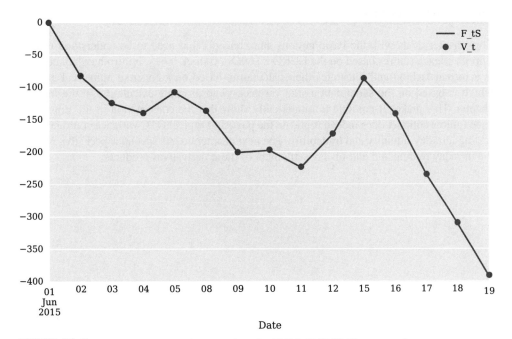

FIGURE 10.4   Variance swap and futures prices for EURO STOXX 50 compared.

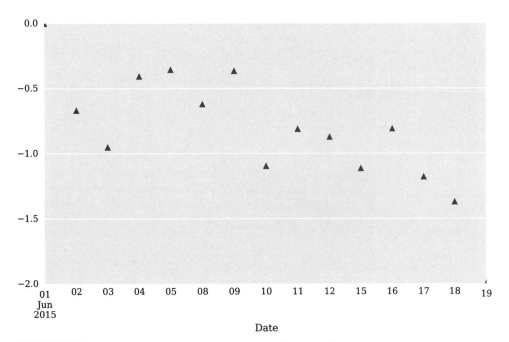

FIGURE 10.5   Differences between variance swap and futures prices.

10.5 CONCLUSIONS

This chapter deals with the basic notions and concepts that need to be understood to trade Eurex variance futures based on the EURO STOXX 50 stock index. It introduces all concepts in a formal fashion and illustrates their calculation based on a concrete numerical example which is based on the same data as the variance swap example calculation in the previous chapter. This makes it possible to numerically show that the construction of the Eurex variance futures contract does indeed replicate the payoff of typical OTC variance contracts while adding intraday liquidity and tradability. The next chapter covers special aspects that relate to the intraday trading and end-of-day settlement of these derivatives products.

## CHAPTER 11

Trading and Settlement

11.1 INTRODUCTION

This chapter covers practical aspects of trading Eurex variance futures. Among others, topics are:

- overview of major variance futures contract terms
- intraday trading and trade conventions
- trade matching at the end of the trading day
- different traded volatilities with their impact on margining
- after the trade matching until maturity
- further details about interest rate calculation and market disruption events.

11.2 OVERVIEW OF VARIANCE FUTURES TERMS

The following list provides an overview of the major terms of the Eurex variance futures contract. All technical terms are explained in chapter 10 *Variance Futures at Eurex*.

- **underlying**: realized variance of EURO STOXX 50 stock index
- **interest rates**: Euribor for present value factor DF_t and Eonia for $ARMVM_t$
- **standard strike**: determined on first trading day and equal to settled implied volatility for the relevant maturity
- **1st settlement price**: equal to 3,000 (i.e. for setting standard strike = settled implied variance)
- **contract value**: 1 EUR per variance futures point
- **minimum price change/tick value**: 0.0001 variance futures points and 0.0001 EUR
- **settlement**: in cash
- **terms**: next three month ends and the next three quarter end months thereafter as well as June and December thereafter
- **last trading day**: one day before final settlement day
- **final settlement day/expiration**: third Friday of maturity month

- **final settlement price**: based on the average index level of EURO STOXX 50 between 11:50 am and 12:00 CET on final settlement day
- **trade matching**: variance futures trade in notional vega at volatility; upon matching notional vega and volatility are converted into variance futures and variance futures prices, respectively
- **continuous trading**: from 9:00 am until 5:30 pm CET on each trading day of Eurex
- **Eurex trade entry services**: from 6:30 pm until 9:00 pm CET on each trading day of Eurex
- **order maintenance**: notional vega at volatility, minimum order size 1 vega, minimum price change 0.05 volatility points.

11.3 INTRADAY TRADING

Variance futures are traded on-exchange in terms of notional vega at volatility. However, intraday there are no live futures prices quoted; they have to be calculated using live volatility quotes and the conversion parameters provided by Eurex. The conversion parameters are those used for the calculation of the settlement price from the previous day, except that the time-to-maturity $(T - t)$ is reduced by 1 day and the number of elapsed days t is increased by 1 day.

Let us get back to the numerical example from section 10.3 *Example Calculation for a Variance Future*. The example simulates the calculation of daily settlement prices for a variance futures contract with inception on June 1, 2015 and a maturity on June 19, 2015 (i.e. 15 trading days). Since we have saved the data, we can continue from where we ended.

```
In [1]: import numpy as np
```

```
In [2]: a = np.random.standard_normal((10))
```

```
In [3]: np.round(a)
Out[3]: array([1., -0., -1., 1., 1., -0., 0., 0., 1., 1.])
```

```
In [4]: import pandas as pd

In [5]: h5 = pd.HDFStore('./source/data/var_data.h5', 'r')

In [6]: data = h5['var_future']

In [7]: h5.close()

In [8]: data.head()
```

```
Out[8]:
                SX5E     V6I1     2w    EONIA      R_t  sigma**2  t       DF_t \
Date
2015-06-01  3575.04  25.8710  -0.108  -0.106      NaN       NaN  1   1.000038
2015-06-02  3561.89  25.9232  -0.109  -0.122  -0.003685  34.220799  2   1.000036
2015-06-03  3583.82  25.7958  -0.109  -0.143   0.006138  64.580457  3   1.000033
2015-06-04  3556.38  26.2418  -0.109  -0.138  -0.007686  92.677552  4   1.000030
2015-06-05  3510.01  27.4496  -0.109  -0.115  -0.013124 178.023718  5   1.000027


            F_tS  ARMVM_t
Date
2015-06-01  3000  0.000000
2015-06-02  2917  0.000000
2015-06-03  2875  0.040173
2015-06-04  2860  0.111062
2015-06-05  2892  0.187647
```

We need to read out two central terms of the variance, namely the time-to-maturity in year fractions and the standard volatility strike.

```
In [9]: T = data['t'][-1]

In [10]: T
Out[10]: 15

In [11]: sigma_K = data['V6I1'][0]

In [12]: sigma_K
Out[12]: 25.870999999999999
```

Similarly to the calculation in section 10.3, *Example Calculation for a Variance Future*, we can now do the following calculation where we use the previous day's input parameters but today's remaining time-to-maturity and today's elapsed time (in days).

```
In [13]: data['F_ti'] = 3000.0

In [14]: for t in data.index[2:]:
   ....:     data.loc[t, 'F_ti'] = data['DF_t'].shift(1)[t] * (
   ....:               (data['t'][t] * data['sigma**2'].shift(1)[t]
   ....:               +(T - data['t'][t]) * data['V6I1'].shift(1)[t]
   ....:               ** 2) / T
   ....:               - sigma_K ** 2) - data['ARMVM_t'].shift(1)[t] + 3000
   ....:
```

The results are shown in the following table in the column F_ti for interim futures prices.

```
In [15]: data
Out[15]:
                SX5E       V6I1       2w     EONIA        R_t      sigma**2    t \
Date
2015-06-01    3575.04    25.8710    -0.108    -0.106        NaN          NaN    1
2015-06-02    3561.89    25.9232    -0.109    -0.122   -0.003685    34.220799    2
2015-06-03    3583.82    25.7958    -0.109    -0.143    0.006138    64.580457    3
2015-06-04    3556.38    26.2418    -0.109    -0.138   -0.007686    92.677552    4
2015-06-05    3510.01    27.4496    -0.109    -0.115   -0.013124   178.023718    5
2015-06-08    3468.31    27.2996    -0.110    -0.127   -0.011951   214.408816    6
2015-06-09    3456.79    26.8020    -0.110    -0.126   -0.003327   183.323049    7
2015-06-10    3526.48    25.8610    -0.111    -0.117    0.019960   300.555651    8
2015-06-11    3551.91    26.3897    -0.111    -0.120    0.007185   279.249096    9
2015-06-12    3502.77    29.7725    -0.113    -0.125   -0.013931   302.564935   10
2015-06-15    3438.07    34.5593    -0.108    -0.119   -0.018644   359.901600   11
2015-06-16    3454.09    36.2222    -0.109    -0.125    0.004649   332.134168   12
2015-06-17    3428.76    34.7235    -0.109    -0.110   -0.007360   315.833038   13
2015-06-18    3450.45    34.7235    -0.109    -0.118    0.006306   299.246550   14
2015-06-19    3455.80    34.7235    -0.108    -0.120    0.001549   278.303868   15

                 DF_t      F_tS    ARMVM_t           F_ti
Date
2015-06-01    1.000038    3000    0.000000    3000.000000
2015-06-02    1.000036    2917    0.000000    3000.000000
2015-06-03    1.000033    2875    0.040173    2875.140910
2015-06-04    1.000030    2860    0.111062    2835.844331
2015-06-05    1.000027    2892    0.187647    2820.555454
2015-06-08    1.000025    2863    0.236836    2853.797523
2015-06-09    1.000022    2799    0.305743    2827.984087
2015-06-10    1.000019    2802    0.406065    2763.381425
2015-06-11    1.000016    2776    0.497784    2778.130966
2015-06-12    1.000014    2827    0.604188    2748.494268
2015-06-15    1.000011    2912    0.689681    2788.339034
2015-06-16    1.000008    2858    0.730901    2856.790440
2015-06-17    1.000005    2764    0.800957    2792.748076
2015-06-18    1.000003    2689    0.903601    2705.047722
2015-06-19    1.000000    2607    1.048771    2629.033294
```

As an example, assume that a trader buys on June 9, intraday 100,000 notional vega at a traded implied volatility level of 26. The number of futures she has bought then is

$$
\begin{aligned}
futures &= \frac{VegaNotional}{2 \cdot \sigma_{ti}} \cdot \frac{T}{T-t} \\
&= \frac{100000}{2 \cdot 26} \cdot \frac{15}{15-7} \\
&= 3605.77
\end{aligned}
$$

```
In [16]: futures = 100000. /(2 * 26) * T / (T - data['t']['2015-06-09'])

In [17]: futures
Out[17]: 3605.769230769231
```

The intraday futures price for the variance futures contract is:

```
In [18]: F_ti = data['F_ti']['2015-06-09']

In [19]: F_ti
Out[19]: 2827.9840866529353
```

The traded variance strike is

$$\sigma_t^2 = \frac{t \cdot \sigma_{0,t}^2 + (T - t) \cdot \sigma_i^2(t, T)}{T}$$

$$= \frac{7 \cdot 13.54^2 + (15 - 7) \cdot 26^2}{15}$$

$$= 446.08$$

```
In [20]: sigma_t2 = (data['t']['2015-06-09'] * data['sigma**2']['2015-06-09']
    ....:           + (T - data['t']['2015-06-09'] ) * 26 ** 2) / T
    ....:

In [21]: sigma_t2
Out[21]: 446.0840897506356
```

The traded futures price then is

$$F_t = DF_t \cdot \left(\sigma_t^2 - \sigma_i^2(t, T)\right) - ARMV\, M_t + 3000 = 2776.47$$

```
In [22]: F_t = (data['DF_t']['2015-06-09'] *
    ....:       (sigma_t2 - data['V6I1']['2015-06-01'] ** 2)
    ....:       - data['ARMVM_t']['2015-06-09'] + 3000)
    ....:

In [23]: F_t
Out[23]: 2776.4648130015858
```

Consequently, the trade has a value of:

```
In [24]: P_ti = futures * F_t

In [25]: P_ti
Out[25]: 10011291.393034564
```

11.4 TRADE MATCHING

At the end of the day, the trade in notional vega and volatility is confirmed. Notional vega and volatility are, however, converted into variance futures at the variance futures settlement price. To this end, the intraday transaction gets cancelled and replaced by a confirmed transaction with the same number of futures but with the variance futures settlement price of the day.

In the example, we have:

```
In [26]: F_tS = data['F_tS']['2015-06-09']

In [27]: F_tS
Out[27]: 2799
```

Consequently, the transaction booked has a value of:

```
In [28]: P_t = futures * F_tS

In [29]: P_t
Out[29]: 10092548.076923078
```

The first margin payment given these numbers then is:

```
In [30]: P_t - P_ti
Out[30]: 81256.683888513595
```

This is roughly the same as vega notional times the difference in settlement and traded volatility:

$$margin = VegaNotional \cdot (\sigma_i - \sigma_i(t, T))$$

```
In [31]: 100000 * (data['V6I1']['2015-06-09'] - 26)
Out[31]: 80199.999999999956
```

11.5 DIFFERENT TRADED VOLATILITIES

Let us now see what impact different traded volatilities have on the first day margining of the same trade as before. The necessary parameters and values can be calculated in vectorized fashion. First, the array with the traded volatilities.

```
In [32]: import numpy as np

In [33]: trad_vols = np.arange(15, 25.01, 1)

In [34]: trad_vols
Out[34]: array([15., 16., 17., 18., 19., 20., 21., 22., 23., 24., 25.])
```

Second, the traded variance strikes.

```
In [35]: sigma_t2 = (data['t']['2015-06-09'] * data['sigma**2']['2015-06-09']
    ....:            + (T - data['t']['2015-06-09']) * trad_vols ** 2) / T
    ....:

In [36]: sigma_t2
Out[36]:
array([205.55075642,  222.08408975,  239.68408975,  258.35075642,
       278.08408975,  298.88408975,  320.75075642,  343.68408975,
       367.68408975,  392.75075642,  418.88408975])
```

Third, the traded futures prices.

```
In [37]: F_t = (data['DF_t']['2015-06-09']
    ....:        *(sigma_t2 - data['V6I1']['2015-06-01'] ** 2)
    ....:         - data['ARMVM_t']['2015-06-09'] + 3000)
    ....:

In [38]: F_t
Out[38]:
array([ 2535.92620765,  2552.45990336,  2570.06028912,  2588.72736492,
        2608.46113077,  2629.26158666,  2651.12873261,  2674.06256859,
        2698.06309463,  2723.13031071,  2749.26421683])
```

Fourth, the first day margins (P&L).

```
In [39]: margins = futures * (F_tS - F_t)

In [40]: margins
Out[40]:
array([ 948583.3858882 ,  888966.69461993,  825503.76520532,
        758194.59764436,  687039.19193707,  612037.54808344,
        533189.66608347,  450495.54593716,  363955.18764451,
        273568.59120552,  179335.75662019])
```

Let us visualize the results. The margins (P&L) are linear in traded volatility with the slope in Figure 11.1 being equal to the vega notional of 100,000.

```
In [41]: import seaborn as sns; sns.set()

In [42]: import matplotlib

In [43]: matplotlib.rcParams['font.family'] = 'serif'

In [44]: results = pd.DataFrame({'margins' : margins}, index=trad_vols)

In [45]: results.plot(figsize=(10, 6));
```

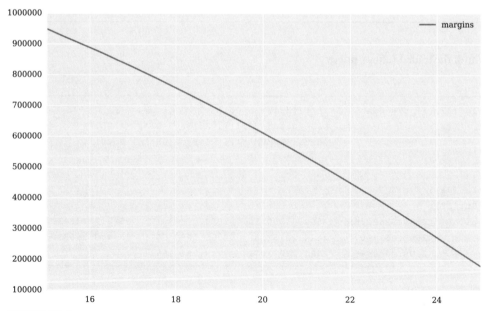

FIGURE 11.1   Variance futures margins.

11.6 AFTER THE TRADE MATCHING

What happens after the trade matching until maturity? To find out, we can calculate the subsequent margins as follows. We start with the differences between settlement prices.

```
In [46]: F_diffs = (data['F_tS'] - data['F_tS'].shift(1))

In [47]: F_diffs
Out[47]:
Date
2015-06-01     NaN
2015-06-02   -83.0
2015-06-03   -42.0
2015-06-04   -15.0
2015-06-05    32.0
2015-06-08   -29.0
2015-06-09   -64.0
2015-06-10     3.0
2015-06-11   -26.0
2015-06-12    51.0
2015-06-15    85.0
2015-06-16   -54.0
2015-06-17   -94.0
2015-06-18   -75.0
2015-06-19   -82.0
Name: F_tS, dtype: float64
```

With these differences, we can calculate the daily margins until maturity.

```
In [48]: margin_t = futures * F_diffs[F_diffs.index >= '2015-06-09']

In [49]: margin_t
Out[49]:
Date
2015-06-09   -230769.230769
2015-06-10     10817.307692
2015-06-11    -93750.000000
2015-06-12    183894.230769
2015-06-15    306490.384615
2015-06-16   -194711.538462
2015-06-17   -338942.307692
2015-06-18   -270432.692308
2015-06-19   -295673.076923
Name: F_tS, dtype: float64
```

The following code generates a pandas `DataFrame` object with the initial margins given the traded volatility strike and the subsequent margins until maturity.

```
In [50]: results = pd.DataFrame(np.tile(margin_t, (len(trad_vols), 1)).T,
    ....:                        index=margin_t.index,
    ....:                        columns=trad_vols)
    ....:

In [51]: results.loc['2015-06-09', :] = margins   # setting the first
                                                    day margins

In [52]: np.round(results)
Out[52]:
                     15.0        16.0        17.0        18.0        19.0        20.0 \
Date
2015-06-09    948583.0    888967.0    825504.0    758195.0    687039.0    612038.0
2015-06-10     10817.0     10817.0     10817.0     10817.0     10817.0     10817.0
2015-06-11    -93750.0    -93750.0    -93750.0    -93750.0    -93750.0    -93750.0
2015-06-12    183894.0    183894.0    183894.0    183894.0    183894.0    183894.0
2015-06-15    306490.0    306490.0    306490.0    306490.0    306490.0    306490.0
2015-06-16   -194712.0   -194712.0   -194712.0   -194712.0   -194712.0   -194712.0
2015-06-17   -338942.0   -338942.0   -338942.0   -338942.0   -338942.0   -338942.0
2015-06-18   -270433.0   -270433.0   -270433.0   -270433.0   -270433.0   -270433.0
2015-06-19   -295673.0   -295673.0   -295673.0   -295673.0   -295673.0   -295673.0


                     21.0        22.0        23.0        24.0        25.0
Date
2015-06-09    533190.0    450496.0    363955.0    273569.0    179336.0
2015-06-10     10817.0     10817.0     10817.0     10817.0     10817.0
2015-06-11    -93750.0    -93750.0    -93750.0    -93750.0    -93750.0
2015-06-12    183894.0    183894.0    183894.0    183894.0    183894.0
2015-06-15    306490.0    306490.0    306490.0    306490.0    306490.0
2015-06-16   -194712.0   -194712.0   -194712.0   -194712.0   -194712.0
2015-06-17   -338942.0   -338942.0   -338942.0   -338942.0   -338942.0
2015-06-18   -270433.0   -270433.0   -270433.0   -270433.0   -270433.0
2015-06-19   -295673.0   -295673.0   -295673.0   -295673.0   -295673.0
```

Figure 11.2 visualizes the cumulative P&L (assuming zero interest rates) for the different traded volatility strikes.

```
In [53]: results.cumsum().plot(figsize=(10, 6), title='cumulative P&L');
```

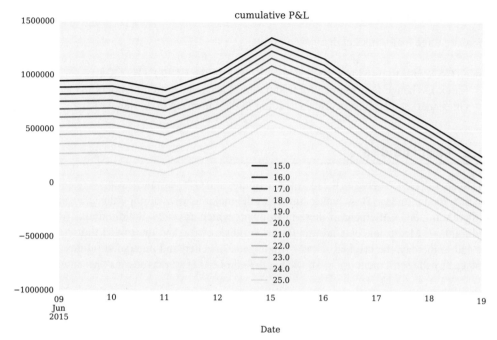

FIGURE 11.2 Cumulative P&L for variance future.

11.7 FURTHER DETAILS

This section briefly discusses some further details of importance for trading in Eurex variance futures.

11.7.1 Interest Rate Calculation

ARMVM is calculated based on the Eonia rate as settled at 7 pm CET on the previous day. The discount factors are calculated using the Euribor rates fixed at 11:00 am CET and interpolated to the respective maturities of the variance futures. The interpolation is done in linear fashion using the following formula:

$$r_i = r(T_i) = \frac{T_{K+1} - T_i}{T_{K+1} - T_K} r(T_K) + \frac{T_i - T_K}{T_{K+1} - T_K} r(T_{K+1})$$

where T_{K+1} is the maturity of the Euribor rate later than the futures maturity T_i and T_K is the maturity of the Euribor rate before the futures maturity T_i.

11.7.2 Market Disruption Events

There are three major market disruption events:

- STOXX fails to provide a market closing level for the EURO STOXX 50
- Eurex Exchange fails to open for trading during scheduled trading hours
- Other market disruption events according to the European OTC standard.

11.8 CONCLUSIONS

The major difference between listed variance futures and OTC variance swaps is that the former can be traded intraday. This chapter illustrates the major aspects of importance when it comes to the trading and settlement of these instruments which are even liquid intraday (during the trading day). Major concepts are the traded variance strike and the traded futures price. At the end of the day, the original intraday trade gets cancelled and the traded futures price gets replaced by the settlement price – however, the number of futures remains the same.

DX Analytics

CHAPTER **12**

DX Analytics – An Overview

12.1 INTRODUCTION

Although Python is arguably a good programming language and ecosystem for financial analytics (see chapter 1, *Derivatives, Volatility and Variance* or chapter 1 of Hilpisch (2014)), dedicated libraries for finance are not that common. This is even more true when it comes to derivatives analytics as a sub-discipline. One exception in this regard is DX Analytics (the "dx library"), written by the author of this book, which has a major focus on advanced derivatives and risk analytics. The central resource to get started with the library is the website http://dx-analytics.com.

This chapter provides an overview of the relevant parts of the library for the purposes of the case studies which follow. The development of the library is guided by two central principles:

- **global valuation approach**: in practice, this approach translates into the non-redundant modeling of all risk factors (e.g. option underlyings like equity indexes) and the valuation of all derivative instruments by a unique, consistent numerical method – which is Monte Carlo simulation in the case of DX Analytics
- **unlimited computing resources**: Monte Carlo simulation is computationally and memory intensive and has therefore often been dismissed as an adequate numerical method to implement, for example, front-office analytics libraries; in 2016, the technical infrastructures available to even smaller players in the financial industry have reached performance levels that 10 years ago seemed impossible or at least not financially feasible; in that sense "unlimited resources" is not to be understood literally but rather as the guiding principle that hardware and computing resources generally are no longer a bottleneck

Among others, DX Analytics provides the following features:

- **models**: models for risk factors include simple ones like geometric Brownian motion as well as more sophisticated ones like stochastic volatility jump diffusion models
- **derivatives**: derivatives models include single risk factor as well as multi risk factor models, both with European and American (Bermudan) exercise

■ **portfolios**: derivatives portfolios can be arbitrarily complex with multiple, correlated risk factors and multiple, diverse derivative instruments (single risk and multi risk); simulations and valuations are implemented in such a way that both value and risk aggregations are consistent for each Monte Carlo path.

The following sections illustrate the use of the library by means of a simple, yet still realistic, example with two correlated risk factors and two different options.

12.2 MODELING RISK FACTORS

First, some necessary imports and in particular the import of the dx library.

```
In [1]: import dx

In [2]: import numpy as np

In [3]: np.random.seed(1000)

In [4]: import pandas as pd

In [5]: import datetime as dt

In [6]: import seaborn as sns; sns.set()

In [7]: import matplotlib as mpl;
```

Usually, the first step is to define a model for the *risk-neutral discounting* since all valuations are based on the risk-neutral (or martingale) pricing approach (see Björk (2009)). Throughout, we will work with a constant short rate model although DX Analytics also provides deterministic yield curve and stochastic short rate models.

```
In [8]: r = dx.constant_short_rate('r', 0.01)
```

The next step is to define a *market environment* containing the parameter specifications needed. Several objects might have different market environments but they might also share market environments. The first risk factor to be modeled is a *geometric Brownian motion* (Black-Scholes-Merton (1973) model). The following market environment object contains all parameters needed for this model. Comments in the code explain the single elements.

```
# instantiation of market environment object
In [9]: me_1 = dx.market_environment('me', dt.datetime(2016, 1, 1))
```

```
# starting value of simulated processes
In [10]: me_1.add_constant('initial_value', 100.)

# volatility factor
In [11]: me_1.add_constant('volatility', 0.2)

# horizon for simulation
In [12]: me_1.add_constant('final_date', dt.datetime(2016, 6, 30))

# currency of instrument
In [13]: me_1.add_constant('currency', 'EUR')

# frequency for discretization (here: weekly)
In [14]: me_1.add_constant('frequency', 'W')

# number of paths
In [15]: me_1.add_constant('paths', 25000)

# short rate model for discount curve
In [16]: me_1.add_curve('discount_curve', r)
```

Equipped with this object, the model object for the risk factor can be instantiated.

```
In [17]: gbm_1 = dx.geometric_brownian_motion('gbm_1', me_1)

In [18]: gbm_1
Out[18]: <dx.dx_models.geometric_brownian_motion at 0x2b20c39c5510>
```

The `get_instrument_values()` method initiates a Monte Carlo simulation and delivers back the simulated paths – given the parametrizations from the market environment object – as a NumPy `ndarray` object.

```
In  [19]: gbm_1.get_instrument_values()
Out [19]:
array([[ 100.        ,  100.        ,  100.        , ...,  100.        ,
         100.        ,  100.        ],
       [ 103.99970675,  100.94138063,  101.87289049, ...,  101.57080458,
         100.82390334,   98.15531921],
       [ 101.93603717,   94.66240389,   91.81649108, ...,  101.20745936,
          99.98530091,  102.49930045],
       ...,
       [  94.34847745,  111.87828236,  105.88943893, ...,   89.84492969,
         109.03063645,  107.8625328 ],
```

```
[  91.01721535,  113.83465258,  102.59432299,  ...,   92.09515398,
   104.17599152,  101.67756176],
[  90.56511589,  113.20730366,  100.79160449,  ...,   90.91965416,
   100.6385713 ,  101.76583508]])
```

Via the `time_grid` attribute one can access the date-time information for the time series data.

```
In [20]: gbm_1.time_grid[:10]
Out[20]:
array([datetime.datetime(2016, 1, 1, 0, 0),
       datetime.datetime(2016, 1, 3, 0, 0),
       datetime.datetime(2016, 1, 10, 0, 0),
       datetime.datetime(2016, 1, 17, 0, 0),
       datetime.datetime(2016, 1, 24, 0, 0),
       datetime.datetime(2016, 1, 31, 0, 0),
       datetime.datetime(2016, 2, 7, 0, 0),
       datetime.datetime(2016, 2, 14, 0, 0),
       datetime.datetime(2016, 2, 21, 0, 0),
       datetime.datetime(2016, 2, 28, 0, 0)], dtype=object)
```

Combining both arrays to a single pandas `DataFrame` object makes plotting straightforward (see Figure 12.1).

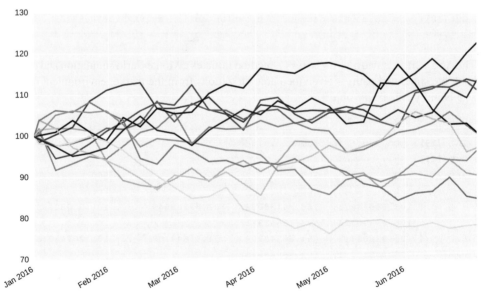

FIGURE 12.1   Simulated paths for the risk factor based on geometric Brownian motion.

```
In [21]: pdf_1 = pd.DataFrame(gbm_1.get_instrument_values(),
                    index=gbm_1.time_grid)

In [22]: pdf_1.ix[:, :10].plot(legend=False, figsize=(10, 6));
```

Next, we define a second risk factor, again based on geometric Brownian motion. We use the market environment information from the first risk factor and only overwrite the volatility value.

```
# instantiate new market environment object
In [23]: me_2 = dx.market_environment('me_2', me_1.pricing_date)

# add complete environment
In [24]: me_2.add_environment(me_1)

# overwrite volatility value
In [25]: me_2.add_constant('volatility', 0.5)
```

Using the updated market environment, define the second risk factor as follows.

```
In [26]: gbm_2 = dx.geometric_brownian_motion('gbm_2', me_2)
```

The plot in Figure 12.2 illustrates the higher volatility of the second risk factor graphically.

```
In [27]: pdf_2 = pd.DataFrame(gbm_2.get_instrument_values(),
                    index=gbm_2.time_grid)

In [28]: ax = pdf_1.ix[:, :10].plot(legend=False, figsize=(10, 6),
                    style=11 * ['b']);

In [29]: pdf_2.ix [:, :10].plot(legend=False, style=11 * ['r'], ax=ax);
```

12.3 MODELING DERIVATIVES

Based on the risk factors, we can define derivatives models for valuation. To this end, we need to add at least one (the `maturity`), in general two (`maturity` and `strike`), parameters to the market environment(s).

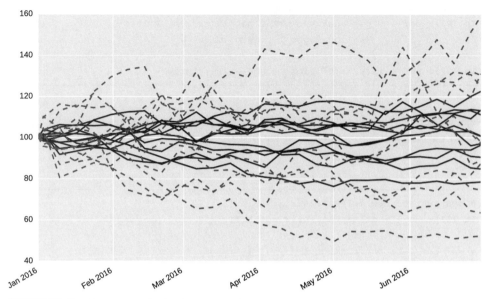

FIGURE 12.2   Simulated paths for the two risk factors; solid lines = low volatility, dashed lines = high volatility.

```
# instantiation of market environment object for option
In [30]: me_opt = dx.market_environment('me_opt', me_1.pricing_date)

# add complete market environment
In [31]: me_opt.add_environment(me_1)

# add maturity date for option
In [32]: me_opt.add_constant('maturity', dt.datetime(2016, 6, 30))

# add strike for option
In [33]: me_opt.add_constant('strike', 110.)
```

The first derivative is an *American put option* on the first risk factor gbm_1.

```
In [34]: am_put = dx.valuation_mcs_american_single(
    ....:                 name='am_put',  # name of the option as string
    ....:                 underlying=gbm_1,  # the risk factor object
    ....:                 mar_env=me_opt,  # the market environment
    ....:                 payoff_func='np.maximum(strike - instrument_values, 0)')
    ....:
```

Let us calculate a Monte Carlo present value estimate and estimates for the Greeks of the American put.

```
In [35]: am_put.present_value()   # Monte Carlo estimator
Out[35]: 11.799

In [36]: am_put.delta()   # delta of the option
Out[36]: -0.6809

In [37]: am_put.gamma()   # gamma of the option
Out[37]: 0.0149

In [38]: 0.5 * am_put.gamma() * am_put.underlying.initial_value ** 2
            # dollar gamma
Out[38]: 74.5

In [39]: am_put.vega()   # vega of the option
Out[39]: 23.8208

In [40]: am_put.theta()   # theta of the option
Out[40]: -3.81

In [41]: am_put.rho()   # rho of the option
Out[41]: -30.113
```

The second derivative is a European call option on the second risk factor gbm_2. It has the same strike and maturity as the American put option.

```
In [42]: eur_call = dx.valuation_mcs_european_single(
   ....:                name='eur_call',
   ....:                underlying=gbm_2,
   ....:                mar_env=me_opt,
   ....:                payoff_func='np.maximum(maturity_value - strike, 0)')
   ....:
```

The major statistics for this option are:

```
In [43]: eur_call.present_value()
Out[43]: 10.364663

In [44]: eur_call.delta()
Out[44]: 0.4174

In [45]: eur_call.gamma()
Out[45]: 0.0121
```

```
In [46]: 0.5 * eur_call.gamma() * eur_call.underlying.initial_value ** 2
Out[46]: 60.5

In [47]: eur_call.vega()
Out[47]: 27.6147

In [48]: eur_call.theta()
Out[48]: -14.1996

In [49]: eur_call.rho()
Out[49]: 18.0684
```

Note that all these values might vary to a greater or lesser extent with the parameters chosen for the Monte Carlo simulation.

To conclude this section, let us analyze the European call option in a bit more detail. We want to estimate and collect the Greeks for different strikes. The following code implements the necessary steps:

```
In [50]: k_list = np.arange(80., 120.5, 2.5)

In [51]: pv = []; de = []; ve = []; th = []; rh = []; ga = []

In [52]: for k in k_list:
    ....:     eur_call.update(strike=k)
    ....:     pv.append(eur_call.present_value())
    ....:     de.append(eur_call.delta())
    ....:     ve.append(eur_call.vega())
    ....:     th.append(eur_call.theta())
    ....:     rh.append(eur_call.rho())
    ....:     ga.append(eur_call.gamma())
    ....:
```

Figure 12.3 shows the results graphically.

```
In [53]: dx.plot_option_stats_full(k_list, pv, de, ga, ve, th, rh)
```

12.4 DERIVATIVES PORTFOLIOS

The previous sections show how convenient and flexible it is to model single derivatives with DX Analytics. The numerical methods used and the API of the library mimic working with the Black-Scholes-Merton closed option pricing formula when it comes to Greeks although the derivative itself might be much more complex than a plain vanilla European call or put option

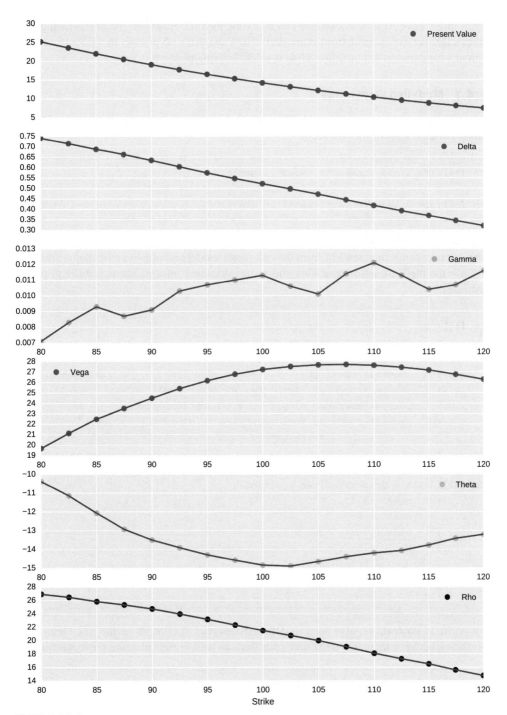

FIGURE 12.3   Greeks of the European call option for different strikes.

(e.g. it might have American exercise and an exotic payoff). However, the area which differentiates DX Analytics most from other derivatives analytics libraries is the global valuation approach for derivatives portfolios. How it works is explained in this section.

12.4.1 Modeling Portfolios

In a *portfolio context*, we need to add information about the model class(es) to be used by the market environments of the risk factors.

```
In [54]: me_1.add_constant('model', 'gbm')

In [55]: me_2.add_constant('model', 'gbm')
```

To compose a portfolio consisting of the two options, we need to define *derivatives positions*. Note that this step is independent from the risk factor model and option model definitions. We only use the market environment data and some additional information needed (e.g. payoff functions).

```
In [56]: put = dx.derivatives_position(
    ....:      name='put',  # name as string
    ....:      quantity=2,  # number of options in the portfolio
    ....:      underlyings=['gbm_1'],  # the underlying(s) as list object
    ....:      mar_env=me_opt,  # the market environment object
    ....:      otype='American single',  # the option type
    ....:      payoff_func='np.maximum(strike - instrument_values, 0)')
    ....:                         # the payoff
    ....:

In [57]: call = dx.derivatives_position(
    ....:      name='call',
    ....:      quantity=3,
    ....:      underlyings=['gbm_2'],
    ....:      mar_env=me_opt,
    ....:      otype='European single',
    ....:      payoff_func='np.maximum(maturity_value - strike, 0)')
    ....:
```

In a portfolio context, we also need to define the *market*. It consists of the risk factors, the correlation between them, the derivatives positions as well as the valuation environment.

```
In [58]: risk_factors = {'gbm_1': me_1, 'gbm_2': me_2}  # as dictionary

In [59]: correlations = [['gbm_1', 'gbm_2', 0.4]]  # as list

In [60]: positions = {'put' : put, 'call' : call}  # as dictionary
```

The *valuation environment* (technically another market environment) contains all those parameters shared by all derivatives positions. This might imply that certain parameters from the market environments of the derivatives get replaced for the portfolio simulations and valuations.

```
In [61]: val_env = dx.market_environment('general', dt.datetime(2016, 1, 1))

In [62]: val_env.add_constant('frequency', 'W')

In [63]: val_env.add_constant('paths', 25000)

In [64]: val_env.add_constant('starting_date', val_env.pricing_date)

In [65]: val_env.add_constant('final_date', val_env.pricing_date)

In [66]: val_env.add_curve('discount_curve', r)
```

These new objects are needed to instantiate a `portfolio` object.

```
In [67]: port = dx.derivatives_portfolio(
    ....:         name='portfolio',  # name as string
    ....:         positions=positions,  # derivatives positions
    ....:         val_env=val_env,  # valuation environment
    ....:         risk_factors=risk_factors, # relevant risk factors
    ....:         correlations=correlations,  # correlation between risk factors
    ....:         parallel=False)  # parallel valuation True/False
    ....:
```

12.4.2 Simulation and Valuation

Simulation and valuation are now as straightforward as in the single option case.

```
In [68]: port.get_values()   # get all present values
Total
pos_value     54.103966
dtype: float64
Out[68]:
   position  name quantity           otype risk_facts      value currency \
0       put   put        2 American single      [gbm_1]  11.804000      EUR
1      call  call        3 European single      [gbm_2]  10.165322      EUR

   pos_value
0  23.608000
1  30.495966
```

```
In [69]: port.get_statistics()   # get major statistics
Totals
pos_value     54.1030
pos_delta      0.0082
pos_vega     130.9992
dtype: float64
Out[69]:
  position  name quantity           otype risk_facts   value currency \
0      put   put        2 American single     [gbm_1]  11.804      EUR
1     call  call        3 European single     [gbm_2]  10.165      EUR


   pos_value  pos_delta  pos_vega
0     23.608    -1.4192   48.7344
1     30.495     1.4274   82.2648
```

12.4.3 Risk Reports

A strength of DX Analytics and the global valuation approach is that one can easily generate consistent risk reports. By this we mean that single parameters are shocked and the effect on the portfolio value is estimated. Think of a larger portfolio containing multiple options on the S&P 500 equity index. By changing the spot value of the index, DX Analytics can estimate in a single step what the impact is on the overall portfolio value (and not only on a single option as in the case of a delta calculation).

When calling the get_port_risk() method you need to define which parameter will be shocked. You get back all hypothetical portfolio values and the benchmark value without shock. The following estimates show the "portfolio deltas."

```
In [70]: deltas, benchvalue = port.get_port_risk(Greek='Delta')

gbm_1
0.8 0.9 1.0 1.1 1.2
gbm_2
0.8 0.9 1.0 1.1 1.2

In [71]: benchvalue
Out[71]: 54.103966

In [72]: deltas
Out[72]:
<class 'pandas.core.panel.Panel'>
Dimensions: 2 (items) x 5 (major_axis) x 2 (minor_axis)
Items axis: gbm_1_Delta to gbm_2_Delta
Major_axis axis: 0.8 to 1.2
Minor_axis axis: factor to value
```

There is a convenience function called `risk_report()` in DX Analytics to nicely print the results.

```
In [73]: dx.risk_report (deltas)  # gives the resulting values ...

gbm_1_Delta
          0.8    0.9    1.0    1.1    1.2
factor  80.00 90.00 100.0 110.00 120.00
value   90.51 70.89  54.1  42.19  35.37

gbm_2_Delta
          0.8    0.9    1.0    1.1    1.2
factor  80.00 90.00 100.0 110.00 120.00
value   33.28 41.94  54.1  69.74  88.39

In [74]: dx.risk_report (deltas.ix[:, :, 'value'] - benchvalue,
   ....:                       gross=False)  # ... as net changes
   ....:
      gbm_1_Delta   gbm_2_Delta
0.8         36.41        -20.83
0.9         16.79        -12.16
1.0          0.00          0.00
1.1        -11.92         15.63
1.2        -18.74         34.28
```

"Portfolio vegas" are calculated in the same way.

```
In [75]: vegas, benchvalue = port.get_port_risk(Greek='Vega', step=0.05)

gbm_1
0.8 0.85 0.9 0.95 1.0 1.05 1.1 1.15 1.2
gbm_2
0.8 0.85 0.9 0.95 1.0 1.05 1.1 1.15 1.2

In [76]: dx.risk_report (vegas)

gbm_1_Vega
          0.80   0.85   0.90   0.95 1.00   1.05   1.10   1.15   1.20
factor    0.16   0.17   0.18   0.19  0.2   0.21   0.22   0.23   0.24
value    52.40 52.85 53.20 53.64 54.1 54.59 55.05 55.52 56.01

gbm_2_Vega
          0.80   0.85   0.90   0.95 1.00   1.05   1.10   1.15   1.20
factor    0.40   0.43   0.45   0.48  0.5   0.53   0.55   0.58   0.60
value    45.92 47.95 50.00 52.05 54.1 56.16 58.22 60.28 62.34
```

```
In [77]: dx.risk_report(vegas.ix[:, :, 'value'] - benchvalue, gross=False)
         gbm_1_Vega  gbm_2_Vega
0.80        -1.70       -8.19
0.85        -1.26       -6.15
0.90        -0.91       -4.11
0.95        -0.47       -2.05
1.00         0.00        0.00
1.05         0.49        2.06
1.10         0.95        4.12
1.15         1.41        6.18
1.20         1.90        8.24
```

12.5 CONCLUSIONS

This chapter provides a quick start with DX Analytics, a Python-based financial analytics library with a focus on derivatives and risk analytics. The library offers many more features than are covered in this brief chapter. It is recommended to check out the main page http://dx-analytics.com and to work through the different parts of the documentation which are all based on executable Jupyter Notebooks.

The focus of this chapter is on the basic tool set and a basic understanding of the API to have a good foundation for the case studies in the two subsquent chapters. The case studies use DX Analytics to model the VSTOXX volatility index by the *square-root diffusion model* from chapter 6, *Valuing Volatility Derivatives* as well as the *square-root jump diffusion model* from chapter 7, *Advanced Modeling of the VSTOXX Index*. The major goal of the case studies is to analyze how well the two models perform over time in replicating the market quotes of traded VSTOXX options.

## CHAPTER 13

DX Analytics – Square-Root Diffusion

13.1 INTRODUCTION

This chapter uses DX Analytics to model the VSTOXX volatility index by a square-root diffusion process as proposed in Grünbichler and Longstaff (1996) and discussed in chapter 6 *Valuing Volatility Derivatives*. It implements a study over a time period of three months to analyze how well the model performs in replicating market quotes for VSTOXX options.

13.2 DATA IMPORT AND SELECTION

The data we are working with is for the first quarter of 2014. The complete data set is contained in the online resources accompanying this book. As usual, some imports first.

```
In [1]: import numpy as np

In [2]: import pandas as pd

In [3]: import datetime as dt
```

Next, we read the data from the source into pandas `DataFrame` objects.

```
In [4]: h5 = pd.HDFStore('./source/data/vstoxx_march_2014.h5', 'r')

In [5]: vstoxx_index = h5['vstoxx_index']    # data for the index itself

In [6]: vstoxx_futures = h5['vstoxx_futures']    # data for the futures

In [7]: vstoxx_options = h5['vstoxx_options']    # data for the options

In [8]: h5.close()
```

Inspecting the data sub-set for the VSTOXX index itself, we see that we are dealing with 63 trading days.

```
In [9]: vstoxx_index.info()
<class 'pandas.core.frame.DataFrame'>
DatetimeIndex: 63 entries, 2014-01-02 to 2014-03-31
Data columns (total 9 columns):
V2TX    63 non-null float64
V6I1    57 non-null float64
V6I2    63 non-null float64
V6I3    61 non-null float64
V6I4    63 non-null float64
V6I5    63 non-null float64
V6I6    62 non-null float64
V6I7    63 non-null float64
V6I8    63 non-null float64
dtypes: float64(9)
memory usage: 4.9 KB

In [10]: vstoxx_index.tail()
Out[10]:
                 V2TX      V6I1      V6I2      V6I3      V6I4      V6I5      V6I6  \
Date
2014-03-25    18.2637   18.2303   18.3078   19.0371   19.8378   20.3065   18.1063
2014-03-26    17.5869   17.4810   17.7009   18.4499   19.4150   19.9961   20.2562
2014-03-27    17.6397   17.5032   17.7608   18.6249   19.4860   20.0477   20.1078
2014-03-28    17.0324   16.6849   17.2864   18.3281   19.3032   19.8332   20.1371
2014-03-31    17.6639   17.6087   17.6879   18.5689   19.4285   20.0430   19.9823


                 V6I7      V6I8
Date
2014-03-25    20.8292   21.2046
2014-03-26    20.4541   20.8563
2014-03-27    20.4865   20.9449
2014-03-28    20.3808   20.8210
2014-03-31    20.4448   20.8994
```

Per trading day, there are eight futures quotes for the eight different maturities of the VSTOXX futures contract. This makes for a total of 504 futures quotes.

```
In [11]: vstoxx_futures.info()
<class 'pandas.core.frame.DataFrame'>
Int64Index: 504 entries, 0 to 503
Data columns (total 5 columns):
DATE         504 non-null datetime64[ns]
```

```
EXP_YEAR      504 non-null int64
EXP_MONTH     504 non-null int64
PRICE         504 non-null float64
MATURITY      504 non-null datetime64[ns]
dtypes: datetime64[ns](2), float64(1), int64(2)
memory usage: 23.6 KB


In [12]: vstoxx_futures.tail()
Out[12]:
          DATE  EXP_YEAR  EXP_MONTH  PRICE   MATURITY
499 2014-03-31      2014          7  20.40 2014-07-18
500 2014-03-31      2014          8  20.70 2014-08-15
501 2014-03-31      2014          9  20.95 2014-09-19
502 2014-03-31      2014         10  21.05 2014-10-17
503 2014-03-31      2014         11  21.25 2014-11-21
```

By far the biggest data sub-set is the one for the VSTOXX options. For each trading day there are market quotes for puts and calls for eight different maturities and a multitude of different strike prices. This makes for a total of 46,960 option quotes for the first quarter of 2014.

```
In [13]: vstoxx_options.info()
<class 'pandas.core.frame.DataFrame'>
Int64Index: 46960 entries, 0 to 46959
Data columns (total 7 columns):
DATE          46960 non-null datetime64[ns]
EXP_YEAR      46960 non-null int64
EXP_MONTH     46960 non-null int64
TYPE          46960 non-null object
STRIKE        46960 non-null float64
PRICE         46960 non-null float64
MATURITY      46960 non-null datetime64[ns]
dtypes: datetime64[ns](2), float64(2), int64(2), object(1)
memory usage: 2.9+ MB


In [14]: vstoxx_options.tail()
Out[14]:
            DATE  EXP_YEAR  EXP_MONTH TYPE  STRIKE  PRICE   MATURITY
46955 2014-03-31      2014         11    P    85.0  63.65 2014-11-21
46956 2014-03-31      2014         11    P    90.0  68.65 2014-11-21
46957 2014-03-31      2014         11    P    95.0  73.65 2014-11-21
46958 2014-03-31      2014         11    P   100.0  78.65 2014-11-21
46959 2014-03-31      2014         11    P   105.0  83.65 2014-11-21
```

Maturity-wise we are dealing with a total of eleven dates. This is due to the fact that at any given time eight maturities for the VSTOXX futures and options contracts are available and we are looking at data for three months.

```
In [15]: third_fridays = sorted(set(vstoxx_futures['MATURITY']))

In [16]: third_fridays
Out[16]:
[Timestamp('2014-01-17 00:00:00'),
 Timestamp('2014-02-21 00:00:00'),
 Timestamp('2014-03-21 00:00:00'),
 Timestamp('2014-04-18 00:00:00'),
 Timestamp('2014-05-16 00:00:00'),
 Timestamp('2014-06-20 00:00:00'),
 Timestamp('2014-07-18 00:00:00'),
 Timestamp('2014-08-15 00:00:00'),
 Timestamp('2014-09-19 00:00:00'),
 Timestamp('2014-10-17 00:00:00'),
 Timestamp('2014-11-21 00:00:00')]
```

When it comes to the calibration of the square-root diffusion model for the VSTOXX, it is necessary to work with a selection from the large set of option quotes. The following function implements such a selection procedure, using different conditions to generate a sensible set of option quotes around the forward at-the-money level. The function srd_get_option_selection() is used in what follows to select the right sub-set of option quotes for each day during the calibration.

```
def srd_get_option_selection(pricing_date, maturity, tol=tol):
    ''' Function to select option quotes from data set.

    Parameters
    ==========
    pricing_date: datetime object
        date for which the calibration shall be implemented
    maturity: datetime object
        maturity date for the options to be selected
    tol: float
        moneyness tolerance for OTM and ITM options to be selected

    Returns
    =======
    option_selection: DataFrame object
        selected options quotes
    forward: float
        futures price for maturity at pricing_date
    '''
    forward = vstoxx_futures[(vstoxx_futures. DATE == pricing_date)
            & (vstoxx_futures.MATURITY == maturity)]['PRICE'].values[0]
```

```
    option_selection = \
        vstoxx_options[(vstoxx_options.DATE == pricing_date)
                     & (vstoxx_options.MATURITY == maturity)
                     & (vstoxx_options.TYPE == 'C')   # only calls
                     & (vstoxx_options.STRIKE > (1 - tol) * forward)
                     & (vstoxx_options.STRIKE < (1 + tol) * forward)]
    return option_selection, forward
```

13.3 MODELING THE VSTOXX OPTIONS

The previous chapter illustrates how European options are modeled with DX Analytics based on a geometric Brownian motion model (dx.geometric_brownian_motion()). To model the VSTOXX options for the calibration, we just need to replace that model with the square-root diffusion model dx.square_root_diffusion(). The respective market environment then needs some additional parameters.

All the code used for the calibration is found in the Python script dx_srd_calibration.py (see sub-section 14.6.1 *dx_srd_calibration.py*). After some imports, the script starts by defining some general parameters and curves for the market environment. During the calibration process, some of these get updated to reflect the current status of the optimization procedure.

```
import dx
import time
import numpy as np
import pandas as pd
import datetime as dt
import scipy.optimize as spo
import matplotlib.pyplot as plt
import seaborn as sns; sns.set()
import matplotlib
matplotlib.rcParams['font.family'] = 'serif'

# importing the data
h5 = pd.HDFStore('../data/vstoxx_march_2014.h5', 'r')
vstoxx_index = h5['vstoxx_index']
vstoxx_futures = h5['vstoxx_futures']
vstoxx_options = h5['vstoxx_options']
h5.close()
# collecting the maturity dates
third_fridays = sorted(set(vstoxx_futures['MATURITY']))

# instantiation of market environment object with dummy pricing date
me_vstoxx = dx.market_environment('me_vstoxx', dt.datetime(2014, 1, 1))
me_vstoxx.add_constant('currency', 'EUR')
me_vstoxx.add_constant('frequency', 'W')
```

```
me_vstoxx.add_constant('paths',  5000)


# constant short rate model with somewhat arbitrary rate
csr = dx.constant_short_rate('csr', 0.01)
me_vstoxx.add_curve('discount_curve', csr)


# parameters to be calibrated later, dummies only
me_vstoxx.add_constant('kappa', 1.0)
me_vstoxx.add_constant('theta', 20)
me_vstoxx.add_constant('volatility', 1.0)


# payoff function for all European call options
payoff_func = 'np.maximum(maturity_value - strike, 0)'


tol = 0.2   # otm & itm moneyness tolerance
```

The function `srd_get_option_models()` creates valuation models for all options in a given selection of option quotes.

```
def srd_get_option_models(pricing_date, maturity, option_selection):
    ''' Function to instantiate option pricing models.

    Parameters
    ==========
    pricing_date: datetime object
        date for which the calibration shall be implemented
    maturity: datetime object
        maturity date for the options to be selected
    option_selection: DataFrame object
        selected options quotes

    Returns
    =======
    vstoxx_model: dx.square_root_diffusion
        model object for VSTOXX
    option_models: dict
        dictionary of dx.valuation_mcs_european_single objects
    '''
    # updating the pricing date
    me_vstoxx.pricing_date = pricing_date
    # setting the initial value for the pricing date
    initial_value = vstoxx_index['V2TX'][ pricing_date]
    me_vstoxx.add_constant('initial_value', initial_value)
    # setting the final date given the maturity date
    me_vstoxx.add_constant('final_date', maturity)
    # instantiating the risk factor (VSTOXX) model
```

```
vstoxx_model = dx.square_root_diffusion('vstoxx_model', me_vstoxx)
# setting the maturity date for the valuation model(s)
me_vstoxx.add_constant('maturity', maturity)

option_models = {}  # dictionary collecting all models
for option in option_selection.index:
    # setting the strike for the option to be modeled
    strike = option_selection['STRIKE'].ix[option]
    me_vstoxx.add_constant('strike', strike)
    # instantiating the option model
    option_models[option] = \
                        dx.valuation_mcs_european_single(
                                'eur_call_%d' % strike,
                                vstoxx_model,
                                me_vstoxx,
                                payoff_func)
return vstoxx_model, option_models
```

13.4 CALIBRATION OF THE VSTOXX MODEL

Calibration of a parametrized model usually boils down to using global and local optimization algorithms to find parameters that minimize a given target function. This process is discussed in detail in Hilpisch (2015, ch. 11). For the calibration process to follow, we use the helper function srd_calculate_model_values() to calculate "at once" the model values for the VSTOXX options at hand. The function parameter p0 is a tuple since this is what the optimization functions provide as input.

```
def srd_calculate_model_values(p0):
    ''' Returns all relevant option values.

    Parameters
    ===========
    p0: tuple/list
        tuple of kappa, theta, volatility

    Returns
    =======
    model_values: dict
        dictionary with model values
    '''
    # read the model parameters from input tuple
    kappa, theta, volatility = p0
    # update the option market environment
    vstoxx_model.update(kappa=kappa,
                        theta=theta,
                        volatility=volatility)
```

```
# estimate and collect all option model present values
results = [option_models[option].present_value(fixed_seed=True)
            for option in option_models]
# combine the results with the option models in a dictionary
model_values = dict(zip(option_models, results))
return model_values
```

The target function to be minimized during the calibration is the *mean-squared error* of the model values given the market quotes of the VSTOXX options. Again, refer to Hilpisch (2015, ch. 11) for details and alternative formulations. The function srd_mean_squared_error() implements this concept and uses the function srd_calculate_model_values() for the option model value calculations.

```
def srd_mean_squared_error(p0, penalty=True):
    ''' Returns the mean-squared error given
    the model and market values.

    Parameters
    ==========
    p0: tuple/list
        tuple of kappa, theta, volatility

    Returns
    =======
    MSE: float
        mean-squared error
    '''
    # escape with high value for non-sensible parameter values
    if p0[0] < 0 or p0[1] < 5. or p0[2] < 0 or p0[2] > 10.:
        return 1000
    # define/access global variables/objects
    global option_selection, vstoxx_model, option_models, first, last
    # calculate the model values for the option selection
    model_values = srd_calculate_model_values(p0)
    option_diffs = {}  # dictionary to collect differences
    for option in model_values:
        # differences between model value and market quote
        option_diffs[option] = (model_values[option]
                                - option_selection['PRICE'].loc[option])
    # calculation of mean-squared error
    MSE = np.sum(np.array(option_diffs.values()) ** 2) / len(option_diffs)
    if first is True:
        # if in global optimization, no penalty
        penalty = 0.0
    else:
        # if in local optimization, penalize deviation from previous
```

```
            # optimal parameter combination
            penalty = (np.sum((p0 - last) ** 2)) / 100
    if penalty is False:
        return MSE
    return MSE + penalty
```

Equipped with the target function to be minimized, we can define the function for the global and local calibration routine itself. The calibration takes place for one or multiple maturities over the pricing date range defined. For example, the function `srd_get_parameter_series()` can calibrate the model (separately) for the two maturities May and June 2014 over the complete first quarter 2014.

```
def srd_get_parameter_series(pricing_date_list, maturity_list):
    ''' Returns parameter series for the calibrated model over time.

    Parameters
    ==========
    pricing_date_list: pd.DatetimeIndex
        object with relevant pricing dates
    maturity_list: list
        list with maturities to be calibrated

    Returns
    =======
    parameters: pd.DataFrame
        DataFrame object with parameter series
    '''
    # define/access global variables/objects
    global option_selection, vstoxx_model, option_models, first, last
    parameters = pd.DataFrame()  # object to collect parameter series
    for maturity in maturity_list:
        first = True
        for pricing_date in pricing_date_list:
            # select relevant option quotes
            option_selection, forward = srd_get_option_selection
                                        (pricing_date, maturity)
            # instantiate all model given option selection
            vstoxx_model, option_models = srd_get_option_models
                        (pricing_date, maturity, option_selection)
            if first is True:
                # global optimization to start with
                opt = spo.brute(srd_mean_squared_error,
                    ((1.25, 6.51, 0.75),   # range for kappa
                    (10., 20.1, 2.5),   # range for theta
                    (0.5, 10.51, 2.5)),   # range for volatility
                    finish=None)
```

```
                # local optimization
                opt = spo.fmin(srd_mean_squared_error, opt,
                            maxiter=550, maxfun=650,
                            xtol=0.0000001, ftol=0.0000001);
                # calculate MSE for storage
                MSE = srd_mean_squared_error(opt, penalty=False)
                # store main parameters and results
                parameters = parameters.append(
                        pd.DataFrame(
                        {'date' :  pricing_date,
                         'maturity' : maturity,
                         'initial_value' :vstoxx_model.initial_value,
                         'kappa' : opt [0],
                         'theta' : opt [1],
                         'sigma' : opt [2],
                         'MSE' : MSE},
                         index = [0]), ignore_index=True)
        first = False  # set to False after first iteration
        last = opt  # store optimal parameters for reference
        print ("Maturity %s" % str(maturity) [:10]
                + " | Pricing Date %s" % str(pricing_date) [:10]
                + " | MSE %6.5f " % MSE)
    return parameters
```

The final step is to start the calibration and collect the calibration results. The calibration we implement is for the April 18, 2014 maturity.

```
if __name__ is '__main__':
    t0 = time.time()
    # define the dates for the calibration
    pricing_date_list = pd.date_range('2014/1/2', '2014/3/31', freq='B')
    # select the maturities
    maturity_list = [third_fridays[3]]   # only 18. April 2014 maturity
    # start the calibration
    parameters = srd_get_parameter_series(pricing_date_list, maturity_list)
    # plot the results
    for mat in maturity_list:
        fig1, ax1 = plt. subplots()
        to_plot = parameters [parameters.maturity ==
                    maturity_list[0]].set_index('date')[
                    ['kappa', 'theta', 'sigma', 'MSE']]
        to_plot.plot(subplots=True, color='b', figsize=(10, 12),
                title='SRD | ' + str(mat) [:10], ax=ax1)
        plt.savefig('../images/dx_srd_cali_1_ %s.pdf' % str(mat) [:10])
        # plotting the histogram of the MSE values
```

```
        fig2,   ax2 = plt. subplots ()
        dat = parameters.MSE
        dat.hist (bins=30, ax=ax2)
        plt.axvline (dat.mean (), color='r', ls='dashed',
                        lw=1.5, label='mean = %5.4f' % dat.mean ())
        plt.legend ()
        plt.savefig ('../images/dx_srd_cali_1_hist_%s.pdf' % str (mat) [:10])
    # measuring and printing the time needed for the script execution
    print "Time in minutes %.2f" % ((time.time () - t0) / 60)
```

A visualization of the calibration results tells the whole story. Figure 13.1 shows the three square-root diffusion parameters over time and the resulting MSE values.

As we can see throughout, the results are quite good given the low MSE values. The mean MSE value is below 0.01 as seen in Figure 13.2.

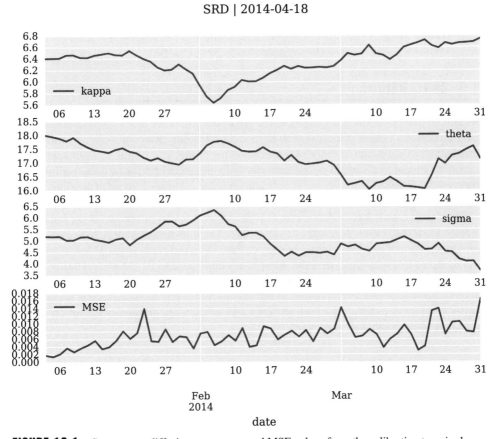

FIGURE 13.1   Square-root diffusion parameters and MSE values from the calibration to a single maturity (April 18, 2015).

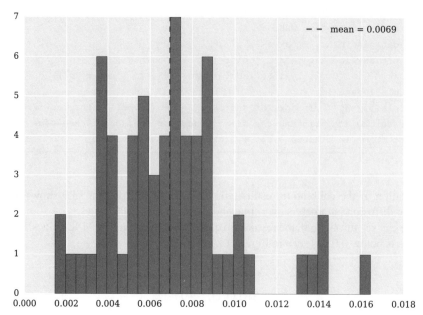

FIGURE 13.2   Histogram of the mean-squared errors for the calibration of the square-root diffusion model to a single maturity (April 18, 2015).

13.5   CONCLUSIONS

This chapter uses DX Analytics to model the VSTOXX volatility index by a square-root dif-fusion process. In similar vein, it is used to model traded European call options on the index to implement a calibration of the VSTOXX model over time. The results show that when cal-ibrating the model to a single options maturity only, the model performs quite well yielding rather low MSE values throughout. The parameter values also seem to be in sensible regions throughout (e.g. theta between 15 and 18) and they evolve rather smoothly.

There exist closed form solutions for the price of a European call option in the square-root diffusion model of Grünbichler and Longstaff (1996) as shown in chapter 6, *Valuing Volatility Derivatives*. For our analysis in this chapter we have nevertheless used the Monte Carlo valu-ation model of DX Analytics since this approach is more general in that we can easily replace one model by another, maybe more sophisticated, one. This is done in the next chapter where the same study is implemented based on the square-root jump diffusion model presented in chapter 7, *Advanced Modeling of the VSTOXX Index*. The only difference is that a few more parameters need to be taken care of.

13.6   PYTHON SCRIPTS

13.6.1   dx_srd_calibration.py

```
#
# Calibration of Grünbichler and Longstaff (1996)
# Square-Root Diffusion (SRD) model to
```

```
# VSTOXX call options with DX Analytics
#
# All data from www.eurexchange.com
#
# (c) Dr. Yves J. Hilpisch
# Listed Volatility and Variance Derivatives
#
import dx
import time
import numpy as np
import pandas as pd
import datetime as dt
import scipy.optimize as spo
import matplotlib.pyplot as plt
import seaborn as sns; sns. set()
import matplotlib
matplotlib.rcParams['font.family'] = 'serif'


# importing the data
h5 = pd.HDFStore('../data/vstoxx_march_2014.h5', 'r')
vstoxx_index = h5['vstoxx_index']
vstoxx_futures = h5['vstoxx_futures']
vstoxx_options = h5['vstoxx_options']
h5.close()
# collecting the maturity dates
third_fridays = sorted(set(vstoxx_futures['MATURITY']))


# instantiation of market environment object with dummy pricing date
me_vstoxx = dx.market_environment('me_vstoxx', dt.datetime(2014, 1, 1))
me_vstoxx.add_constant('currency', 'EUR')
me_vstoxx.add_constant('frequency', 'W')
me_vstoxx.add_constant('paths', 5000)


# constant short rate model with somewhat arbitrary rate
csr = dx.constant_short_rate('csr', 0.01)
me_vstoxx.add_curve ('discount_curve', csr)


# parameters to be calibrated later, dummies only
me_vstoxx.add_constant('kappa', 1.0)
me_vstoxx.add_constant('theta', 20)
me_vstoxx.add_constant('volatility', 1.0)


# payoff function for all European call options
payoff_func = 'np.maximum(maturity_value - strike, 0)'


tol = 0.2  # otm & itm moneyness tolerance
```

```python
def srd_get_option_selection (pricing_date, maturity, tol=tol):
    ''' Function to select option quotes from data set.

    Parameters
    ==========
    pricing_date: datetime object
        date for which the calibration shall be implemented
    maturity: datetime object
        maturity date for the options to be selected
    tol: float
        moneyness tolerace for OTM and ITM options to be selected

    Returns
    =======
    option_selection: DataFrame object
        selected options quotes
    forward: float
        futures price for maturity at pricing_date
    '''
    forward = vstoxx_futures[(vstoxx_futures.DATE == pricing_date)
                & (vstoxx_futures.MATURITY == maturity)]\
                                                ['PRICE'].values[0]
    option_selection = \
        vstoxx_options[(vstoxx_options.DATE == pricing_date)
                    &(vstoxx_options.MATURITY == maturity)
                    &(vstoxx_options.TYPE == 'C')   # only calls
                    &(vstoxx_options.STRIKE > (1 - tol) * forward)
                    &(vstoxx_options.STRIKE <(1 + tol) * forward)]
    return option_selection, forward

def srd_get_option_models (pricing_date, maturity, option_selection):
    ''' Function to instantiate option pricing models.

    Parameters
    ==========
    pricing_date: datetime object
        date for which the calibration shall be implemented
    maturity: datetime object
        maturity date for the options to be selected
    option_selection: DataFrame object
        selected options quotes

    Returns
    =======
    vstoxx_model: dx.square_root_diffusion
        model object for VSTOXX
    option_models: dict
```

```
            dictionary of dx.valuation_mcs_european_single objects
    '''
    # updating the pricing date
    me_vstoxx.pricing_date = pricing_date
    # setting the initial value for the pricing date
    initial_value = vstoxx_index['V2TX'][pricing_date]
    me_vstoxx.add_constant('initial_value', initial_value)
    # setting the final date given the maturity date
    me_vstoxx.add_constant('final_date', maturity)
    # instantiating the risk factor (VSTOXX) model
    vstoxx_model = dx.square_root_diffusion('vstoxx_model', me_vstoxx)
    # setting the maturity date for the valuation model(s)
    me_vstoxx.add_constant('maturity', maturity)

    option_models = {}  # dictionary collecting all models
    for option in option_selection.index:
        # setting the strike for the option to be modeled
        strike = option_selection['STRIKE'].ix[option]
        me_vstoxx.add_constant('strike', strike)
        # instantiating the option model
        option_models[option] = \
                        dx.valuation_mcs_european_single(
                                'eur_call_%d' % strike,
                                vstoxx_model,
                                me_vstoxx,
                                payoff_func)
    return vstoxx_model, option_models

def srd_calculate_model_values(p0):
    ''' Returns all relevant option values.

    Parameters
    ==========
    p0: tuple/list
        tuple of kappa, theta, volatility

    Returns
    =======
    model_values: dict
        dictionary with model values
    '''
    # read the model parameters from input tuple
    kappa, theta, volatility = p0
    # update the option market environment
    vstoxx_model. update(kappa=kappa,
                    theta=theta,
                    volatility=volatility)
```

```python
    # estimate and collect all option model present values
    results = [option_models[option].present_value(fixed_seed=True)
               for option in option_models]
    # combine the results with the option models in a dictionary
    model_values = dict(zip(option_models, results))
    return model_values


def srd_mean_squared_error(p0, penalty=True):
    ''' Returns the mean-squared error given
    the model and market values.

    Parameters
    ===========
    p0: tuple/list
        tuple of kappa, theta, volatility

    Returns
    =======
    MSE: float
        mean-squared error
    '''
    # escape with high value for non-sensible parameter values
    if p0[0] < 0 or p0[1] < 5. or p0[2] < 0 or p0[2] > 10.:
        return 1000
    # define/access global variables/objects
    global option_selection, vstoxx_model, option_models, first, last
    # calculate the model values for the option selection
    model_values = srd_calculate_model_values(p0)
    option_diffs = {}  # dictionary to collect differences
    for option in model_values:
        # differences between model value and market quote
        option_diffs[option] = (model_values[option]
                         - option_selection['PRICE'].loc[option])
    # calculation of mean-squared error
    MSE = np.sum(np.array(option_diffs.values()) ** 2) / len(option_diffs)
    if first is True:
        # if in global optimization, no penalty
        penalty = 0.0
    else:
        # if in local optimization, penalize deviation from previous
        # optimal parameter combination
        penalty = (np.sum((p0 - last) ** 2)) / 100
    if penalty is False:
        return MSE
    return MSE + penalty
```

```
def srd_get_parameter_series(pricing_date_list, maturity_list):
    '''Returns parameter series for the calibrated model over time.

    Parameters
    ==========
    pricing_date_list: pd.DatetimeIndex
        object with relevant pricing dates
    maturity_list: list
        list with maturities to be calibrated

    Returns
    =======
    parameters: pd.DataFrame
        DataFrame object with parameter series
    '''
    # define/access global variables/objects
    global option_selection, vstoxx_model, option_models, first, last
    parameters = pd.DataFrame()  # object to collect parameter series
    for maturity in maturity_list:
        first = True
        for pricing_date in pricing_date_list:
            # select relevant option quotes
            option_selection, forward = srd_get_option_selection
                                        (pricing_date, maturity)
            # instantiate all model given option selection
            vstoxx_model, option_models = srd_get_option_models
                        (pricing_date, maturity, option_selection)
            if first is True:
                # global optimization to start with
                opt = spo.brute(srd_mean_squared_error,
                    ((1.25, 6.51, 0.75),  # range for kappa
                     (10., 20.1, 2.5),  # range for theta
                     (0.5, 10.51, 2.5)),  # range for volatility
                    finish=None)
            # local optimization
            opt = spo.fmin(srd_mean_squared_error, opt,
                        maxiter=550, maxfun=650,
                        xtol=0.0000001, ftol=0.0000001);
            # calculate MSE for storage
            MSE = srd_mean_squared_error(opt, penalty=False)
            # store main parameters and results
            parameters = parameters.append(
                    pd.DataFrame(
                    {'date' : pricing_date,
                     'maturity' : maturity,
                     'initial_value' : vstoxx_model.initial_value,
                     'kappa' : opt[0],
```

```python
                            'theta' : opt[1],
                            'sigma' : opt[2],
                            'MSE' : MSE},
                            index=[0]), ignore_index=True)
            first = False  # set to False after first iteration
            last = opt  # store optimal parameters for reference
            print ("Maturity %s" %str(maturity)[:10]
                        + " | Pricing Date %s" % str(pricing_date)[:10]
                        + " | MSE %6.5f " % MSE)
    return parameters


if __name__ is '__main__':
    t0 = time.time()
    # define the dates for the calibration
    pricing_date_list = pd.date_range('2014/1/2', '2014/3/31', freq='B')
    # select the maturities
    maturity_list = [third_fridays[3]]  # only 18. April 2014 maturity
    # start the calibration
    parameters = srd_get_parameter_series(pricing_date_list,
                                            maturity_list)

    # plot the results
    for mat in maturity_list:
        fig1, ax1 = plt.subplots()
        to_plot = parameters[parameters.maturity ==
                        maturity_list[0]].set_index('date')[
                        ['kappa', 'theta', 'sigma', 'MSE']]
        to_plot.plot(subplots=True, color='b', figsize=(10, 12),
                title='SRD | ' + str(mat)[:10], ax=ax1)
        plt.savefig('../images/dx_srd_cali_1_%s.pdf' % str(mat)[:10])
        # plotting the histogram of the MSE values
        fig2, ax2 = plt. subplots()
        dat = parameters.MSE
        dat.hist(bins=30, ax=ax2)
        plt.axvline(dat.mean(), color='r', ls='dashed',
                        lw=1.5, label='mean = %5.4f' %dat.mean())
        plt.legend()
        plt.savefig('../images/dx_srd_cali_1_hist_%s.pdf' % str(mat)[:10])
    # measuring and printing the time needed for the script execution
    print "Time in minutes %.2f" % ((time.time()- t0)/ 60)
```

## CHAPTER 14

DX Analytics – Square-Root
Jump Diffusion

14.1 INTRODUCTION

Similarly to the previous chapter, this chapter again uses DX Analytics to model the VSTOXX index, but this time by the square-root jump diffusion (SRJD) process as introduced in chapter 7, *Advanced Modeling of the VSTOXX Index*. The study this chapter implements is actually the same as in the previous one using the very same data set. However, the challenge is increased in that we require multiple VSTOXX option maturities to be calibrated simultaneously and over time.

14.2 MODELING THE VSTOXX OPTIONS

DX Analytics provides a class for the deterministic shift square-root jump diffusion model. It is called `dx.square_root_jump_diffusion()`. Although the calibration we are implementing in this chapter is more or less the same as in the previous one, we need nevertheless to adjust the code significantly in many places. Therefore, we are stepping through the single elements again in what follows. All the code used in this chapter is found in the Python script `dx_srjd_calibration.py` (see sub-section 14.6.1, *dx_srjd_calibration.py*).

The beginning of the script is rather similar to the one implementing the calibration of the square-root diffusion model. A major difference is that we need three additional parameters `lambda`, `mu` and `delta`.

```
import dx
import time
import numpy as np
import pandas as pd
import datetime as dt
import scipy.optimize as spo
import matplotlib.pyplot as plt
import seaborn as sns; sns.set()
```

```python
import matplotlib
matplotlib.rcParams['font.family'] = 'serif'
from copy import deepcopy


# importing the data
h5 = pd.HDFStore('../data/vstoxx_march_2014.h5', 'r')
vstoxx_index = h5['vstoxx_index']
vstoxx_futures = h5['vstoxx_futures']
vstoxx_options = h5['vstoxx_options']
h5.close()


# collecting the maturity dates
third_fridays = sorted(set(vstoxx_futures['MATURITY']))


# instantiation of market environment object with dummy pricing date
me_vstoxx = dx.market_environment('me_vstoxx', dt.datetime(2014, 1, 1))
me_vstoxx.add_constant('currency', 'EUR')
me_vstoxx.add_constant('frequency', 'W')
me_vstoxx.add_constant('paths', 5000)


# constant short rate model with somewhat arbitrary rate
csr = dx.constant_short_rate('csr', 0.01)
me_vstoxx.add_curve('discount_curve', csr)


# parameters to be calibrated later, dummies only
# SRD part
me_vstoxx.add_constant('kappa', 1.0)
me_vstoxx.add_constant('theta', 20)
me_vstoxx.add_constant('volatility', 1.0)
# jump part
me_vstoxx.add_constant('lambda', 0.5)
me_vstoxx.add_constant('mu', -0.2)
me_vstoxx.add_constant('delta', 0.1)


# payoff function for all European call options
payoff_func = 'np.maximum(maturity_value - strike, 0)'


tol = 0.2  # otm & itm moneyness tolerance
first = True  # flag for first calibration
```

The function `srjd_get_option_selection()` selects the options used for the calibration. In the current case, we can choose multiple option maturities to be included.

```python
def srjd_get_option_selection(pricing_date, tol=tol):
    ''' Function to select option quotes from data set.
```

```
    Parameters
    ==========
    pricing_date: datetime object
        date for which the calibration shall be implemented
    tol: float
        moneyness tolerance for OTM and ITM options to be selected


    Returns
    =======
    option_selection: DataFrame object
        selected options quotes
    futures: DataFrame object
        futures prices at pricing_date
    '''
    option_selection = pd.DataFrame()
    mats = [third_fridays[3],]  # list of maturity dates
    # select the relevant futures prices
    futures = vstoxx_futures[(vstoxx_futures.DATE == pricing_date)
            & (vstoxx_futures.MATURITY.apply(lambda x: x in mats))]
    # collect option data for the given option maturities
    for mat in mats:
        forward = futures[futures.MATURITY == mat]['PRICE'].values[0]
        option_selection = option_selection.append(
            vstoxx_options[(vstoxx_options.DATE == pricing_date)
                    & (vstoxx_options.MATURITY == mat)
                    & (vstoxx_options.TYPE == 'C')  # only calls
                    & (vstoxx_options.STRIKE > (1 - tol) * forward)
                    & (vstoxx_options.STRIKE < (1 + tol) * forward)])
    return option_selection, futures
```

The calibration of the SRJD model consists of two steps:

- **term structure calibration**: using the futures prices at a given pricing date, this step calibrates the forward rates of the model
- **option quote calibration**: using market quotes of traded options, this step calibrates the model parameters to optimally reflect the market quotes.

Two functions are used to implement the first step. The function `srd_forward_error()` calculates the mean-squared error (MSE) for the futures term structure given a set of model parameters.

```
def srd_forward_error(p0):
    ''' Calculates the mean-squared error for the
    term structure calibration for the SRD model part.

    Parameters
    ===========
```

```
    p0: tuple/list
        tuple of kappa, theta, volatility

    Returns
    =======
    MSE: float
        mean-squared error
    '''
    global initial_value, f, t
    if p0[0] < 0 or p0[1] < 0 or p0[2] < 0:
        return 100
    f_model = dx.srd_forwards(initial_value, p0, t)
    MSE = np.sum((f - f_model) ** 2) / len(f)
    return MSE
```

The second function is called `generate_shift_base()` and calculates the single deterministic shift values to match the futures term structure perfectly – after the minimization of the term structure MSE. Note that the perfect shift gets lost again later on when the SRD parameters are updated during the calibration to the option quotes.

```
def generate_shift_base(pricing_date, futures):
    ''' Generates the values for the deterministic shift for the
    SRD model part.

    Parameters
    ==========
    pricing_date: datetime object
        date for which the calibration shall be implemented
    futures: DataFrame object
        futures prices at pricing_date

    Returns
    =======
    shift_base: ndarray object
        shift values for the SRD model part
    '''
    global initial_value, f, t
    # futures price array
    f = list(futures['PRICE'].values)
    f.insert(0, initial_value)
    f = np.array(f)
    # date array
    t = [_.to_pydatetime() for _ in futures['MATURITY']]
    t.insert(0, pricing_date)
    t = np.array(t)
    # calibration to the futures values
    opt = spo.fmin(srd_forward_error, (2., 15., 2.))
```

```
# calculation of shift values
f_model = dx.srd_forwards(initial_value, opt, t)
shifts = f - f_model
shift_base = np.array((t, shifts)).T
return shift_base
```

As in the SRD calibration case, the function `srjd_get_option_models()` creates the valuation models for all selected options.

```
def srjd_get_option_models(pricing_date, option_selection, futures):
    ''' Function to instantiate option pricing models.

    Parameters
    ==========
    pricing_date: datetime object
        date for which the calibration shall be implemented
    maturity: datetime object
        maturity date for the options to be selected
    option_selection: DataFrame object
        selected options quotes

    Returns
    =======
    vstoxx_model: dx.square_root_diffusion
        model object for VSTOXX
    option_models: dict
        dictionary of dx.valuation_mcs_european_single objects
    '''
    global initial_value
    # updating the pricing date
    me_vstoxx.pricing_date = pricing_date
    # setting the initial value for the pricing date
    initial_value = vstoxx_index['V2TX'][pricing_date]
    me_vstoxx.add_constant('initial_value', initial_value)
    # setting the final date given the maturity dates
    final_date = max(futures.MATURITY).to_pydatetime()
    me_vstoxx.add_constant('final_date', final_date)
    # adding the futures term structure
    me_vstoxx.add_curve('term_structure', futures)
    # instantiating the risk factor (VSTOXX) model
    vstoxx_model = dx.square_root_jump_diffusion_plus('vstoxx_model',
                                                      me_vstoxx)
    # generating the shift values and updating the model
    vstoxx_model.shift_base = generate_shift_base(pricing_date, futures)
    vstoxx_model.update_shift_values()
```

```
    option_models = {}  # dictionary collecting all models
    for option in option_selection.index:
        # setting the maturity date for the given option
        maturity = option_selection['MATURITY'].ix[option]
        me_vstoxx.add_constant('maturity', maturity)
        # setting the strike for the option to be modeled
        strike = option_selection['STRIKE'].ix[option]
        me_vstoxx.add_constant('strike', strike)
        # instantiating the option model
        option_models[option] = \
                            dx.valuation_mcs_european_single(
                                    'eur_call_%d' % strike,
                                    vstoxx_model,
                                    me_vstoxx,
                                    payoff_func)
    return vstoxx_model, option_models
```

14.3 CALIBRATION OF THE VSTOXX MODEL

The function `srjd_calculate_model_values()` only differs from the SRD case in
that three more parameters need to be taken care of.

```
def srjd_calculate_model_values(p0):
    ''' Returns all relevant option values.

    Parameters
    ===========
    p0: tuple/list
        tuple of kappa, theta, volatility, lamb, mu, delt

    Returns
    =======
    model_values: dict
        dictionary with model values
    '''
    # read the model parameters from input tuple
    kappa, theta, volatility, lamb, mu, delt = p0
    # update the option market environment
    vstoxx_model.update(kappa=kappa,
                        theta=theta,
                        volatility=volatility,
                        lamb=lamb,
                        mu=mu,
                        delt=delt)
    # estimate and collect all option model present values
```

```
        results = [option_models[option].present_value(fixed_seed=True)
                       for option in option_models]
        # combine the results with the option models in a dictionary
        model_values = dict(zip(option_models, results))
        return model_values
```

The same holds true for the function `srjd_mean_squared_error()` which now also penalizes certain parameter ranges for the additional parameters of the SRJD model.

```
def srjd_mean_squared_error(p0, penalty=True):
    ''' Returns the mean-squared error given
    the model and market values.

    Parameters
    ==========
    p0: tuple/list
        tuple of kappa, theta, volatility
    Returns
    =======
    MSE: float
        mean-squared error
    '''
    # escape with high value for non-sensible parameter values
    if (p0[0] < 0 or p0[1] < 5. or p0[2] < 0 or p0[2] > 10.
        or p0[3] < 0 or p0[4] < 0 or p0[5] < 0):
        return 1000
    # define/access global variables/objects
    global option_selection, vstoxx_model, option_models, first, last
    # calculate the model values for the option selection
    model_values = srjd_calculate_model_values(p0)
    option_diffs = {}  # dictionary to collect differences
    for option in model_values:
        # differences between model value and market quote
        option_diffs[option] = (model_values[option]
                                - option_selection['PRICE'].loc[option])
    # calculation of mean-squared error
    MSE = np.sum(np.array(option_diffs.values()) ** 2) / len(option_diffs)
    if first is True:
        # if in first optimization, no penalty
        penalty = 0.0
    else:
        # if 2, 3, ... optimization, penalize deviation from previous
        # optimal parameter combination
        penalty = (np.sum((p0 - last) ** 2))
    if penalty is False:
        return MSE
    return MSE + penalty
```

The function `srjd_get_parameter_series()` implementing the calibration routines then takes on the form:

```python
def srjd_get_parameter_series(pricing_date_list):
    ''' Returns parameter series for the calibrated model over time.

    Parameters
    ==========
    pricing_date_list: pd.DatetimeIndex
        object with relevant pricing dates

    Returns
    =======
    parameters: pd.DataFrame
        DataFrame object with parameter series
    '''
    # define/access global variables/objects
    global initial_value, futures, option_selection, vstoxx_model, \
            option_models, first, last
    parameters = pd.DataFrame()  # DataFrame object to collect parameter series
    for pricing_date in pricing_date_list:
        # setting the initial value for the VSTOXX
        initial_value = vstoxx_index['V2TX'][pricing_date]
        # select relevant option quotes
        option_selection, futures = srjd_get_option_selection(pricing_date)
        # instantiate all model given option selection
        vstoxx_model, option_models = srjd_get_option_models(pricing_date,
                                                              option_selection,
                                                              futures)
        # global optimization to start with
        opt = spo.brute(srjd_mean_squared_error,
            ((1.25, 6.51, 0.75),   # range for kappa
             (10., 20.1, 2.5),     # range for theta
             (0.5, 10.51, 2.5),    # range for volatility
             (0.1, 0.71, 0.3),     # range for lambda
             (0.1, 0.71, 0.3),     # range for mu
             (0.1, 0.21, 0.1)),    # range for delta
            finish=None)
        # local optimization
        opt = spo.fmin(srjd_mean_squared_error, opt,
                       maxiter=550, maxfun=650,
                       xtol=0.0000001, ftol=0.0000001);
        # calculate MSE for storage
        MSE = srjd_mean_squared_error(opt, penalty=False)
        # store main parameters and results
        parameters = parameters.append(
                pd.DataFrame(
                {'date' : pricing_date,
```

```
                'initial_value' : vstoxx_model.initial_value,
                'kappa' : opt[0],
                'theta' : opt[1],
                'sigma' : opt[2],
                'lambda' : opt[3],
                'mu' : opt[4],
                'delta' : opt[5],
                'MSE' : MSE},
                index=[0]), ignore_index=True)
        first = False  # set to False after first iteration
        last = opt  # store optimal parameters for reference
        print ("Pricing Date %s" % str(pricing_date)[:10]
               + " | MSE %6.5f" % MSE)
    return parameters
```

Finally, the function `srjd_plot_model_fit()` plots the results for the last pricing date of the calibration procedure and compares the model values to the market quotes.

```
def srjd_plot_model_fit(parameters):
    # last pricing date
    pdate = max(parameters.date)
    # optimal parameters for that date and the maturity
    opt = np.array(parameters[parameters.date == pdate][[
        'kappa', 'theta', 'sigma', 'lambda', 'mu', 'delta']])[0]
    option_selection, futures = srjd_get_option_selection(pdate, tol=tol)
    vstoxx_model, option_models = srjd_get_option_models(pdate,
                                                   option_selection,
                                                   futures)
    model_values = srjd_calculate_model_values(opt)
    model_values = pd.DataFrame(model_values.values(),
                            index=model_values.keys(),
                            columns=['MODEL'])
    option_selection = option_selection.join(model_values)
    mats = set(option_selection.MATURITY.values)
    mats = sorted(mats)
    # arranging the canvas for the subplots
    height = max(8, 2 * len(mats))
    if len(mats) == 1:
        mat = mats[0]
        fig, axarr = plt.subplots(2, figsize=(10, height))
        os = option_selection[option_selection.MATURITY == mat]
        strikes = os.STRIKE.values
        axarr[0].set_ylabel('%s' % str(mat)[:10])
        axarr[0].plot(strikes, os.PRICE.values, label='Market Quotes')
        axarr[0].plot(strikes, os.MODEL.values, 'ro', label='Model Prices')
        axarr[0].legend(loc=0)
```

```
        wi = 0.3
        axarr[1].bar(strikes - wi / 2, os.MODEL.values - os.PRICE.values,
                     width=wi)
        axarr[0].set_xlabel('strike')
        axarr[1].set_xlabel('strike')
    else:
        fig, axarr = plt.subplots(len(mats), 2, sharex=True,
                                  figsize=(10, height))
        for z, mat in enumerate(mats):
            os = option_selection[option_selection.MATURITY == mat]
            strikes = os.STRIKE.values
            axarr[z, 0].set_ylabel('%s' % str(mat)[:10])
            axarr[z, 0].plot(strikes, os.PRICE.values, label='Market Quotes')
            axarr[z, 0].plot(strikes, os.MODEL.values, 'ro', label='Model
                                                              Prices')
            axarr[z, 0].legend(loc=0)
            wi = 0.3
            axarr[z, 1].bar(strikes - wi / 2,
                            os.MODEL.values - os.PRICE.values, width=wi)
        axarr[z, 0].set_xlabel('strike')
        axarr[z, 1].set_xlabel('strike')
    plt.savefig('../images/dx_srjd_cali_1_fit.pdf')
```

The final step is to start the calibration, collect the calibration results and to plot them. Remember that the maturities in this case are selected in the function `srjd_get_option_selection()`.

```
if __name__ is '__main__':
    t0 = time.time()
    # selecting the dates for the calibration
    pricing_date_list = pd.date_range('2014/3/1', '2014/3/31', freq='B')
    # conducting the calibration
    parameters = srjd_get_parameter_series(pricing_date_list)
    # storing the calibration results
    date = str(dt.datetime.now())[:10]
    h5 = pd.HDFStore('../data/srjd_calibration_%s_%s_%s' %
                     (me_vstoxx.get_constant('paths'),
                      me_vstoxx.get_constant('frequency'),
                      date.replace('-', '_')), 'w')
    h5['parameters'] = parameters
    h5.close()
    # plotting the parameter time series data
    fig1, ax1 = plt.subplots(1, figsize=(10, 12))
    to_plot = parameters.set_index('date')[
                   ['kappa', 'theta', 'sigma',
                    'lambda', 'mu', 'delta', 'MSE']]
```

```
        to_plot.plot(subplots=True, color='b', title='SRJD', ax=ax1)
        plt.savefig('../images/dx_srjd_cali_1.pdf')
        # plotting the histogram of the MSE values
        fig2, ax2 = plt.subplots()
        dat = parameters.MSE
        dat.hist(bins=30, ax=ax2)
        plt.axvline(dat.mean(), color='r', ls='dashed',
                    lw=1.5, label='mean = %5.4f' % dat.mean())
        plt.legend()
        plt.savefig('../images/dx_srjd_cali_1_hist.pdf')
        # plotting the model fit at last pricing date
        srjd_plot_model_fit(parameters)
        # measuring and printing the time needed for the script execution
        print "Time in minutes %.2f" % ((time.time() - t0) / 60)
```

14.4 CALIBRATION RESULTS

This section presents calibration results for three different calibration runs. The first run implements a calibration to a single maturity, the second to two maturities simultaneously while the third run does the same for five maturities of the VSTOXX options. The final run shows the effects of not using penalties for deviations from previous optimal parameters which in general would be used to get smoother parameter time series.

14.4.1 Calibration to One Maturity

First, we calibrate the SRJD model to a single maturity, April 18, 2014. The calibration takes place for all trading days in the first quarter of 2014. Figure 14.1 shows the time series data for the parameters of the square-root jump diffusion over time and the resulting MSE values.

The MSE values are all quite low in general with a mean of about 0.1 and one outlier as Figure 14.2 illustrates.

Figure 14.3 shows the calibration results for the last pricing date, i.e. on March 31, 2014.

14.4.2 Calibration to Two Maturities

Let us have a look at the results for the calibration to two maturities where the VSTOXX futures term structure comes into play. Figure 14.4 shows the parameter time series data for this case.

In this case, the resulting MSE values are even slightly lower on average with a mean of about 0.05 as seen in Figure 14.5.

Figure 14.6 shows the calibration results for the last pricing date, i.e. on March 31, 2014.

14.4.3 Calibration to Five Maturities

Finally, let us have a look at the calibration to five maturities simultaneously. This is the largest number of maturities for which there is data over the whole time range from January to March 2014. Figure 14.7 shows the results for the model parameters and the MSE values.

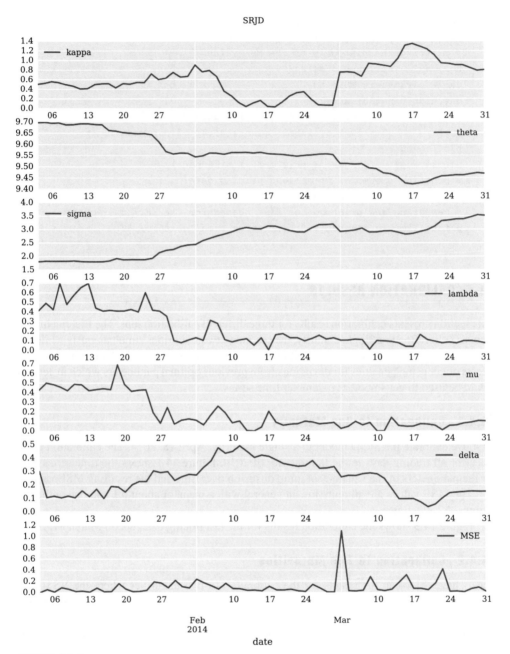

FIGURE 14.1 Square-root jump diffusion parameters and MSE values from the calibration to two maturities.

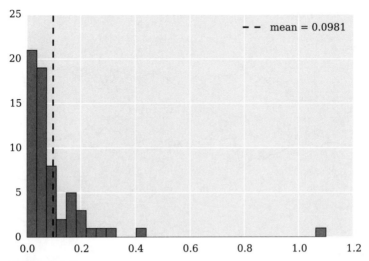

FIGURE 14.2   Histogram of MSE values for SRJD calibration to two maturities.

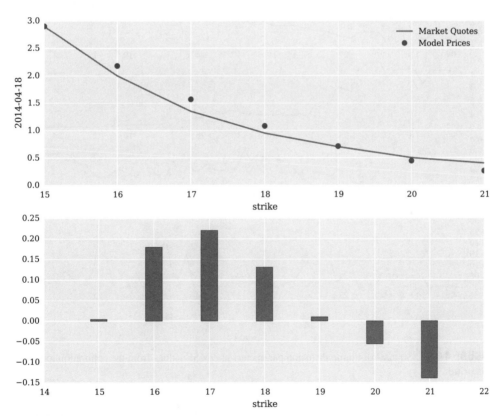

FIGURE 14.3   Model values from the SRJD calibration vs. market quotes as well as pricing errors (bars) on March 31, 2014 (one maturity).

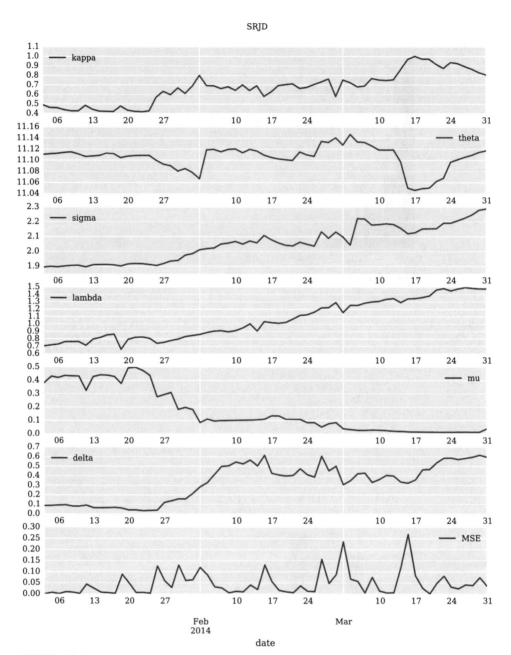

FIGURE 14.4 Square-root jump diffusion parameters and MSE values from the calibration to five maturities.

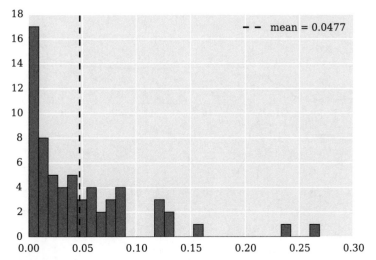

FIGURE 14.5 Histogram of MSE values for SRJD calibration to five maturities.

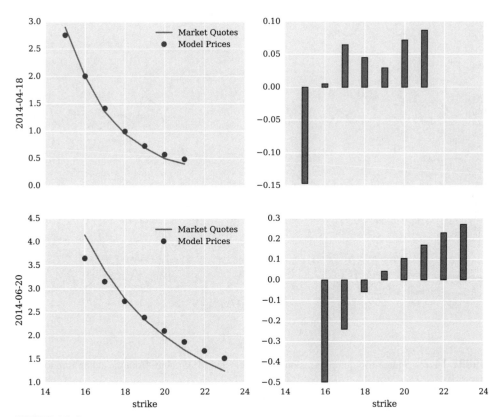

FIGURE 14.6 Model values from the SRJD calibration vs. market quotes as well as pricing errors (bars) on March 31, 2014 (two maturities).

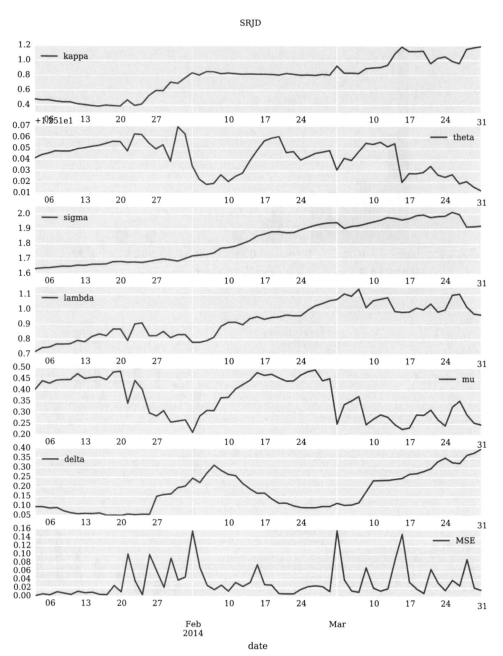

FIGURE 14.7 Square-root jump diffusion parameters and MSE values from the calibration to five maturities.

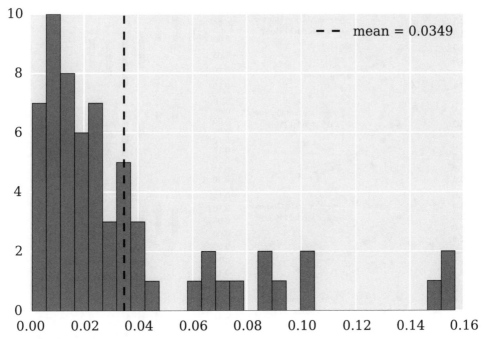

FIGURE 14.8   Histogram of MSE values for SRJD calibration to five maturities.

The resulting MSE values are again slightly lower on average. The mean MSE value is about 0.035 (see Figure 14.8).

The final plot (see Figure 14.9) again shows the calibration results at the last pricing date, March 31, 2014. Given that the calibration includes options with different moneyness levels over five different maturity months, the performance of the SRJD model is satisfactory.

14.4.4 Calibration without Penalties

It might be surprising that the highest average MSE value is observed for the calibration case with one maturity only. This is mainly due to the fact that we penalize deviations from previous optimal parameter values quite heavily and also to the existence of one outlier. The advantage of this is rather smooth time series for the single parameters, i.e. without too much variation. This is usually desirable, for example, when such a model is used for hedging purposes and hedge positions (indirectly) depend on the parameter values.

In this sub-section we therefore want to illustrate what changes when we do not penalize deviations from the previous optimal parameter values. Figure 14.10 shows the results for the model parameters and the MSE values from a calibration to one maturity (April 18, 2014) without penalization. Inspection of the figure reveals how erratically the parameter time series can behave in this case.

However, the advantage here is that there are excellent model fits to the market data with a mean MSE value of 0.0007 only (see Figure 14.11).

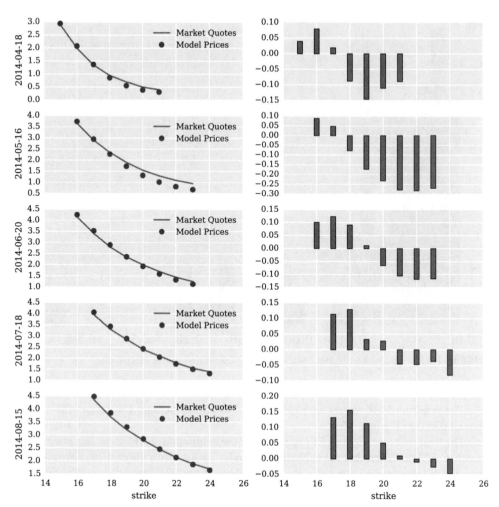

FIGURE 14.9 Model values from the SRJD calibration vs. market quotes as well as pricing errors (bars) on March 31, 2014 (five maturities).

14.5 CONCLUSIONS

This chapter calibrates the square-root jump diffusion (SRJD) model to both the VSTOXX futures term structure and for multiple maturities for the VSTOXX options. It uses DX Analytics as in the previous chapter which provides flexible modeling capabilities for volatility-based derivatives based, among other things, on square-root diffusions and square-root jump diffusions.

The results we achieve are quite good in that the typical mean-squared error values are relatively low for all cases covered – and this over the complete three month period for which we are updating the calibration with only a few outliers.

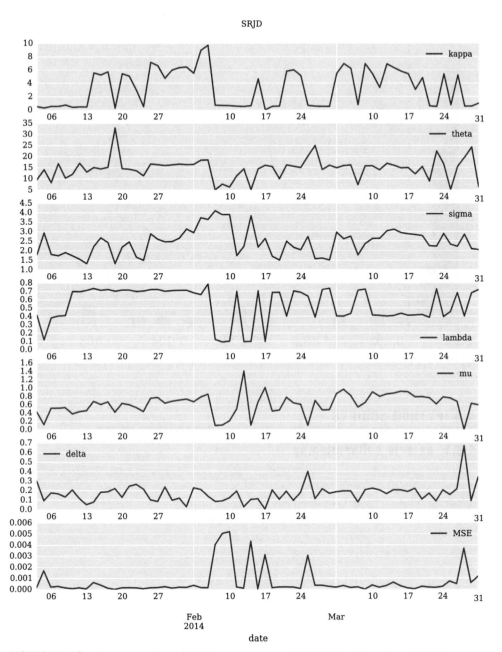

FIGURE 14.10 Square-root jump diffusion parameters and MSE values from the calibration to one maturity without penalization.

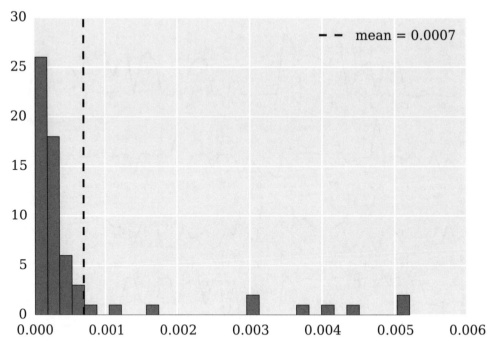

FIGURE 14.11   Histogram of MSE values for SRJD calibration to one maturity without penalization.

14.6 PYTHON SCRIPTS

14.6.1 dx_srjd_calibration.py

```
#
# Calibration of Square-Root Jump Diffusion (SRJD)
# model to VSTOXX call options with DX Analytics
#
# All data from www.eurexchange.com
#
# (c) Dr. Yves J. Hilpisch
# Listed Volatility and Variance Derivatives
#
import dx
import time
import numpy as np
import pandas as pd
import datetime as dt
import scipy.optimize as spo
import matplotlib.pyplot as plt
import seaborn as sns ; sns.set()
import matplotlib
```

```python
matplotlib.rcParams['font.family'] = 'serif '
from copy import deepcopy


# importing the data
h5 = pd.HDFStore('../data/vstoxx_march_2014.h5', 'r')
vstoxx_index = h5['vstoxx_index']
vstoxx_futures = h5['vstoxx_futures']
vstoxx_options = h5['vstoxx_options']
h5.close()
# collecting the maturity dates
third_fridays = sorted(set(vstoxx_futures['MATURITY']))


# instantiation of market environment object with dummy pricing date
me_vstoxx = dx.market_environment('me_vstoxx', dt.datetime(2014, 1, 1))
me_vstoxx.add_constant('currency', 'EUR')
me_vstoxx.add_constant('frequency', 'W')
me_vstoxx.add_constant('paths', 5000)
# constant short rate model with somewhat arbitrary rate
csr = dx.constant_short_rate('csr', 0.01)
me_vstoxx.add_curve('discount_curve', csr)


# parameters to be calibrated later, dummies only
# SRD part
me_vstoxx.add_constant('kappa', 1.0)
me_vstoxx.add_constant('theta', 20)
me_vstoxx.add_constant('volatility', 1.0)
# jump part
me_vstoxx.add_constant('lambda', 0.5)
me_vstoxx.add_constant('mu', -0.2)
me_vstoxx.add_constant('delta', 0.1)


# payoff function for all European call options
payoff_func = 'np.maximum(maturity_value - strike, 0)'

tol = 0.2  # otm & itm moneyness tolerance
first = True  # flag for first calibration


def srjd_get_option_selection(pricing_date, tol=tol):
    ''' Function to select option quotes from data set.

    Parameters
    ==========
    pricing_date: datetime object
        date for which the calibration shall be implemented
    tol: float
        moneyness tolerace for OTM and ITM options to be selected
    Returns
```

```
    =======
    option_selection: DataFrame object
        selected options quotes
    futures: DataFrame object
        futures prices at pricing_date
    '''
    option_selection = pd.DataFrame()
    mats = [third_fridays[3],]  # list of maturity dates
    # select the relevant futures prices
    futures = vstoxx_futures[(vstoxx_futures.DATE == pricing_date)
            & (vstoxx_futures.MATURITY.apply(lambda x: x in mats))]
    # collect option data for the given option maturities
    for mat in mats:
        forward = futures[futures.MATURITY == mat]['PRICE'].values[0]
        option_selection = option_selection.append(
            vstoxx_options[(vstoxx_options.DATE == pricing_date)
                        & (vstoxx_options.MATURITY == mat)
                        & (vstoxx_options.TYPE == 'C')   # only calls
                        & (vstoxx_options.STRIKE > (1 - tol) * forward)
                        & (vstoxx_options.STRIKE < (1 + tol) * forward)])
    return option_selection, futures


def srd_forward_error(p0):
    ''' Calculates the mean-squared error for the
    term structure calibration for the SRD model part.

    Parameters
    ==========
    p0: tuple/list
        tuple of kappa, theta, volatility

    Returns
    =======
    MSE: float
        mean-squared error
    '''
    global initial_value, f, t
    if p0[0] < 0 or p0[1] < 0 or p0[2] < 0:
        return 100
    f_model = dx.srd_forwards(initial_value, p0, t)
    MSE = np.sum(( f - f_model) ** 2) / len(f)
    return MSE


def generate_shift_base(pricing_date, futures):
    ''' Generates the values for the deterministic shift for the
    SRD model part.
```

```
    Parameters
    ==========
    pricing_date: datetime object
        date for which the calibration shall be implemented
    futures: DataFrame object
        futures prices at pricing_date

    Returns
    =======
    shift_base: ndarray object
        shift values for the SRD model part
    '''
    global initial_value, f, t
    # futures price array
    f = list(futures['PRICE'].values)
    f.insert(0, initial_value)
    f = np.array(f)
    # date array
    t = [_.to_pydatetime() for _ in futures['MATURITY']]
    t.insert(0, pricing_date)
    t = np.array(t)
    # calibration to the futures values
    opt = spo.fmin(srd_forward_error, (2., 15., 2.))
    # calculation of shift values
    f_model = dx.srd_forwards(initial_value, opt, t)
    shifts = f - f_model
    shift_base = np.array(( t, shifts)).T
    return shift_base


def srjd_get_option_models(pricing_date, option_selection, futures):
    ''' Function to instantiate option pricing models.

    Parameters
    ==========
    pricing_date: datetime object
        date for which the calibration shall be implemented
    maturity: datetime object
        maturity date for the options to be selected
    option_selection: DataFrame object
        selected options quotes

    Returns
    =======
    vstoxx_model: dx.square_root_diffusion
        model object for VSTOXX
```

```
    option_models: dict
        dictionary of dx.valuation_mcs_european_single objects
    '''
    global initial_value
    # updating the pricing date
    me_vstoxx.pricing_date = pricing_date
    # setting the initial value for the pricing date
    initial_value = vstoxx_index['V2TX'][pricing_date]
    me_vstoxx.add_constant('initial_value', initial_value)
    # setting the final date given the maturity dates
    final_date = max(futures.MATURITY).to_pydatetime()
    me_vstoxx.add_constant('final_date', final_date)
    # adding the futures term structure
    me_vstoxx.add_curve('term_structure', futures)
    # instantiating the risk factor (VSTOXX) model
    vstoxx_model = dx.square_root_jump_diffusion_plus('vstoxx_model',
                                                      me_vstoxx)
    # generating the shift values and updating the model
    vstoxx_model.shift_base = generate_shift_base(pricing_date, futures)
    vstoxx_model.update_shift_values()

    option_models = {}  # dictionary collecting all models
    for option in option_selection.index:
        # setting the maturity date for the given option
        maturity = option_selection['MATURITY'].ix[option]
        me_vstoxx.add_constant('maturity', maturity)
        # setting the strike for the option to be modeled
        strike = option_selection['STRIKE'].ix[option]
        me_vstoxx.add_constant('strike', strike)
        # instantiating the option model
        option_models[option] = \
                        dx.valuation_mcs_european_single(
                                'eur_call_ %d' % strike,
                                vstoxx_model,
                                me_vstoxx,
                                payoff_func)
    return vstoxx_model, option_models


def srjd_calculate_model_values(p0):
    ''' Returns all relevant option values.

    Parameters
    ==========
    p0: tuple/list
        tuple of kappa, theta, volatility, lamb, mu, delt
```

```
    Returns
    =======
    model_values: dict
        dictionary with model values
    '''
    # read the model parameters from input tuple
    kappa, theta, volatility, lamb, mu, delt = p0
    # update the option market environment
    vstoxx_model.update(kappa=kappa,
                        theta=theta,
                        volatility=volatility,
                        lamb=lamb,
                        mu=mu,
                        delt=delt)
    # estimate and collect all option model present values
    results = [option_models[option].present_value(fixed_seed=True)
            for option in option_models]
    # combine the results with the option models in a dictionary
    model_values = dict(zip(option_models, results))
    return model_values


def srjd_mean_squared_error(p0, penalty=True):
    ''' Returns the mean-squared error given
    the model and market values.

    Parameters
    ==========
    p0: tuple/list
        tuple of kappa, theta, volatility

    Returns
    =======
    MSE: float
        mean-squared error
    '''
    # escape with high value for non-sensible parameter values
    if (p0[0] < 0 or p0[1] < 5. or p0[2] < 0 or p0[2] > 10.
        or p0[3] < 0 or p0[4] < 0 or p0[5] < 0):
        return 1000
    # define/access global variables/objects
    global option_selection, vstoxx_model, option_models, first, last
    # calculate the model values for the option selection
    model_values = srjd_calculate_model_values(p0)
    option_diffs = {}  # dictionary to collect differences
    for option in model_values:
        # differences between model value and market quote
```

```python
        option_diffs[option] = (model_values[option]
                              - option_selection['PRICE'].loc[option])
    # calculation of mean-squared error
    MSE = np.sum(np.array(option_diffs.values()) ** 2) / len(option_diffs)
    if first is True:
        # if in first optimization, no penalty
        penalty = 0.0
    else:
        # if 2, 3, ... optimization, penalize deviation from previous
        # optimal parameter combination
        penalty =(np.sum(( p0 - last) ** 2))
    if penalty is False:
        return MSE
    return MSE + penalty


def srjd_get_parameter_series(pricing_date_list):
    ''' Returns parameter series for the calibrated model over time.

    Parameters
    ==========
    pricing_date_list: pd.DatetimeIndex
        object with relevant pricing dates

    Returns
    =======
    parameters: pd.DataFrame
        DataFrame object with parameter series
    '''
    # define/access global variables/objects
    global initial_value, futures, option_selection, vstoxx_model, \
           option_models, first, last
    parameters = pd.DataFrame()  # DataFrame object to collect
                                 # parameter series
    for pricing_date in pricing_date_list:
        # setting the initial value for the VSTOXX
        initial_value = vstoxx_index['V2TX'][pricing_date]
        # select relevant option quotes
        option_selection, futures = srjd_get_option_selection
                                        (pricing_date)
    # instantiate all model given option selection
    vstoxx_model, option_models = srjd_get_option_models(pricing_date,
                                                option_selection,
                                                futures)
    # global optimization to start with
    opt = spo.brute(srjd_mean_squared_error,
        ((1.25, 6.51, 0.75),  # range for kappa
```

```
             (10., 20.1, 2.5),   # range for theta
             (0.5, 10.51, 2.5),  # range for volatility
             (0.1, 0.71, 0.3),   # range for lambda
             (0.1, 0.71, 0.3),   # range for mu
             (0.1, 0.21, 0.1)),  # range for delta
          finish=None)
     # local optimization
     opt = spo.fmin(srjd_mean_squared_error, opt,
                   maxiter=550, maxfun=650,
                   xtol=0.0000001, ftol=0.0000001);
     # calculate MSE for storage
     MSE = srjd_mean_squared_error(opt, penalty=False)
     # store main parameters and results
     parameters = parameters.append(
             pd.DataFrame(
             {'date' : pricing_date,
              'initial_value' : vstoxx_model.initial_value,
              'kappa' : opt[0],
              'theta' : opt[1],
              'sigma' : opt[2],
              'lambda' : opt[3],
              'mu' : opt[4],
              'delta' : opt[5],
              'MSE' : MSE},
             index=[0]), ignore_index=True)
     first = False  # set to False after first iteration
     last = opt  # store optimal parameters for reference
     print ("Pricing Date %s" % str(pricing_date)[:10]
             + " | MSE %6.5f" % MSE)
     return parameters


def srjd_plot_model_fit(parameters):
    # last pricing date
    pdate = max(parameters.date)
    # optimal parameters for that date and the maturity
    opt = np.array(parameters[parameters.date == pdate][[
        'kappa', 'theta', 'sigma', 'lambda', 'mu', 'delta']])[0]
    option_selection, futures = srjd_get_option_selection(pdate, tol=tol)
    vstoxx_model, option_models = srjd_get_option_models(pdate,
                                                    option_selection,
                                                    futures)
    model_values = srjd_calculate_model_values(opt)
    model_values = pd.DataFrame(model_values.values(),
                               index=model_values.keys(),
                               columns=['MODEL'])
    option_selection = option_selection.join(model_values)
```

```python
    mats = set(option_selection.MATURITY.values)
    mats = sorted(mats)
    # arranging the canvas for the subplots
    height = max(8, 2 * len(mats))
    if len(mats) == 1:
        mat = mats[0]
        fig, axarr = plt.subplots(2, figsize=(10, height))
        os = option_selection[option_selection.MATURITY == mat]
        strikes = os.STRIKE.values
        axarr[0].set_ylabel('%s' % str(mat)[:10])
        axarr[0].plot(strikes, os.PRICE.values, label='Market Quotes')
        axarr[0].plot(strikes, os.MODEL.values, 'ro', label='Model Prices')
        axarr[0].legend(loc=0)
        wi = 0.3
        axarr[1].bar(strikes - wi / 2, os.MODEL.values os.PRICE.values,
                     width=wi)
        axarr[0].set_xlabel('strike')
        axarr[1].set_xlabel('strike')
    else:
        fig, axarr = plt.subplots(len(mats), 2, sharex=True,
                     figsize=(10, height))
        for z, mat in enumerate(mats):
            os = option_selection[option_selection.MATURITY == mat]
            strikes = os.STRIKE.values
            axarr[z, 0].set_ylabel('%s' % str(mat)[:10])
            axarr[z, 0].plot(strikes, os.PRICE.values, label='Market Quotes')
            axarr[z, 0].plot(strikes, os.MODEL.values, 'ro', label='Model
                                                               Prices')
            axarr[z, 0].legend(loc=0)
            wi = 0.3
            axarr[z, 1].bar(strikes - wi / 2,
                            os.MODEL.values - os.PRICE.values, width=wi)
        axarr[z, 0].set_xlabel('strike')
        axarr[z, 1].set_xlabel('strike')
    plt.savefig('../images/dx_srjd_cali_1_fit.pdf')


if __name__ is '__main__':
    t0 = time.time()
    # selecting the dates for the calibration
    pricing_date_list = pd.date_range('2014/3/1', '2014/3/31', freq='B')
    # conducting the calibration
    parameters = srjd_get_parameter_series(pricing_date_list)
    # storing the calibation results
    date = str(dt.datetime.now())[:10]
    h5 = pd.HDFStore('../data/srjd_calibration_%s_%s_%s' %
                (me_vstoxx.get_constant('paths'),
```

```
                    me_vstoxx.get_constant('frequency'),
                    date.replace('-', '_')), 'w')
    h5['parameters'] = parameters
    h5.close()
    # plotting the parameter time series data
    fig1, ax1 = plt.subplots(1, figsize =(10, 12))
    to_plot = parameters.set_index('date')[
                    ['kappa', 'theta', 'sigma',
                     'lambda', 'mu', 'delta', 'MSE']]
    to_plot.plot(subplots=True, color='b', title='SRJD', ax=ax1)
    plt.savefig('../images/dx_srjd_cali_1.pdf')
    # plotting the histogram of the MSE values
    fig2, ax2 = plt.subplots()
    dat = parameters.MSE
    dat.hist(bins=30, ax=ax2)
    plt.axvline(dat.mean(), color='r', ls='dashed',
                    lw=1.5, label='mean = %5.4f' % dat.mean())
    plt.legend()
    plt.savefig('../images/dx_srjd_cali_1_hist.pdf')
    # plotting the model fit at last pricing date
    srjd_plot_model_fit(parameters)
    # measuring and printing the time needed for the script execution
    print "Time in minutes %.2f" % (( time.time() - t0) / 60)
```

Bibliography

Bennett, Collin and Miguel Gil (2012) *Volatility Trading – Trading Volatility, Correlation, Term Structure and Skew.* Banco Santander.

Björk, Tomas (2009) *Arbitrage Theory in Continuous Time.* 3rd ed., Oxford University Press, Oxford.

Black, Fischer (1976) "The Pricing of Commodity Contracts." *Journal of Financial Economics*, Vol. 3, 167–179.

Black, Fischer and Myron Scholes (1973) "The Pricing of Options and Corporate Liabilities." *Journal of Political Economy*, Vol. 81, No. 3, 637–654.

Bossu, Sebastian (2014) *Advanced Equity Derivatives: Volatility and Correlation.* Wiley Finance.

Bossu, Sebastien, Eva Strasser, Regis Guichard (2005) "Just What You Need To Know About Variance Swaps." JPMorgan.

Breeden, Douglas and Robert Litzenberger (1978) "Prices of State-Contingent Claims Implicit in Option Prices." *Journal of Business*, Vol. 51, No. 4, 621–651.

Brenner, Menachem and Dan Galai (1989) "New Financial Instruments for Hedging Changes in Volatility." *Financial Analysts Journal*, Jul/Aug, Vol. 45, No. 4.

Brigo, Damiano and Fabio Mercurio (2001) "On Deterministic-Shift Extensions of Short-Rate Models." Working Paper, Banca IMI, Milano, www.damianobrigo.it.

Carr, Peter and Roger Lee (2009) "Volatility Derivatives." *Annual Review of Financial Economics*, Vol. 1, 1–21.

Chicago Board Options Exchange (2003) "The CBOE Volatility Index – VIX." White Paper.

Cohen, Guy (2005) *The Bible of Options Strategies.* Pearson Education, Upper Saddle River.

Cox, John, Jonathan Ingersoll and Stephen Ross (1985) "A Theory of the Term Structure of Interest Rates." *Econometrica*, Vol. 53, No. 2, 385–407.

Duffie, Darrell, Jun Pan and Kenneth Singleton (2000) "Transform Analysis and Asset Pricing for Affine Jump-Diffusions." *Econometrica*, Vol. 68, No. 6, 1343–1376.

Fleming, Jeff, Barbara Ostdiek and Rober Whaley (1995) "Predicting Stock Market Volatility: A New Measure." *The Journal of Futures Markets*, Vol. 15, No. 3, 265–302.

Gatheral, Jim (2006) *The Volatility Surface – A Practitioner"s Guide.* John Wiley & Sons, Hoboken, New Jersey.

Grünbichler, Andreas and Francis Longstaff (1996) "Valuing Futures and Options on Volatility." *Journal of Banking and Finance*, Vol. 20, 985–1001.

Guobuzaite, Renata and Lionel Martellini (2012) "The Benefits of Volatility Derivatives in Equity Portfolio Management." EDHEC Risk Institute, http://www.eurexchange.com/exchange-en/about-us/news/60036/.

Haenel, Valentin, Emmanuelle Gouillart and Gaël Varoquaux (2013) "Python Scientific Lecture Notes." http://scipy-lectures.github.com.

Hilpisch, Yves (2015) *Derivatives Analytics with Python – Data Analysis, Models, Simulation, Calibration and Hedging.* Wiley Finance, http://derivatives-analytics-with-python.com.

Hilpisch, Yves (2014) *Python for Finance — Analyze Big Financial Data.* O'Reilly, http://python-for-finance.com.

Langtangen, Hans Petter (2009) *A Primer on Scientific Programming with Python*. Springer Verlag, Berlin.

Lord, Roger, Remmert Koekkoek and Dick van Dijk (2008) "A Comparison of Biased Simulation Schemes for Stochastic Volatility Models." Working Paper, Tinbergen Institute, Amsterdam, www.ssrn.com.

McKinney, Wes (2012) *Python for Data Analysis – Data Wrangling with Pandas, NumPy, and IPython*. O"Reilly, Beijing.

Merton, Robert (1973) "Theory of Rational Option Pricing." *Bell Journal of Economics and Management Science*, Vol. 4, No. 1, 141–183.

Psychoyios, Dimitris (2005) "Pricing Volatility Options in the Presence of Jumps." Working Paper, Athens University of Economics and Business, Athens.

Psychoyios, Dimitris, George Dotsis and Raphael Markellos (2010) "A Jump Diffusion Model for VIX Volatility Options and Futures." *Review of Quantitative Finance and Accounting*, Vol. 35, No. 3, 245–269.

Sepp, Artur (2008) "VIX Option Pricing in a Jump-Diffusion Model." *Risk Magazine*, April, 84–89.

Sinclair, Euan (2008) *Volatility Trading*. John Wiley & Sons, Hoboken.

Todorov, Viktor and George Tauchen (2011): "Volatility Jumps." *Journal of Business & Economic Statistics*, Vol. 29, No. 3, 356–371.

Whaley, Robert (1993) "Derivatives on Market Volatility: Hedging Tools Long Overdue." *The Journal of Derivatives*, Vol. 1, No. 1, 71–84.

Index